Will, Imagination and Reason

Irving Babbitt and the Problem of Reality

by Claes G. Ryn

Regnery Books

Chicago   Washington, DC

Regnery Books is a Division of Regnery Gateway, Inc.
All inquiries concerning this book should be directed to
Regnery Books, 700 E Street, SE, Washington, DC 20003.

Library of Congress Cataloging-in-Publication Data

Ryn, Claes G., 1943-
    Will, imagination, and reason.

    Bibliography: p.
    1. Babbitt, Irving, 1865-1933. I. Title.
B945.B124R96 1986   191   86-6588
ISBN 0-89526-807-8

To the Memory of Folke Leander,
Optimus Doctor

Bibliographical Note

When a work by Irving Babbitt or Benedetto Croce is cited below, the complete bibliographical reference will be given in a footnote where the work is first cited in each chapter. Otherwise, the reference will be in the form of an abbreviation of the particular title in the text itself, as follows:

Irving Babbitt,	*Democracy and Leadership* = DL
	The Dhammapada = D
	Literature and the American- * College* = LAC
	The Masters of Modern French * Criticism* = MFC
	The New Laokoon = NL
	On Being Creative = OBC
	Rousseau and Romanticism = RR
	Spanish Character = SC
Benedetto Croce,	*Aesthetic* = A
	Logic = L
	Nuovi saggi di estetica = NSE
	The Philosophy of the Practical = PP
	Ultimi saggi = US

Contents

Prefatory Note

This book has deep roots in the intellectual friendship between the late Swedish philosopher Folke Leander (1910-1981) and myself. I first came in contact with Dr. Leander in my home city of Norrköping, Sweden, when I was his student in philosophy in the Latin Gymnasium during the 1962-63 academic year. At the time I did not know that he was a widely published philosopher with a considerable reputation outside of his own country, but I was much impressed by his teaching and immediately felt an affinity between the ideas he articulated and my own emerging view of man and the world. I would later discover that Dr. Leander's work had been read and praised by such scholars as Ernst Cassirer (the director of his Ph.D. dissertation), Eugenio Coseriu, John Dewey, Robert Nisbet, Russell Kirk, Arthur Lovejoy, Herbert W. Schneider, and Austin Warren. In Sweden, Dr. Leander had been denied a well-deserved appointment to a university chair in philosophy because he did not adhere to positivism and formal logic.

When I became a student at Uppsala University and later in the United States, Dr. Leander and I stayed in touch about intellectual matters. Our association intensified as my own scholarly direction crystallized, and it lasted until his final illness. Among our interests was the thought of Irving Babbitt. We regretted that the lack of systematic philosophical study of Babbitt's ideas had hampered an adequate absorption and assessment of his important contribution. We felt compelled to help remedy this situation.

The idea of this book was conceived in preliminary form about a decade ago. Dr. Leander had published *The Inner Check* (1974), which provides some of the needed explication of the ethical doctrine common to Babbitt and Paul Elmer More, his close friend and intellectual ally. I was preparing some writing of my own related to Babbitt's thought, including *Democracy and the Ethical Life* (1978). An important remaining task was to explore the relationship between Babbitt's ethical and aesthetical ideas and the implications of that relationship for how we understand reality and the knowledge of reality. Here were to be found Babbitt's perhaps most original insights. To demonstrate their significance they had to be placed in philosophical context and subjected to careful analysis. Babbitt's ideas, as partly revised and supplemented, constituted the key ingredient for a new approach to the epistemology of the humanities and social sciences.

Having retired from teaching in 1975, Dr. Leander wished to do what he could to advance the needed philosophical work. With me as correspondent and critic he started to write down analyses of some of the pertinent questions. But, because of health problems and advancing age, he wanted it understood that any writing for publication would have to be my task. He asked me to make whatever use I could of his outlines and suggestions. I set for myself the goal of preparing a book-length study of the problems of reality and knowledge. Dr. Leander cautioned me that I would be dealing with some very difficult philosophical issues that had been left largely unexplored by earlier scholars; indeed, the complexity of the subject matter, combined with protracted hostility to Babbitt, might delay publication indefinitely.

In the summer of 1981 I completed and sent to Dr. Leander a first manuscript draft of this book. I had reworked and developed his original materials and incorporated them into a larger whole. By the time he received the manuscript his health had rather sharply deteriorated, and he had been hospitalized; he would die about two months later. But according to his wife, Asta, he read and seemed very pleased with the draft.

In the years since Dr. Leander's death the manuscript in its entirety has been extensively revised; it has, in effect, been rewritten. Hence, I cannot claim the approval of my friend for what is now offered to the reader. Except for the Introduction,

Chapter 1, and Chapter 7, the present chapters all contain at least some material that could be traced back to the outlines he left me; however, with the passage of time, these early drafts have blended into the whole and become virtually indistinguishable from my own thought and writing.

My work on this book took a large step forward during a sabbatical leave from The Catholic University of America in the academic year 1980-81. I gratefully acknowledge grants from the Earhart Foundation and the Marguerite Eyer Wilbur Foundation that made possible concentrated research and writing. A grant from His Majesty the King of Sweden aided me at a later stage of the preparation of the book.

Without forgetting others who have encouraged my work and made valuable suggestions, I should like to thank especially Professors George Panichas, Ellis Sandoz, Paul Gottfried, and Peter Stanlis. I am also indebted to my former graduate student Mr. Joseph Baldacchino, the President of the National Humanities Institute, who provided perceptive editorial assistance and other support. My sincere thanks and warm personal regards go to Dr. Leander's widow, Asta.

Claes G. Ryn
Washington, D.C.

Introduction

It is a controversial assumption of this book that the work of Irving Babbitt (1865-1933), the Harvard literary scholar and cultural thinker, will always stand as a monument to American intellectual culture at its finest. Though frequently misunderstood and even maligned, Babbitt is likely to live on after most of his critics have faded from memory.

One reason Babbitt has not yet acquired the general reputation he deserves is that his central doctrines went contrary to the intellectual currents of his time. He subjected to sharp and sustained criticism dispositions on which many of his most influential contemporaries were basing their claims to moral and aesthetical sensibility. Indiscriminate benevolence toward mankind, translated into various "progressive" egalitarian schemes in education and politics, he viewed as a caricature of ethics and love as understood in traditional Christianity and other high religions. He insisted that a genuinely moral concern for others presupposes difficult self-discipline on the part of the bearer and a keen awareness of both the lower and the higher potentialities in self and others. In aesthetics, Babbitt similarly went against the tide by arguing that various doctrines of *l'art pour l'art* are blind to the ultimate purpose of art. Truly great works of the imagination are such not by virtue of their intuitive coherence alone but by virtue of the moral quality of experience they convey. These and other highly inopportune themes, which were not always formulated with diplomatic tact but sometimes with sharpness, irony and ridicule, were not designed to spare him intense, emotional opposition.

Babbitt's ideas were the subject of much controversy in the 1920s and '30s. They often served as the focal point for criticism of the so-called New Humanism, inspired in large part by his work. This controversy involved at one time or another practically every leading figure in American literature and scholarship. Unfortunately, discussion of Babbitt was characterized more by vague generalities or vituperation than by careful and dispassionate examination of his ideas. The influence of Babbitt's numerous opponents—including such men as Edmund Wilson, Joel Spingarn, R. P. Blackmur, Oscar Cargill, H. L. Mencken, Sinclair Lewis and Ernest Hemingway—was sufficient to deny his arguments a real hearing. Because of the animosity that he and his disciples encountered, it sometimes seemed dangerous even to mention his name. Babbitt himself cautioned his students accordingly.

This is not to suggest that Irving Babbitt has lacked prominent admirers in the United States and abroad. Besides Paul Elmer More (1864-1937), who became his close friend and intellectual ally, he deeply influenced individuals as diverse as T. S. Eliot, Walter Lippmann, Gordon Keith Chalmers, Louis Mercier, Austin Warren and, in a younger generation, Russell Kirk, Nathan Pusey and Peter Viereck. He had many admirers in Europe, perhaps especially in France, and also as far outside the West as China. In 1960 Harvard University inaugurated the Irving Babbitt Chair of Comparative Literature.

Irving Babbitt was born in 1865 in Dayton, Ohio. On his father's side he was descended from an Englishman who settled in Plymouth, Massachusetts, in 1643. Irving's father was a physician of diverse and sometimes crankish interests. Babbitt was to see in the sentimental and pseudo-scientific predilections of his father examples of what ailed the modern age. Irving's mother, Augusta, died when he was eleven years old. During his childhood and early youth he lived, much of the time with relatives, in many different places, including New York City; East Orange, New Jersey; and farms in Ohio and Wyoming. Babbitt entered Harvard College in 1885. He was already well-grounded in the classics and was, as he says, generally "overprepared" for his studies. Dissatisfied with the pedantry and narrowness of much of the instruction at Harvard, he would not attend class regularly. He spent his junior year in Europe and graduated with Final Honors in Classics in 1889. Babbitt wanted to delve deeper into oriental subjects. After teaching for two years at the College of Montana, he spent a year in Paris working under Professor Sylvain Lévi. He continued his oriental studies with Professor Charles Lanman at Harvard. Babbitt received the A.M. degree in 1893. Out of contempt for what he saw as the German-inspired requirements for the doctoral degree he refused to acquire that academic credential.

Babbitt taught French, Spanish and Italian at Williams College before being appointed to the faculty of Harvard University in 1894. There he was to remain until his death in 1933. Although deeply knowledgeable in and attracted to the Greek and Roman classics, he was allowed to teach only in the Department of Romance Languages and Literature and in the Department of Comparative Literature. His teaching soon earned him considerable opposition from his colleagues. His open criticism of the educational ideas of President Charles W. Eliot did not strengthen Babbitt's position, but his growing reputation as a scholar and teacher and his large number of good students finally led to his promotion to full professor in 1912. Babbitt was a Visiting Professor at the Sorbonne in 1923. He became a corresponding member of the Institute of France, and in the United States he was elected to the American Academy of Arts and Letters.

Babbitt's first book, *Literature and the American College* (1908), defines and defends the classical discipline of *humanitas* as an answer to the erosion of ethical and cultural standards brought on by scientific naturalism and sentimental humanitarianism. In *The New Laokoon* (1910) he examines at greater length the weaknesses and dangers of modern conceptions of art. *The Masters of Modern French Criticism* (1912) develops Babbitt's critical standards and applies them in assessments of leading French literary critics and aestheticians mainly in the nineteenth century. Perhaps the most important of Babbitt's works is *Rousseau and Romanticism* (1919). Here he describes and criticizes in depth various aspects of romanticism with special reference to one of its seminal and most brilliant minds. *Democracy and*

Leadership (1924) relates Babbitt's ethical and cultural philosophy to issues of politics. *On Being Creative* (1932) and *The Spanish Character*, published posthumously in 1940, contain essays in literary and cultural criticism. Babbitt's original translation of *The Dhammapada*, the Buddhist holy text, was published together with a long interpretive essay in 1936.

These brief biographical and bibliographical remarks cannot convey the scope of Babbitt's mind. His thinking defies academic boundaries. He is far more than a literary and cultural critic, as those terms are ordinarily meant. His particular subjects become the occasion for developing a comprehensive view of life. His thought is marked by cosmopolitan breadth and vast literary, historical and philosophical learning.

A legendary Harvard teacher of wit and humor as well as strong conviction and assertiveness, Babbitt made a deep impression on many of his students. Austin Warren refers to Babbitt in the classroom as "an experience not before encountered nor ever to be forgotten."[1] Friends and students of Babbitt's contributed to the valuable collection of memoirs edited by F. Manchester and O. Shepard, *Irving Babbitt, Man and Teacher* (1941). Babbitt's ideas and their historical influence are examined in David Hoeveler's *The New Humanism: A Critique of Modern America 1900-1940* (1977), which is broadly informative and sometimes quite perceptive but not consistently reliable in details and matters of interpretation.

Babbitt has continued to have a not insubstantial influence, although it is one often formally unacknowledged in footnotes and other references. Examining Babbitt's influence on various well-known writers, some of whom have also been his critics, sometimes becomes a psychologically interesting study of the covert assimilation of ideas. Walter Lippmann was a young socialist when he took a course with Babbitt at Harvard. There was an understandable element of irritation and hurt pride in Lippmann's early reaction to his teacher, yet Babbitt made a lasting impression. Lippmann's famous book *The Public*

---

1. Austin Warren, A Memoir, in Frederick Manchester and Odell Shepard (eds.), *Irving Babbitt, Man and Teacher* (New York: Greenwood Press, 1969; first published in 1941), 209.

Philosophy (1955) is unmistakably imbued with Babbitt's ideas; still, it does not once mention his name. Other erstwhile critics, such as Arthur Lovejoy and Jacques Barzun, seem to have been similarly affected by Babbitt. Whether submerged or cited openly, Babbitt somehow remains present in the American intellectual consciousness. Perhaps the most telling sign of his presence is the hostility that has greeted attempts to take a new look at his ideas long after his death. That his critics generally have been unwilling to contend with his real arguments, as distinguished from long-circulating caricatures, may indicate that, intuitively, the critics do recognize the importance of his ideas and their potential for unsettling accustomed ways of thinking.

An important reason why Babbitt has not yet received the widespread attention he deserves is that, with very few exceptions, his interpreters have not attempted a philosophical explication and assessment of his work. Babbitt was well versed in many aspects of philosophy and brought to most of his subjects the kind of comprehensiveness that is characteristic of good philosophy. Yet he was not a professional, "technical" philosopher. Profound though many of his insights are, he did not always develop them systematically and with conceptual precision. The intellectual power and coherence of his work are sometimes obscured by fragmentary argumentation or by ambiguous, cryptic or overly compressed statements of ideas. The real import of Babbitt's central insights can be demonstrated by careful philosophical analysis of his work as a whole. There is a strong need to lift his thought out of the sphere of rather general discussion in which friendly and unfriendly commentators alike have placed it. The renewed and growing interest in Babbitt in recent years underscores the scholarly necessity of relating his ideas to the enduring concerns of philosophy proper.

The plan of this book does not quite conform to any established genre of scholarship. Literary scholars who are most likely to be familiar with Babbitt may be disappointed to find in this study, which aims first of all at conceptual clarification, little of the stylistic flavor and concrete illustrations expected of a more literary or historical work. Some professional philosophers, on the other hand, will perhaps feel uneasiness about the many references to writers and subjects that have been primarily the concern of literary scholarship.

This book seeks to demonstrate the significance of Babbitt's work for understanding and dealing with the problem of reality. Babbitt has much to contribute to broadening and deepening the epistemology of the humanities, including philosophy itself and the social disciplines. His most original insight relating to the theory of knowledge may be his view of the relationship between imagination (intuition) and moral character. The book is structured to explain in depth the epistemological importance of Babbitt's doctrine of the ethical and unethical imagination. His ideas in this area address a neglected aspect of modern aesthetics, but they also have profound implications for our understanding of the process of knowledge, including the work of reason.

Babbitt's contribution to the theory of knowledge can be brought fully into view by examining it within a philosophical frame of reference in some respects broader than his own. Much can be gained by drawing selectively from the work of the Italian philosopher Benedetto Croce (1866-1952). Croce's name is everywhere known, but his importance has been insufficiently understood, especially outside of his home country. He is famous for his early aesthetical ideas, particularly as expressed in *Aesthetic* (1902). Far less known but of similar philosophical weight are his ideas on logic and ethics, developed most importantly in *Logic* (1908) and *Philosophy of the Practical* (1908).

Many of Croce's ideas correspond or run parallel to Babbitt's. Although this book will argue that Croce's work has serious weaknesses and that he is not Babbitt's equal where it counts most, he expresses himself with a philosophical precision rarely matched by Babbitt. Croce's philosophy, because it develops systematically and at length some ideas which are left vague in Babbitt's writings, is helpful in bringing Babbitt's ideas to greater conceptual clarity. An examination of Croce also suggests the need to revise and supplement Babbitt in some areas, particularly in his view of reason.

A comparative critical analysis of these representatives of

two continents is well-suited to rethinking the fundamental problems of epistemology. The emphases and ideas of Babbitt and Croce are sufficiently different to require discrimination and choice but also are sufficiently related to make possible some fruitful syntheses. The book will seek to forge their respective strengths into a systematic whole, thus developing a new approach to the problem of knowledge.

Readers sympathetic to Babbitt may be suspicious of an attempt to synthesize his work and Croce's. Did not Babbitt express strong reservations about the Italian philosopher? How could Babbitt's ethical dualism, his belief in the reality of evil as well as good, be reconciled with Croce's idealistic monism, closely related to Hegel's? How could Babbitt's insistence on the ethical dimension of art be reconciled with Croce's emphatic insistence, at least before 1917, that art is indifferent to morality? But it is possible to draw on Croce's ideas in logic and ethics without accepting his monism; and one can learn a great deal from his aesthetics without accepting his early insensitivity to art's ethical quality. After 1917 his aesthetical ideas became virtually indistinguishable from Babbitt's. Philosophical discussions are never served by rigid prejudgments of what is to be found in various thinkers. Ideas contain potentialities for development in sometimes unexpected directions.

This book offers some extensive criticisms of Babbitt, many of them along lines suggested by Croce's philosophy. Part One is devoted mainly to identifying weaknesses in Babbitt's position and to supplementing his ideas. Attention is drawn in particular to deficiencies in Babbitt's understanding of the nature of reason. This criticism and revision is needed in part to explicate the main strengths of Babbitt's general position, which is done in Part Two. Because of the order of presentation, the impression may initially prevail that Croce is the superior thinker. Rather, the net effect of comparing and synthesizing the two men's ideas is to demonstrate the essential soundness of Babbitt's thought where it matters most. Not only are the weaknesses in his treatment of epistemological issues balanced by significant insights in that same field; it can also be argued that, in the search for reality, technical philosophical brilliance

is less important in the end than having ethical wisdom. Babbitt reveals a deep and subtle awareness of the fundamental
problem of ethics and its relationship to the problem of knowledge. That Babbitt pays inadequate attention to some questions
of epistemology and is disinclined to take up sustained technical philosophical analyses can be attributed in large measure
to his belief that grasping reality is ultimately dependent on
man's *willing* what he ought to will. For all of Croce's intellectual brilliance, he betrays a lack of ethical sensitivity. Even
though a critic of much of Hegel's work, Croce is a captive still
of the German philosopher's monistic-pantheistic tendency to
explain away the reality of evil. According to Babbitt, Croce
"combines numerous peripheral merits with a central wrong-
ness and at times with something that seems uncomfortably
like a central void."[2] Read as an assessment of Croce's work
as a whole, this is an unfair and exaggerated statement; most
of Croce's philosophical insights are anything but peripheral.
The statement is typical of Babbitt's habit of judging thinkers
primarily by their ability to discern adequately the ethical
dimension of problems, a habit which sometimes makes him
discount—or seem to discount—merits in other areas. Yet his
comment on Croce is not without truth. In respect to what is
most important to the central soundness of a philosophy of life,
the synthesis of Babbitt and Croce must be achieved largely on
the terms of the former. Croce is regarded here as providing
a very enlightening supplement and corrective to Babbitt, rather
than vice versa.

Through the explication and critical assessment of Babbitt,
with special reference to Croce, this book develops a theory of
reality and knowledge. The central thesis presented is that
knowledge of reality rests upon a certain orientation of the will
and upon the corresponding quality of imagination (intuition)
that the will begets. Reason is dependent for the truth and comprehensiveness of its concepts on the depth and scope of the
material that it receives from the imagination. Babbitt's important contribution is the doctrine that only the highest form of

2. Irving Babbitt, *Spanish Character and Other Essays* (Boston: Houghton Mifflin,
1940), 66.

the imagination—which he regards as sustained and anchored in ultimate reality by ethical will—pulls man towards a comprehensive and proportionate view of life. Conversely, immoral desire distorts our imaginative vision and, hence, our sense of reality. Synthesizing Babbitt's ethico-aesthetical ideas and elements of Croce's logic, the book argues that an important source of faulty philosophical reasoning is misleading intuition which misdirects the attention of reason. Because man's grasp of life is seen as enhanced or distorted according to the underlying orientation of the will, considerable attention is given to Babbitt's ethical doctrine and Croce's philosophy of the practical. If the book puts much emphasis on the intuitive and practical aspects of knowing as something poorly understood in contemporary philosophy, it also argues for renewed confidence in reason. An integral part of the epistemological thesis is a revised understanding of the nature of reason. The philosophy of human life, it is suggested, employs reason of a different kind than pragmatic or positivistic rationality. Genuinely philosophical reason has the capacity for discerning and formulating the universal dimensions of life. Still, reason is not ahistorical. This book rejects prevalent formal and abstract notions of logic in favor of dialectical logic. Philosophical reason joins the universal and the historical. The coexistence in philosophical reason of the universal and the concrete particular points to the aforementioned bond between reason and intuition.

The human consciousness forms an organic whole. A philosophical account of a particular element of experience must set it in the larger context of life and hence relate it, implicitly or explicitly, to other elements. An adequate understanding of either will, imagination or reason requires that they be viewed together—that is, systematically. The universals of philosophy are distinct categories within a larger whole. The essence of the theory of knowledge here developed lies in the theory's definitions of will, imagination and reason, and of their relations to each other.

The complexity of the subject matter presents unusually difficult problems of organization. The intricacy of the relationship between the relevant problems of ethics, aesthetics and logic requires much movement back and forth between these areas. Because philosophy is systematic, all the chapters in a philosophical treatise in a way presuppose each other. Insight is not gained by a process of mere addition. Concepts formulated in certain pages are ideas in the making, anticipations of the clearer view which can be provided only by the work in its entirety. Particular formulations are seen in hindsight to have been manifestations of the overall thesis and to be in this sense indistinguishable from ideas presented later or earlier. Attempts fully to explain the placing of a chapter or section here or there are attempts to write the entire work before it is written. The reader of this book, if sometimes wondering about the order of exposition, may rest assured that the material has been carefully arranged to make as clear as possible the distinctions and relations which constitute the book's philosophical substance.

Part One of the book develops the notion of philosophical reason. It does so by distinguishing this reason from will and imagination, as well as from pragmatic rationality. These discussions set the stage for Part Two, which concentrates on explaining the epistemological significance of Babbitt's understanding of the relationship between will and imagination.

Babbitt's grounding of the search for reality in a transcendent moral order has some parallels or counterparts among thinkers of recent decades, as exemplified by American social and political thought. With varying emphases and degrees of success, this line of inquiry has been pursued by thinkers as diverse as John Hallowell, Russell Kirk, Reinhold Niebuhr, Leo Strauss, Peter Viereck, Eliseo Vivas and Eric Voegelin. The efforts of these writers appear to have had little influence on the development of philosophy in the broader and stricter sense. With rare exceptions, they have not formed part of a sustained attempt to develop a comprehensive and precisely formulated philosophy.

Because of what usually passes as reason in most contemporary philosophy, technical philosophical inquiries are often viewed with suspicion as likely to play into the hands of moral nihilism or relativism. It is not uncommon, as in the case of

Viereck, Kirk and even Voegelin, to appeal to experience or intuition rather than to conceptual reason as support for the existence of a universal moral order, a position that is not false but insufficient. If experience gives evidence of a transcendent moral order, it needs to be explained how we gain *knowledge* of that order. How is the moral order related to conceptual thought? And what is the relationship of both of these to intuition? The need to explore these issues in depth runs counter to a rather common prejudice, particularly in the Anglo-Saxon countries, against "systematic" thought. Speculation of that type is believed to be indicative of a closed, dogmatic system. But no claim to final knowledge need be implied in the view that philosophy proper studies its subjects within the context of the larger whole to which they belong. On the contrary, the complexity and limited transparency of that whole induces intellectual humility.

Strauss and most of his followers are among those who affirm a distinction between good and evil in the name of reason and philosophy. But what they call philosophy is usually rather narrow in scope and quite general in formulation. Hence, one may question whether they have really come to philosophical grips with the deepest challenges of modernity. Are the epistemologies of Plato or Aristotle still essentially adequate? Or have the more than two thousand years of philosophical speculation since their time yielded substantial new insight adding to or making necessary the rearticulation and revision of their central ideas? The laudable wish to uphold the existence of universal values is hardly best served by attempting a return to premodern ways of thought. Being philosophically modern does not have to mean espousal of what undermines universality. The most truly modern thinker may be one who is profoundly respectful of ancient insights while understanding that philosophical knowledge is a grasp of the universal forever in need of clarification and restatement.

In order to gain a strong foothold in philosophy, contemporary intellectual efforts to restore a sense of man's transcendent moral purpose need to give more attention to fundamental philosophical problems and particularly to questions of epistemology. A willingness to consider that the last two centuries have brought forward some very fruitful new ideas, as well as much decadence, may produce results surprisingly compatible with central classical and medieval beliefs. Since all genuine philosophy is systematic, attempts to develop a theory of knowledge are likely to give greater depth and precision also to our understanding of the transcendent moral order.

Part One

Chapter 1
The Ethical Will and Reality

Babbitt's view of human existence is anchored in his idea of the higher will. He regards the higher will as ultimately constitutive not only of man's happiness but of his ability to gain knowledge of the essence of life. An examination of Babbitt's ethical doctrine is hence given priority in the task of defining will, imagination and reason and their interaction in the acquisition of knowledge.

According to Babbitt, attempts by modern philosophy to solve the problem of knowledge rest on a vain belief in abstract rationality as the way to truth. These attempts signify a failure to understand that, in the end, man will attach himself only to a standard of reality that has immediacy and concreteness—that is, one firmly established in experience. Thinking specifically of the failure of epistemology, Babbitt is moved to the sweeping and indiscriminate statement that "modern philosophy is bankrupt, not merely from Kant, but from Descartes." Babbitt's doctrine of the ethical (and aesthetical) basis of man's search for reality is, among other things, a contribution to the development of a new theory of knowledge. (RR,9)[1]

Instead of taking ideas on authority, modern man proposes to submit them to the test of experience. Babbitt is willing to accept this challenge and to adopt what he calls "the positive and critical spirit." He also insists that what is typically meant by "experience" in the modern world is artificially restricted. Babbitt accuses representatives of the modern project of being

1. Irving Babbitt, *Rousseau and Romanticism* (Austin: University of Texas Press, 1977; first published in 1919), 9; hereinafter referred to in the text as "RR." The introduction to this book is one of many places where Babbitt calls attention to the epistemological relevance of his ethical and aesthetical ideas.

"incomplete positivists." They are not really attentive to the full range of human experience but arbitrarily select fragments of it or distort it through methodological reductionism. Babbitt points out that human experience, now and over the centuries, provides a vast array of evidence regarding the nature of man, including evidence of a universal moral order. This experience must be examined on its own ground.

More than anywhere else, man discovers the essence of reality in ethical action. Such action, Babbitt contends, realizes the ultimate meaning of life and is its own reward. An admirer of Plato and especially of Aristotle, Babbitt is at the same time critical of the Greek tendency to equate virtue and intellectual knowledge. He sees in Christianity a deeper ethical wisdom, more fully attuned to the centrality of will and to the need for man to take on the discipline of a higher will. As a representative of the Orient rather than the more intellectualistic West, Jesus of Nazareth does not present man with a new philosophy, to be tested on abstract intellectual grounds. Jesus asks men to follow him—that is, to perform Christ-like actions. Genuine religion and morality, Babbitt argues, is most importantly exercise of good will, a path of striving. Without in some way entering upon that path, and thus undertaking a gradual transformation of character, the individual will be unable to perceive the reality of the path, which is first of all a reality of practice.

In contrast to theories that tend to make moral virtue a problem of intellection, Babbitt's thesis stresses the human proclivity for moral procrastination, the lethargy or intractability of the will that keeps the individual from moral action. Theorizing about the nature of moral virtue will not bring the individual much closer to understanding those values unless he also has some experience of them in concrete action. Philosophizing about the good can easily become an excuse or pretext for not doing what is always more difficult, namely getting on with the task of good action. The crux of the ethical life, Babbitt argues, is not acquiring definitive theoretical knowledge of the good, which is beyond man, but the ability to *act* on whatever ethical insight one does have. As man grows in character and performs new good actions, the light of reality streaming forth from these actions will brighten. Theoretical doubts regarding the existence or nature of the universal good will tend to evaporate. Summarizing the contribution of the Christian teaching of the Incarnation to solving the problem of knowledge, Babbitt observes, "The final reply to all the doubts that torment the human heart is not some theory of conduct, however perfect, but the man of character." The man of good action embodies, or "incarnates," in himself the reality of the eternal. (DL, 197)[2]

Babbitt agrees with Aristotle that truly virtuous action finds its own justification in the satisfaction of happiness, which must be carefully distinguished from passing moments of mere pleasure. In the specifically religious sphere, the result of moral striving is peace. In both cases, man comes to know concretely something of the ultimate purpose and meaning of human existence. What is meant by happiness or peace cannot be understood by anyone wholly lacking in personal experience of moral action. The happy life of the mean described in *The Nicomachean Ethics* is achieved gradually, not simply through intellectual deliberation, but primarily through ethical action that transforms character. Volumes of good ethical philosophy will mean little to their reader unless the terms used find referents in personal life and help the reader better to understand his own experience. What is true of humanistic self-understanding is true also of religious self-understanding. In Babbitt's words, "Knowledge in matters religious waits upon will." (D)[3] To submit questions of truth or falsity to the test of experience means to judge them ultimately from the point of view of life's completion in good action. To Babbitt, the final

2. Irving Babbitt, *Democracy and Leadership* (Boston: Houghton Mifflin, 1952; first published in 1924), 171-72; hereinafter referred to in the text as "DL." On the ultimacy of will in Babbitt's thought, see Folke Leander, *Humanism and Naturalism* (Göteborg: Göteborgs Högskola, 1937), Ch. X. For a discussion of the historical concretization of what is ethically universal, see Claes G. Ryn, "History and the Moral Order," in Francis J. Canavan (ed.), *The Ethical Dimension of Political Life* (Durham: Duke University Press, 1983).

3. *The Dhammapada*, Translated and with an Essay by Irving Babbitt (New York: New Directions, 1965; first published in 1936), 109; hereinafter referred to in the text as "D."

criterion of reality is the special type of willing that by its very nature satisfies man's deepest yearning. This is the meaning of his statement that the epistemological problem, "though it cannot be solved abstractly or metaphysically, can be solved practically and in terms of actual conduct." (RR, 9)

As "the supreme maxim" for a modern respect for experience Babbitt proposes the words of Jesus, "By their fruits shall ye know them." Thinkers who are hostile to all traditional authority and who blindly reject the insights common to the great religious and ethical systems of mankind will produce certain practical consequences. As their ideas are put into practice, these theorists will bring upon others and themselves a sense of life's absurdity and misery. Those, by contrast, who are willing to undertake some of the action called for by the older traditions (if not to accept the literal meaning of inherited dogmas) will grow to appreciate the ultimate reality and happiness of life. If absolute knowledge must forever elude man, Babbitt writes, "we may still determine on experimental grounds to what degree any particular view of life is sanctioned or repudiated by the nature of things and rate it accordingly as more or less real." (DL, 14)

It must be left for later treatment but may be noted in passing that in stressing the ultimacy of the practical criterion of reality, Babbitt sometimes unduly discounts—or at least appears to discount—the contribution of reason to man's search for reality. Speaking of the path of religious striving, he says, "The end of this path and the goal of being cannot be formulated in terms of the finite intellect, any more than the ocean can be put into a cup." (RR, 125) This statement would appear to push intellectual humility to an extreme. Yet, if reason is so utterly powerless as Babbitt indicates here, by what faculty is he observing and articulating the shortcomings of the "finite intellect"? In his essay on the *Dhammapada* and in other places, Babbitt does formulate the nature of the religious "path and goal of being." Does he then not have at his disposal a reason which is more powerful and more comprehensive than the "finite intellect" mentioned in the quotation? All of the arguments and concepts presented in his various books—the prac-

tical criterion of reality, the higher and the lower will, etc.
—assume an intellect capable of significant observation.

Inasmuch as Babbitt regards ethical action as the final answer
to questions of reality, it is necessary to examine in some depth
his idea of the higher will, or "inner check," a subject poorly
understood by most of his interpreters. Babbitt's doctrine is
summed up in these words: "I do not hesitate to affirm that
what is specifically human in man and ultimately divine is a
certain quality of will, a will that is felt in its relation to his ordinary self as a will to refrain." In most of Babbitt's work, the
main emphasis is on defining the higher will in its humanistic
manifestation. In *Democracy and Leadership*, he explains that his
"interest in the higher will and the power of veto it exercises
over man's expansive desires is humanistic rather than religious." (DL, 6) Babbitt's ideas regarding the humanistic role
of the higher will are similar in some respects to the traditional
doctrine of natural law. The latter recognizes a standard of good
intrinsic to human life to which man has access independently
of special revelation. But while the tradition of natural law tends
to conceive what is universal and normative in terms of principles of reason, Babbitt conceives what is universal and normative in terms of will. In the ethical life the authority to which
man ultimately defers is not a set of conceptual propositions
but a special power of will which finally transcends efforts at
exhaustive intellectual definition.

Babbitt develops a dualistic view of human nature. Life
presents us with the mystery of the One and the Many. Our
most immediate awareness of reality is simultaneous order and
disorder. Life is not a flux of unrelated impressions; it is an
ordered flux. "Life does not give here an element of oneness
and there an element of change. It gives a *oneness that is always
changing*. The oneness and the change are inseparable." (RR,
7) Set apart from the flux, and yet also in it, is a power which
orders life to a purpose. Man is a unity of opposing inclinations.
He is, in Babbitt's terminology, a lower and a higher self. He
is drawn, on the one hand, into impulses destructive of
individual and social harmony, but he is able, on the other
hand, to structure his impulses toward the opposite goal of

community. Of primary importance to Babbitt, as to Plato, is the moral dimension of the tension at the core of existence. Standing against the human desires in their endless diversity is an unvarying sense of higher moral purpose which transcends all particular impulses. The same in all men, this sense harmonizes the individual circumstances of each. By restraining the merely partisan, particularistic wishes present in human society, it brings men together at a common center of value. This moral ordering of life, in its aspect as a civilizing force, Babbitt calls humanistic self-control.

How is it that man is not just swept along by the stream of desires? The appearance of the inner check, Babbitt maintains, is finally a mystery, but it is an indisputable fact nevertheless. Although our finite intellect cannot fathom the "ultimate nature" of this ordering principle, it is known to us in immediate experience. "The higher will must simply be accepted as a mystery that may be studied in its practical effects . . ."[4] This special quality of will is experienced as a restraint on man's "ordinary self." The latter is Babbitt's term for the impulsive life as unordered by moral considerations. The tendency to act in a self-indulgent manner, without regard for the good of the whole, he also calls, depending on the context, the "lower," "natural," or "temperamental" self. To the extent that man rises above his ordinary self by acting from inside the inner check, the latter becomes more firmly established, not only as an irrefutable fact of experience, but as the very source and center of meaningful life.

Babbitt's theory of the "inner check" has led to vast misunderstanding. Does he mean that morality consists of completely negative action, some sort of ascetic self-denial? One of the reasons why the concept of the inner check has caused so much confusion is that Babbitt's readers have frequently failed to put it in the proper context. He employs the term in opposition to ethical doctrines that would forget the duality of human nature

---

4. Irving Babbitt, "Humanism: An Essay at Definition," in Norman Foerster (ed.), *Humanism and America* (Port Washington, N.Y.: Kennikat Press, 1967; first published in 1930), 40.

and identify the moral good with particular human sentiments and intentions. He is sharply critical, for instance, of the school of moral sense associated with Shaftesbury. Another of his main opponents is Jean-Jacques Rousseau, whose morality of the heart he sees as identifying the good with unrestrained impulse. Our moral will, Babbitt asserts repeatedly, must not be confused with gushes of "sympathy" or "pity." It is better described as an inhibition on our outgoing impulses. Arguing against "expansionists of every kind" (DL, 6), he distinguishes the ordering universal principle from what is ordered. Not only is the urge of the moment frequently in conflict with the good, so that morality requires an act of self-restraint; but when our impulses do harmonize with the moral end, which means that they are not censured by the inner check, they are still transcended by that ordering power itself. Morality, Babbitt insists, is a creation of will, an overcoming of obstacles. It is through spiritual activity, not through some easy yielding to the impulses of the moment, that good is brought into the world. Using the word "civilization" to describe the quality of existence made possible by the higher will, he writes: "Civilization is something that must be deliberately willed; it is not something that gushes up spontaneously from the depths of the unconscious. Furthermore, it is something that must be willed first of all by the individual in his own heart." (DL, 229) There are no shortcuts to the genuine values of social life. Tradition and social reform can aid, but never replace, individual moral effort.

In spite of Babbitt's emphasis on civilization and happiness as the fruits of humanistic exercise of the higher will, it has been alleged often that he has a purely negative conception of the good. A comment by Edmund Wilson is typical of this strangely unperceptive and careless reading of Babbitt: ". . . how can one take seriously a philosophy which enjoins nothing but negative behavior?"[5] In a similar vein, Allen Tate believes that he has exposed "the negative basis of Professor

5. Edmund Wilson, "Notes on Babbitt and More," in C. Hartley Grattan (ed.), *The Critique of Humanism* (New York: Brewer and Warren, 1930), 46.

Babbitt's morality. The good man is he who 'refrains from doing' what the 'lower nature dictates,' and he need do nothing positive.''[6] Henry Hazlitt writes, ''The insistence, you will notice, is always on the purely *negative* virtues.''[7] To some extent, this mistaken impression has been caused by Babbitt's repeated use of a particular term, ''the inner check,'' to describe the ethical will. His actual theory is that morality has two aspects, the renunciation and the affirmation of impulse. They form part of one and the same effort to realize good. In its relation to impulses that are destructive of our spiritual unity and hence of our happiness, the higher will is felt as a check; the moral purpose is advanced by censuring what is opposed to it. That Babbitt pays much attention to the ''negative'' side of morality is due to his assessment of what our time needs to hear the most. The main threat to the values of civilization today is not an excess of renunciation of the world, but an excessive, indiscriminate release of the ''expansive desires.'' Modern Western man has the greatest need to learn not that the good is achieved through affirmation of impulse (although that is a part of the truth), but that man's true humanity lies in his ability to put checks on his desires. In the Middle Ages, with its emphasis on otherworldliness, the point that good can be advanced through positive human acts would have deserved more attention.

In the person who, having followed Aristotle's admonition to develop sound habits, has acquired a taste for morality, the impulsive life tends to merge, without special effort, with the higher will. Realizing its intent through particular actions, the higher will becomes a feeling of acting in consonance with one's own true humanity. The result of bringing one's character into harmony with the universal good, Babbitt and Aristotle agree, is the special satisfaction of happiness. The creation of particular acts having universal value is the affirmative, ''posi-

6. Allen Tate, ''The Fallacy of Humanism,'' in Grattan (ed.), *Critique of Humanism*, 141.

7. Henry Hazlitt, ''Humanism and Value,'' in Grattan (ed.), *Critique of Humanism*, 95 (emphasis in original).

tive" side of the moral life. Even here, however, there is some justification for using the term "inner check" to describe man's higher will, for human acts are not simply identical to or exhaustive of what gives them ethical direction. Higher than particular instances of moral behavior, higher even than man's most noble acts, is the ultimate standard of perfection itself. The tension between immanent and transcendent is never completely removed. It should be noted also that willing is always an act of selection. To affirm what is moral is to negate possibilities of a different quality.[8]

Granted that self-discipline of some kind is necessary if man is not to get lost in chaos, must not that discipline be tied to some standard external to man himself? The principle of moral order, Babbitt contends, is found within the human self. But without an external norm of perfection, does not self-discipline have to be exercised at random? Throwing up his arms in puzzlement, T.S. Eliot exclaims, "What is the higher will to *will* . . .? If this will is to have anything on which to operate, it must be in relation to external objects and to objective values."[9] Eliot is familiar with Babbitt's view that, in its humanistic dimension, the inner check is "a will to civilization," but he has great difficulty finding any definite meaning in this idea. Babbitt's "civilization" appears to leave the goal of life an empty form.

It seems, on the face of it, to mean something definite; it is, in fact, merely a frame to be filled with definite objects, not a definite object itself. I do not believe that I can sit down for three minutes to will civilization without my mind's wandering to something else. I do not mean that civilization is a mere word; the word means something quite real. But the minds of the individuals who can be said to "have willed civilization" are minds filled with a great variety of objects of will, according to place, time, and individual constitution; what they have in common is rather a habit in the same direction

8. A more extensive analysis of the inner check as happiness and of its implications for social and political life is given in Claes G. Ryn, *Democracy and the Ethical Life* (Baton Rouge: Louisiana State University Press, 1978), esp. 75-80.
9. T.S. Eliot, *Selected Essays* (New York: Harcourt, Brace, 1960), 425 (emphasis in original).

than a will to civilization.[10]

This passage is clear evidence that Eliot has not grasped the meaning of Babbitt's "inner check." Ironically, Babbitt would agree almost completely with these sentences, which Eliot believes to be a refutation of his position. Babbitt wholeheartedly agrees that civilization is marked by the diversity of emphasis and perspective of those who contribute to it. Those who will civilization can indeed be said to be joined by "a habit in the same direction." Babbitt would say that it is a habit which brings unity into a multiplicity of activity. Eliot's mistake is opposing this "habit" to what Babbitt calls "the will to civilization." What Eliot has not understood is that civilization, as Babbitt understands it, is defined in its most important dimension by the special quality of will that brings it into existence, namely, "the inner check." This unifying ethical ordering can be described adequately also as "a habit in the same direction."

Perhaps "the inner check" can best be explained as the spirit in which men should act. In respect to ethics, two general ways of structuring conduct may be discerned. Immoral action is to insist on one's own merely private advantage or the advantage of one's own group to the detriment or neglect of everybody else. An infinite variety of particular choices may have this inspiration. A special case of the same basic category is to seek one's own selfish advantage in an enlightened manner. The intelligent egotist is sometimes willing to compromise with others as a means of securing his own maximum satisfaction over time. The other way to act, also containing within itself an infinite diversity of possible particular choices, is inspired by the genuine wish (in the sense of a "divine discontent") to

10. *Ibid.*, 426. Eliot's various criticisms of Babbitt should not conceal that he was also profoundly impressed and influenced by Babbitt as a thinker and as a person. A former student of his at Harvard, Eliot has commented as follows on Babbitt's forceful, idea-oriented instruction and work as a whole: "I do not believe that any pupil who was ever deeply impressed by Babbitt, can ever speak of him with that mild tenderness one feels towards something one has outgrown or grown out of. If one has once had that relationship with Babbitt, he remains permanently an active influence; his ideas are permanently with one, as a measurement and test of one's own." From a Memoir by T.S. Eliot in Frederick Manchester and Odell Shepard (eds.), *Irving Babbit, Man and Teacher* (New York: Greenwood Press, 1969; first published in 1941), 104.

rise above all partisanship and hence to act so as to elevate our common life in the direction of what is good for its own sake. The two ways of human action are thus defined in contradistinction to each other. There is a self in man whose nature it is to put individuals and groups in conflict with each other, be it peaceful or violent; and there is another self that tends to draw men into a more than apparent harmony with all who are similarly motivated. It is the spirit of the latter self, at once individual and supra-individual, that Babbitt terms ''the inner check.''

It should be made explicit that in viewing the inner check as the unifying principle of civilization, Babbitt takes it for granted that there are other aspects of the work of civilization than moral effort. But to him the final measure of progress is the extent to which the various pursuits of society, such as science, art and politics, advance the moral end of goodness.

The goal of civilization does stay forever indefinite or ''open'' in the sense that the higher will is manifested in the unique circumstances of emerging situations. It is not possible to predefine the concrete specifics of good actions. In another sense, however, the end is *not* indefinite. All truly moral acts are performed in one and the same spirit—that is, with the same intent. Man's higher self always wills the same special quality of life, which can be created when selfishness is restrained. Civilization refers to something quite definite: the good life of community. But the particulars of that quality of life depend on the circumstances out of which the higher will is trying to shape good. The universal higher will does not work in the abstract, but rather through the concrete material of given situations.

The moral effort of individual men is likely to be aided by their ability to work in the context of sound tradition. The individual is never saved from moral perplexity by such favorable conditions; he has to create his own moral synthesis out of the universal imperative experienced by him and the unique situation he faces. Still, that synthesis is helped along by the general directives contained in the inherited norms of the civilized society, which carry forward the insights of generations. The individual's attempt to articulate ethical intuition in particular situations can draw on these earlier attempts to give concrete form to man's sense of higher purpose. In the process, tradition is transcended and renewed. What Babbitt calls "the will to civilization" is the eternal spirit of good in which man should create new behavior. It is itself the "external" standard for which Eliot sees a need. Though "internal" in the sense that it is concretely experienced by individual men, it is "external" in that it transcends the past and all individual circumstances and in that it is never exhausted by human action.

A particularly confused rendering of Babbitt's thought has been offered by Allen Tate. Babbitt's morality, Tate alleges, "is only an arbitrarily individualistic *check upon itself*. . . ."[11] This interpretation, insofar as it is intelligible, is wholly misleading. T.S. Eliot, too, although reading Babbitt more sympathetically, is suspicious of his view that man's humanity has its own intrinsic standard of perfection, which can be ascertained without relying on "outer" authority, such as Church doctrine. This notion, Eliot argues, is an invitation to arbitrariness. The source of order must be outside the individual. "The sum of a population of individuals, all ideally and efficiently checking and controlling themselves, will never make a whole. And if you distinguish so sharply between 'outer' and 'inner' checks as Mr. Babbitt does, then there is nothing left for the individual to check himself by but his own private notions and his judgment, which is pretty precarious."[12]

Babbitt agrees that there is always a tendency in man to act according to his own "private notions" and generally with an egocentric bias. What Eliot fails to grasp is that *it is on precisely this inclination that the higher will is a check*. In other words, it is by virtue of the inner check that man becomes aware of his partisan ego. The higher will is the universal good reaching into

11. Tate, "Fallacy of Humanism," 145 (emphasis in original). This polemical essay compares unfavorably with interpretations of Babbitt by other Catholic writers. Although Tate gave the impression of criticizing Babbitt in the name of Christianity, he was apparently only nominally a Christian when he wrote what has been quoted. On Tate's religious development, see Monroe Spear, "The Criticism of Allen Tate," in Radcliffe Squires (ed.), *Allen Tate and His Work* (Minneapolis: University of Minnesota Press, 1972).

12. Eliot, *Selected Essays*, 424.

individual men and pulling them toward itself. Censuring what is selfish and arbitrary, this will is the very principle of truly communal relations. To the extent that it is active, it does have the effect of turning "a population of individuals" into "a whole." "The individual who is practising humanistic control is really subordinating to the part of himself which he possesses in common with other men, that part of himself which is driving him apart from them."[13] Those who take on that discipline are harmonizing their lives with reference to the same center of value and moving toward communion. A specifically Christian way of describing this same self-discipline would be to speak of men being unified in love. Like the higher will, Christian love is not some arbitrary individual power but a transcendent spirit in which men can act and which defines what is arbitrary and selfish by shunning it.

Babbitt readily grants that the higher will is external to man in the sense of his "ordinary" or "natural" self. But our humanity, Babbitt argues, is not just man's "ordinary" self. To be human is to be able to impose order on the flux, most importantly to give moral structure to life. Traditional Christianity—particularly Protestantism—maintains that it is by God's grace that man is able to rise out of sin. Babbitt makes it clear that within the context of Christianity the doctrine of grace is indispensable to the moral life. When speaking within that framework, he even equates his notion of the higher will with grace.[14] The idea of grace is a special Christian theological formulation of the experience of a higher power inspiring human action.

In the United States, attempts to understand Babbitt's idea of a self-validating higher will frequently have centered on his view of religion. Because Babbitt tries to deal with religious truth in a positive and critical manner, without relying on dogma, and because, like the tradition of natural law, he also ascribes a certain moral autonomy to the humanistic level of life, critics

13. Babbitt, "Humanism," 49.
14. See the "Introduction" to Irving Babbitt, *On Being Creative* (New York: Biblo and Tannen, 1968; first published in 1932); hereinafter referred to in the text as "OBC."

like Eliot and Tate have accused him of deprecating religion and
the transcendent. Such interpretations miss the point of Babbitt's approach to ethical questions. He explicitly states: "It is
an error to hold that humanism can take the place of religion.
Religion indeed may more readily dispense with humanism
than humanism with religion. Humanism gains greatly by having a religious background . . . whereas religion, for the man
who has actually renounced the world, may very conceivably
be all in all."[15] Babbitt also spends much time explicating the
specifically religious spirit of otherworldliness. What he questions is not the reality of the divine but the necessity, and the
prudence in modern intellectual circumstances, of tying it
closely to inherited creeds or dogmas. Those who complain that
Babbitt does not embrace a particular theology ignore the difference between revelation and philosophic-scientific observation,
devotional literature and scholarship. Although a sharp, definitive distinction cannot be drawn between them, special criteria
of knowledge obtain for the scholar. The truth of religion, Babbitt believes, does not have to be taken on doctrinal authority;
it can be judged critically, by its fruits. If it were necessary, in
order to speak meaningfully about religion, first to adopt a particular formal creed—say, that of Christianity—all real discussion with Jews, Buddhists, Hindus and others would have to
await their conversion to that creed. The obstacle to serious
debate would be even greater, for Christians themselves would
have to reach agreement on the precise meaning of the creed.
But religious dogmas, Babbitt points out, are in part an attempt
to express what is also a living reality of practice and intuition.
In matters of religion, as in matters of humanism, a vast body
of historical experience is available to the scholar which provides the basis for an ecumenical knowledge and wisdom.

Religious denominations claiming a privileged insight beyond
what can be verified in the actual experience of mankind have
no reason to feel threatened by such philosophic-scientific
examination of the spiritual evidence; they can add to the latter their own revelatory vision. Babbitt freely admits that the-

15. Babbitt, "Humanism," 43-44. Similar statements are made by Babbitt elsewhere,
e.g., in *Rousseau and Romanticism*, 287.

ological dogmas may contain truth beyond what can be established critically on the basis of experience. "Many other things are true, no doubt, in addition to what one may affirm positively; and 'extra-beliefs' are in any case inevitable." (DL, 225) Babbitt recognizes the possible value of dogmas and creeds in bringing forth the fruits of religion. Man's religious symbols sometimes convey a deep sense of the mystery beyond themselves, and, as material for the ethical imagination, they may inspire right conduct. But religious symbols can also succumb to fundamentalistic reification. Formalistic and literalistic hardening is a sign that they are losing contact with reality. Here, as in many other respects, Babbitt anticipates Eric Voegelin. Discussing what he sees as legitimate discontent with Christian metaphysics and theology in the eighteenth and nineteenth centuries, Voegelin points to "the gulf between symbols and experiences" and the concomitant "atrophied dogma." In general Voegelin warns of "deforming doctrinalization" which separates symbols from "the originating experiences."[16]

Babbitt raises the important question, "whether one's religiousness is to be measured by the degree to which one brings forth the 'fruits of the spirit' or by one's theological affirmations." (OBC, xxxiii) Submitting to an external religious authority is not necessarily an act of devotion. It may express a flaw of character in individuals of unstable and relativistic romantic temperament. Inner uncertainty and flux crave outer certainty and order. Babbitt speaks of the affinity of the jellyfish for the rock. Seemingly pious adherence to external norms may in fact signify an escape from what is more difficult, the actual improvement of character. Behind the reverential pose there is no genuine conversion, but all the more chronic self-pity and half-heartedness. Professions of sinfulness can be a delicious enjoyment of what, with one's lips, one feigns to deplore. At the extreme, "faith" becomes everything, "works" nothing. Peter Viereck, a thinker deeply influenced by Babbitt, says of the "pious intolerance" of certain modern proponents of religious orthodoxy that it can be seen as an attempt by per-

16. Eric Voegelin, *The Ecumenic Age* (Baton Rouge: Louisiana State University Press, 1974), 266; 58.

sons who are still at bottom relativists "to shout down that nagging inner voice of doubt."[17] An individual who is more secure in his own character will not feel quite the same need to submit formalistically to external authority. Obviously, Babbitt's concern is not to do away with authority; the importance of sound leadership is a central theme in his work. His reservations here pertain to doctrinal and personal rigidity born of neglect of the primacy of ethical effort. He offers the educated guess that Buddhism, with its non-dogmatic religiosity, has had as many saints as Christianity. He adds that it has been "less marred than Christianity by intolerance and fanaticism." (OBC, xxxiv) An ethically maturing person may well derive a heightened sense of reality from the rich religious traditions of mankind, or of a particular Church, but this is because their symbols and practices find referents in actual experience and can expand and deepen that experience.

A person of fundamentalist inclination may feel compelled to say that in religious matters we can defer only to God, never to man, not even to what Babbitt calls man's higher will. That kind of reaction is indicative of misunderstanding Babbitt's argument or failing to view it in its own terms. To be able to defer to the authority of God, man must somehow be aware of that authority. To exist for man as a living concrete reality, the authority of God must have entered human consciousness. To that extent it is a part of man's self-awareness. It is to indicate the universal authority of that power within human experience that Babbitt calls it man's higher self or higher will. If that use of words is objected to because it appears to build up man at the expense of God, the effect of the complaint is to draw attention away from the experiential facts themselves and to substitute statements of faith for philosophical inquiry. Babbitt is less interested in how to name the presence of the good than in accurately describing its observable influence on man. What others, relying on theological assumptions, might

17. Peter Viereck, *Shame and Glory of the Intellectuals* (New York: Capricorn, 1965), 46. Viereck has in mind, among others, the clerical-minded T.S. Eliot, who is seen as having within himself also a romantic modernist. Cf. Babbitt, *Rousseau and Romanticism*, 205.

prefer to call the work of divine grace in man, Babbitt speaks of ecumenically and non-dogmatically as the exercise of the higher will.

Many modern Westerners reject Christianity because inherited creeds have no authority for them. According to Babbitt these Westerners must, if they are to be true to "the positive and critical spirit," still consider the experiential evidence. In his explication of the prerequisites for bringing forth the "fruits of the spirit," Babbitt not only prepares the way for a modern recovery of religious and ethical truth but also for a recovery that is as free as possible of aesthetic posturing and of secret reservations and doubts.

In most of his writing Babbitt is concerned "less with the meditation in which true religion always culminates, than in the mediation or observance of the law of measure that should govern man in his secular relations." (DL, 6) Babbitt's reason for giving more attention to the elements of humanistic discipline than to the specifically religious discipline of the saintly life is his belief that "the world would have been a better place if more persons had made sure they were human before setting out to be superhuman."[18] To be civilized is difficult enough —indeed, has frequently proved too difficult even for those who have had at their disposal the guidance of sound tradition.

As humanistic discipline, the inner check establishes those secular relations which harmonize and enrich man's "worldly" existence. But the exercise of the higher will "may be carried much further until it amounts to a turning away from the desires of the natural man altogether—the 'dying to the world' of the Christian."[19] The heart of religion is the spirit of other-worldliness as embodied in Christ and the saints. "My kingdom is not of this world." The charity in which religion culminates is a special manifestation of the inner check beyond even the highest moral aspirations of civilization. Given the flawed nature of man, the good life of civilization and justice means something less exalted than turning the other cheek or

18. Babbitt, "Humanism," 28-29.
19. *Ibid.*, 47.

walking the extra mile.

Though humanism and religion both lie on the same ascending path from the naturalistic flux, one must insist that each has its separate domain. . . . [T]he man who sets out to live religously in the secular order without having recourse to the wisdom of the humanist is likely to fall into vicious confusions—notably, into a confusion between the things of God and the things of Caesar. The Catholic Church has therefore been well inspired in rounding out its religious doctrine with the teaching of Aristotle and other masters of the law of measure.[20]

Those who have not sufficiently experienced and acted on the higher will in either of its two manifestations will forever dispute its final reality, claiming that there are only subjective or conventional standards of good. On the other hand, for those who seek to exercise that special quality of will, life is a growth in happiness or peace. To them, denial of the reality of the higher self becomes the height of unreality.

In summarizing this chapter's findings, it should be stressed, first, that Babbitt finds the ultimate criterion of reality in the universal ordering power of the higher will. To know the essence of life man must act to change his character. Without the sense of reality that comes with the exercise of the higher will no adequate perception of life is possible. Second, while Babbitt affirms a universal standard of good, he emphasizes the scholarly need in the modern world of establishing its existence on "experimental" grounds. According to Babbitt, the proper procedure in refuting modern positivists "is not to appeal to some dogma or outer authority but rather to turn against them their own principles." (RR, 5)

The modernists have broken with tradition partly because it is not sufficiently immediate, partly because it is not sufficiently experimental. Why not meet them on their own ground and, having got rid of every ounce of unnecessary metaphysical and theological baggage, oppose to them some-

---

20. *Ibid.*, 43-44. For a more extensive discussion of the relationship between humanism and specifically religious life which is related to Babbitt's approach, see Claes G. Ryn, "The Things of Caesar," *Thought*, Vol. 55 (December 1980).

thing that is both immediate and experimental—namely the presence in man of a higher will or power of control? I use the word experimental deliberately by way of protest against the undue narrowing of this word by the scientific naturalists to observation of the phenomenal order and of man only in so far as he comes under this order.[21]

The reality of our "inner life," including the higher will, is more securely established in immediate experience than are the assumptions of behavioral or physical science. In a later chapter it will be necessary to question Babbitt's claim to be turning against the positivists their own principles; his "experimental" approach and appeal to experience is "positivist" only in the loosest sense. Here it should only be noted that Babbitt disapproves of an ethical and religious traditionalism that does not come to terms with the modern commitment to critical inquiry.

According to Mr. Walter Lippmann, the conviction the modern man has lost is that "there is an immortal essence presiding like a king over his appetites." But why abandon the affirmation of such an "essence" or higher will, to the mere traditionalist? Why not affirm it first of all as . . . one of the immediate data of consciousness, a perception so primordial that, compared with it, the deterministic denials of man's moral freedom are only a metaphysical dream? One would thus be in a position to perform a swift flanking movement on the behaviourists and other naturalistic psychologists who are to be regarded at present as among the chief enemies of human nature.[22]

Babbitt wants to retain the modern emphasis on experiential verification. Yet he broadens and transforms that emphasis by giving primary attention to the knowledge of our own humanity that presents itself directly and from within, rather than indirectly and through externally applied schemes of causal explanation.

21. Babbitt, "Humanism," 44-45.
22. *Ibid.*, 39.

Chapter 2
The Challenge of Modern Aesthetics

The epistemological thesis of this book requires defining the nature and interaction of will, imagination and reason. The analysis of Babbitt's ethical doctrine in relation to problems of reality and knowledge has provided a working definition of the role of will. It is time to turn to the imagination. That subject receives much penetrating attention in the modern aesthetical doctrines discussed by Babbitt. By examining his relationship to the modern notion of the imagination, especially as influenced by German thought, this chapter takes the first step in explaining Babbitt's aesthetical position. It advances the epistemological objective by starting to criticize and supplement his thought and lay the groundwork for the proposed synthesis of Babbitt and Croce.

The chief accomplishment of modern aesthetics is probably the notion of the creative imagination. This doctrine breaks in important ways with long–dominant theories centered on a mimetic notion of art. Greek philosophy was too rationalistic to offer more than vague and scattered anticipations of the aesthetical doctrine that began to emerge in the eighteenth century. Contrary to what is widely assumed, Irving Babbitt accepts the idea of the creative imagination; indeed, with his own amendments, he emphatically affirms it. His thought is influenced in this respect, as in others, by modern philosophy. Yet, he seems unaware of the extent of his indebtedness. He does not do justice to the philosophical developments, including the work of Kant, which prepared the way for the new idea of imagination. His failure to do so accounts in part for his indiscriminate condemnation of "romanticism." The unfortunate prejudice against anything smacking of romanticism makes

Babbitt overreact also against his contemporary, Croce, who is far closer to him than he imagines.

In *History of Europe in the Nineteenth Century,* Croce distinguishes between two aspects of what historically has been called romanticism. One of these Ernest Seillière has labelled *le mal romantique;* the other aspect comprises certain philosophical truths which were being discovered at the end of the eighteenth and the beginning of the nineteenth centuries. Croce intimates that these two sides of romanticism were essentially separate, and that they have been grouped together only because they coincided in time. The student of Irving Babbitt may think of Edmund Burke and his influence, although Croce does not mention him. Burke's insights are not diminished because they were often twisted into a "romantic," reactionary medievalism, especially in Germany. Croce views as a very fruitful development the sowing of the seeds for a new aesthetics in the eighteenth century. No matter how "romantic" in the bad sense was the inspiration of many of the individuals who worked out this new aesthetics, what was true in their arguments cannot be brushed aside. Highly sensitive to and critical of the element of decadence in romanticism, Babbitt does not give adequate attention to possibly valid philosophical insights associated with the same movement. To his many dichotomies Babbitt should have added one of the word romanticism. There are hints toward such a dichotomy in his work, but they are not sufficient to dispel an impression of onesidedness.

In 1925 Babbitt published a review essay dealing with books by Croce and an Introduction contributed by Croce to a work by Gentile. Babbitt writes, "Croce . . . seems to be aware of something seriously wrong with the present situation. In the Introduction to *The Reform of Education* by his fellow 'idealist' Giovanni Gentile, he makes a plea for a 'new Christianity' or a 'new Humanism,' and goes on to express the hope that we may thus be rescued 'from intellectual anarchy, from unbridled individualism, from sensualism, from skepticism, from pessimism, from every aberration which for a century and a half has been harassing the soul of man and the society of mankind

under the name of Romanticism.''' (SC, 67-68)[1] Croce's words
are from the Introduction especially added to the *American* edition of Gentile's book. Considering also that in 1921 Croce had
written a very friendly and appreciative article about Babbitt's
The New Laokoon (1910), it is virtually certain that Croce had Babbitt in mind when writing this passage.[2] He wanted to express
his sympathy for Babbitt's campaign, perhaps in order to initiate
an exchange of opinions on issues still separating the two men.
A writer less dogged than Babbitt in exposing romantic leanings would have responded to Croce in an encouraging manner, but Babbitt's review continues as follows.

> This is a ringing manifesto; unfortunately, coming from
> Croce, it does not ring true. The Hegelian idea of devel-
> opment which he has adopted in an extreme form is, as he
> himself points out, a culminating expression of the roman-
> tic movement in philosophy. Moreover, the work of Vico,
> perhaps his chief spiritual ancestor next to Hegel, is in his
> own phrase a "rich and organic anticipation of romantic
> thought." In general, nothing could be more romantic than
> Croce's cult of intuition in the sense of pure spontaneity and
> untrammeled expression, his tendency to reduce art to a sort
> of lyrical overflow that is not disciplined to any permanent
> center of judgment in either creator or critic and the conse-
> quent identification of genius and taste. (SC, 68)

If Babbitt had kept up with Croce's writings, he would have
known that already in 1917 Croce had thoroughly modified his
view of poetry and art in a way that made it virtually the same
as Babbitt's. French anti-romantic writers may have influenced
Croce, and although he did not publish a review of Babbitt's
The New Laokoon until 1921, he may well have been influenced

1. Irving Babbitt, *Spanish Character and Other Essays* (Boston: Houghton Mifflin,
1940), 67-68; hereinafter referred to in the text as "SC." Babbitt's review essay was
first published in *The Yale Review*, January 1925.

2. Croce's article on *The New Laokoon* was published in *La Critica* (1921). Croce and
Gentile had important philosophical and political disagreements that would soon
drive them apart. They sharply differed about political developments in Italy. In
May of 1925 Croce published an anti-fascist manifesto. At considerable personal
risk, he remained a critic of the fascist regime, protected only by his national and
international stature.

by it long before. Babbitt's severe criticism of Croce's aesthetics applies only with important qualifications to Croce's work after 1917. Croce then shows considerable willingness to do justice to some classical insights he had previously neglected. Even if this had not been the case, Babbitt would have done well to consider more carefully what might be valid in Croce's early aesthetics, that is, in quintessentially modern, post- classical aesthetics. If this modern tendency of thought contains any truth, it must be good that Croce (and after him Dewey and many others) systematized these insights, even though the complementary and indispensable ideas that Babbitt insists upon were neglected.

Babbitt's training in technical philosophy was too spotty to permit him to read Croce with full comprehension. The evidence suggests that he never made an attempt to do so. Paul Elmer More evinces a still more compromising negligence in an essay published in 1928. Ostensibly dealing with Croce's aesthetics as developed in *Nuovi saggi di estetica* (1920), the essay attacks Croce most unfairly and without taking note of changes in his views.[3] It is hard to believe that More could have read the book carefully and yet written as he did. More's acquaintance with technical philosophy was by all indications better than Babbitt's, and if he had set his mind to it, he would certainly have understood Croce's philosophy. If Croce had lived a few centuries earlier, More would perhaps have made the effort. Croce had the misfortune of being a contemporary, and, to make matters worse, More was prejudiced against Italians.[4] Of course, from then on Croce ignored Babbitt and More.

Around the same time that More wrote his unfortunate pages on Croce, he completed *Christ the Word* (1927). It is a work of great learning but written *invita Minerva;* and it seems to have had little influence on theology. Perhaps More would have

3. See the essay on "The Fetish of Pure Art" in Paul Elmer More, *The Demon of the Absolute*, Vol. I of *New Shelburne Essays* (3 Vols.; Princeton: Princeton University Press, 1928-36). Given the weakness of More's evaluation of Croce, Norman Foerster showed questionable judgment including these pages in *Humanism and America* (1930).

4. See the excellent biography by A. Hazard Dakin, *Paul Elmer More* (Princeton: Princeton University Press, 1960), 229-30.

made better use of his exceptional gifts helping to get Humanism out of its intellectual isolation.[5] He could have done so by giving the younger Humanists some training in philosophy and by exploring opportunities for fruitful interaction with leading philosophers of the day. Surprising though it sounds, it is possible that, besides Croce, John Dewey might have been receptive to a restrained and courteous exchange of views. Because of Dewey's reputation as a naturalist and his attacks on the "classical tradition," the potentialities in his philosophy for enriching and broadening that tradition have gone largely unnoticed. *Human Nature and Conduct* (1922) reads in part as a sympathetic answer to Babbitt's *Rousseau and Romanticism* (1919), and *Experience and Nature* (1925) contains passages on romanticism that are strikingly Babbittian. Commenting on Bergson in *Human Nature and Conduct*, Dewey writes: "A blind creative force is as likely to turn out to be destructive as creative; the vital *élan* may delight in war rather than in the laborious arts of civilization, and a mystic intuition of an ongoing splurge be a poor substitute for the detailed work of an intelligence embodied in custom and institution." In another context, Dewey adds, "To view institutions as enemies of freedom, and all conventions as slaveries, is to deny the only means by which positive freedom in action can be secured . . . . Convention and custom are necessary to carrying forward impulse to any happy conclusion. A romantic return to nature . . . finds its terminus in chaos."[6] Whether in any way due to the

5. Dakin quotes from one of More's letters: "To pass the time I am working hard at the revision of my MS. [of *Christ the Word*]. But, do you know, I cannot for the life of me, get up any genuine enthusiasm for the work. I keep asking myself *cui bono*." Dakin, *Paul Elmer More*, 243.

6. John Dewey, *Human Nature and Conduct* (New York: Henry Holt, 1922), 74, 166. Dewey's critical comments on romanticism are discussed in Folke Leander, *The Philosophy of John Dewey* (Göteborg: Elanders boktryckeri, 1939). In further support of Dewey's possible willingness to give a hearing to Babbitt, the following may be noted: Leander's book contains a critique of Dewey's moral philosophy from a largely Babbittian point of view. Still, the reaction to the book on the part of Dewey himself and some of his followers, including Herbert W. Schneider and Max Otto, was highly appreciative and courteous. See, for example, Schneider's review in *The Journal of Philosophy*, XXXVI (1939), 586-87. It may be due to academic departmental barriers that the Humanists, who were mostly professors of literature, appear not to have taken cognizance of Leander's book.

influence of Babbitt, the difference in tone is marked between these books and an earlier work such as *The Influence of Darwin on Philosophy* (1910).

A recent historian is right in pointing out that, on the whole, the debate about Humanism that did take place cannot be taken very seriously intellectually. "What might have been one of the most interesting engagements of the period simply did not come off." But the same historian does not relate this missed opportunity to another fact, recorded elsewhere in his book: "Babbitt, and indeed all the Humanists, were disinclined to establish their credo in a precise and technical philosophical framework, and this characteristic is troublesome to some readers who will be sensitive to the imprecision of language and concepts employed by the Humanists."[7] One of Babbitt's chief critics, the philosopher Arthur O. Lovejoy, was no doubt antipathetic and unjust to Babbitt. But he was notorious as a gadfly. Part of his motivation for criticizing Babbitt may have been simply to goad him to greater clarity of statement, as Lovejoy had already spurred many other thinkers. Some of the theses thrown out by Lovejoy are so paradoxical, he can hardly have meant them quite seriously. And when *The Great Chain of Being* was published in 1936, his view of romanticism turned out to be almost exactly the same as Babbitt's.[8]

The best philosophers of Babbitt's and More's time, whatever their antipathies or sympathies, were rational men. At least in part, Babbitt and More had themselves to blame for their isolation. Perhaps the saddest example is their rude treatment of Croce. They could read Italian and were not blocked or misled by poor translations of his books. If, before writing on Croce, they had carefully studied his *Filosofia della pratica* and *Logica*, they would have found in the former a doctrine of the moral will similar to theirs and in the latter ideas unknown to them

7. J.D. Hoeveler, *The New Humanism* (Charlottesville: The University of Virginia Press, 1977), 26, 37.

8. When Lovejoy reviewed a book, strongly supportive of Babbitt but above all attempting a conceptual clarification of his thought, he was friendly to it. After expressing a few reservations, he ended up calling the book "a learned and *gedankenreich* volume." See Lovejoy's review of Folke Leander, *Humanism and Naturalism* (1937) in *Modern Language Notes*, LIV (1939), 372-74.

but most valuable as a complement to their own. They would certainly have been led to the discovery that Croce's aesthetics and other work after 1917 had a great deal in common with their own critical and historical endeavors.

But not even Croce's aesthetics before 1917 could be rejected out of hand. Ideas may be true even if they can be described as "romantic." Babbitt's attitude toward the distinctively modern aesthetics is inconsistent. On the one hand, he hails the idea of the creative imagination as an important advance. He praises Coleridge for having provided perhaps the best statement of this idea in the English language. (DL, 13)[9] On the other hand, Babbitt calls the new discipline of aesthetics founded by Baumgarten "a nightmare subject." (RR, 166)[10] These positions are difficult to reconcile, considering the new aesthetics is characterized precisely by the discovery of the creative imagination.

This is not the place to give an account of the many and complex influences that produced the doctrine of the creative imagination. A large and growing body of literature, exemplified by such American literary scholars as Abrams, Brooks, Warren and Wellek, describes an often intricate historical development. Babbitt's and Croce's own books are filled with discussions of the sources of the new aesthetics.

Simply put, the older view made the imagination consist of sense impressions associated into images and of the fortuitous emergence and combination of these images of memory. The imagination was thought to be essentially passive. The active power of the mind was the intellect. Crucial to the emergence of the new interpretation of the imagination was starting to view it as a synthetic activity, intermediary between sense and intellect. Gradually, the view gained ground that synthetic wholes are primary, and that so-called sense impressions, far from being primary, are really products of a process of intellectual abstraction which cuts a part out of its context in a larger

---

9. Irving Babbitt, *Democracy and Leadership* (Boston: Houghton Mifflin, 1952), 13; hereinafter referred to in the text as "DL."

10. Irving Babbitt, *Rousseau and Romanticism* (Austin: The University of Texas Press, 1977; first published in 1919), 166; hereinafter referred to in the text as "RR."

whole and labels it an "impression."

The discovery of wholes, and the primacy of wholes, occurred also in fields other than aesthetics. An example is the criticism of atomistic individualism in social philosophy. This criticism meant the revival, although in a strengthened form, of the classical idea of the social nature of man: The individual is conceivable only as a part of human society, not *per se*, as an isolated atom. This is a significant insight, whether proclaimed by an Edmund Burke or by a thinker of primitivistic romantic leanings. The same may be said of another aspect of the Hegelian idea of development, the "dialectic." What is so labeled cannot be rejected *en bloc* as romantic extravagance but needs to be carefully examined and broken up into constituent parts. Babbitt says about Vico's work that it is a rich and organic anticipation of romantic thought. But if there is romantic *thought*, the proper question to ask is whether Vico's ideas are true or false. The question is not answered by calling them "romantic." In his use of that word Babbitt is sometimes guilty of what he so often, and with so much justification, criticizes in others — the indiscriminate use of general terms.

To elaborate on the difficulties with Babbitt's position and, more generally, to advance the epistemological argument, special attention needs to be given to his attitude towards aesthetical developments which can be traced back, at least in part, to the work of Immanuel Kant. Babbitt's insensitivity to the possibly beneficial effects of this influence is evident from his negative statements about Kant, but can also be studied in his writings about thinkers who have been directly or indirectly influenced by Kant, notably Coleridge.[11] Perhaps it should be

11. The aesthetical ideas of Kant, Coleridge and related writers in Germany and elsewhere is the subject of an extensive modern literature which cannot be evaluated here. Besides Babbitt and Croce, contributors to this body of scholarship who are well-known in the United States include M.A. Abrams, W.J. Bate, I. Berlin, C. Brooks, E. Cassirer, H.H. Clark, F.R. Leavis, A. Warren and R. Wellek. Their diverse and sometimes conflicting interpretations and historical accounts attest to the complexity and richness of the subject. Broadly informative standard works which do not necessarily agree in all respects with the interpretations here set forth are René Wellek, *A History of Modern Criticism 1750-1950*, Vols. I-II (New Haven: Yale University Press, 1955) and M.A. Abrams, *The Mirror and the Lamp* (New York: Oxford University Press, 1953).

made explicit that the following selective exemplification of opportunities missed by Babbitt is not intended to give a rounded estimate of Kant or suggest the extent of his influence.

Babbitt's tone whenever he mentions Kant is markedly hostile. What he writes is not precisely wrong, but it does not give Kant credit for having contributed in any way to the quest for synthesis and wholes. Babbitt fails more generally to explain Kant's historical importance. What repels Babbitt is Kant's excessive rationalism (about which much will be said later). Ethical conscience becomes the thinking of a *Vernunftbegriff*. It disturbs Babbitt that for Kant even the sense of beauty is in part rationality. The intuitive side of human nature seems to be denied. According to Kant, nature is Newton's physics dogmatically fixed in an "unearthly ballet" of deterministic categories.[12] The reality of organic nature becomes questionable, as physics alone is held to give reality. The world we can know is governed by mechanical law. Human freedom appears to evaporate into a noumenal *Vernunftbegriff*. To Babbitt there is something spectral and unreal about Kant's philosophy. More is equally hostile to it.

Croce's reaction to Kant is anything but uncritical, but it is more constructive. Croce works out a revised version of Kant's basic ideas which is more attentive to immediate experience. Croce's notion of the ethical will is in some ways derived from the categorical imperative, but like Babbitt's inner check it is an immediate intuition prior to the formulation of rules or precepts. And there is nothing rationalistic about Croce's idea of beauty, however unsatisfactory it may have been to Babbitt in another respect: its disregard, at least in its early form, of the ethical dimension of beauty. Croce also disputes that the Kantian categories, which are largely Newtonian, are really categorial in nature. As will be explained at the appropriate time, Croce recognizes as genuinely categorial only those basic forms of human activity whose respective intrinsic standards

12. See F.H. Bradley, *The Principles of Logic* (New York: G.E. Stechert, 1920; reprint of the 1883 edition), 533: "The sensuous curtain is a deception and a cheat, if it hides some colourless movement of atoms, some spectral woof of impalpable abstractions, or unearthly ballet of bloodless categories."

are beauty, truth, utility and morality. The concepts of modern physical science Croce interprets as pragmatic constructions, which are most useful in giving us mastery of nature, but which are in a deeper sense unreal. Owing to these Crocean reforms, biological life as well as human freedom—which are both unsatisfactorily treated by Kant—could come into their own. Breaking up the rationalistic encrustations of Kant's thought, Croce's revisions reveal a deeper stratum in his work. Babbitt and More never get behind the repugnant mask of cold and abstract rationalism which is usually first encountered by the student of Kant. Croce removes the mask and shows a human face.

If Babbitt and More had not been antipathetically inclined towards things German (an understandable inclination given the Teutonic arrogance of their day), their study of Coleridge in particular might have suggested to them some similar way of dealing with Kant. Coleridge had reacted against such influences as Hartley's sensationalistic materialism, which dissolved experience into impressions and associations. In his inquiry into the synthetic and creative function of the human mind Coleridge had derived immense benefit from reading Kant and others influenced by Kant. But in spite of his deep appreciation for much in Coleridge, Babbitt remains hostile to the German: "Though the philosophy of Kant supplies the freedom and synthetic element that were absent from a philosophy like that of Hume, it supplies them in an abstract and rationalistic way." (DL, 326) Babbitt refers to "the insubstantial transcendence of Kant." (DL, 225) But these and similar comments fail to explain Coleridge's admiration for "the venerable Sage of Koenigsberg." Should it not have told Babbitt something that Coleridge, the student of Kant, was able to restore the "synthetic element" to philosophy in a way that was neither abstract nor rationalistic? Emerson, who is often cited in Babbitt's early works, could derive his intuitive and immediate Over-Soul in large part from Coleridge and other influences stemming directly or indirectly from Kant. These were only a few of the indications that Kant's rationalism is a shell around some rather different and very fruitful philosophical potentialities. Also when writing his essay on "Schiller as Aesthetic Theorist," Babbitt might have been led to see deeper into Kant.[13] Unfortunately, Babbitt says little about Schiller's contribution to the work of liberating Kantianism from excessive rationalism. Characteristically, he is more interested in those elements in Schiller which seem to him to anticipate aestheticism and *l'art pour l'art*. Babbitt's essay on Coleridge offered perhaps the most promising opportunity for reassessing Kant; but in that essay, which does not mention Coleridge's progress beyond Kantian rationalism or beyond the temptation of aestheticism, Babbitt seems oblivious of the possibility that Coleridge is actually right in saying that he has learned much from the German. In general, Babbitt disregards those important modifications of Kant in later thought which largely remove his objections. He dwells instead on Kant's obvious weakness, his rationalistic pedantry. This one-sided attitude is paradoxical, for it appears that the ideas of Babbitt and More themselves would not have been possible without Kant's influence, not least via Coleridge and Emerson.[14]

According to Kant, *Verstand* and *Vernunft* (the latter especially as connected with the sublime) play a considerable role in our experience of beauty and art. Babbitt objects that "there is nothing abstract in our estimates of beauty." (OBC, 142) Croce's way of disposing of misplaced rationality in Kant is to interpret art and beauty as the product of *intuizione*, of creative imagination. What Kant views as an aggregate of faculties Croce "deduces" as a distinct category — the creative imagination. According to Croce, Kant does not really have such an idea.

A profound concept of imagination was entirely lacking to Kant's system and his philosophy of the spirit. Glancing over the table of faculties of the spirit which precedes his *Critique of Judgment*, we see that Kant distinguishes between the cognitive faculty, the feeling of pleasure and pain, and the appeti-

---

13. Irving Babbitt, *On Being Creative* (New York: Biblo and Tannen, 1968; reprint of the 1932 original); hereinafter referred to in the text as "OBC."

14. There are close to 50 references to Emerson in Babbitt's *The Masters of Modern French Criticism* (New York: Noonday Press, 1963; reprint of the 1912 original); hereinafter referred to in the text as "MFC."

tive faculty; to the first corresponds intellect, to the second, judgment (teleological and aesthetic), to the third, reason; but he finds no place for the imagination among the powers of the spirit and it is left among the facts of sensation. He knows a reproductive imagination and an associative, but he knows nothing of a genuinely productive imagination, imagination in the proper sense. (A, 277)[15]

Kant's system also contains something called Transcendental Aesthetic, but this, Croce contends, is merely the doctrine of space and time:

. . . sometimes Kant had an inkling that intellectual activity is preceded by something which is not mere sensational material, but is an independent non-intellectual theoretical form. He obtained a glimpse of this latter form not when he was reflecting on art in the strict sense but when he was examining the process of knowledge: he does not treat it in his *Critique of Judgment,* but in the first section of his *Critique of Pure Reason* . . . . Now, what name does Kant confer upon this science whose existence he has deduced? None other than Transcendental Aesthetic. . . . The characterizing or qualifying imagination which is aesthetic activity ought to have occupied in the *Critique of Pure Reason* the pages devoted to the discussion of space and time, and would thus have constituted a real Transcendental Aesthetic, a real prologue to the transcendental Logic. (A, 277-79)

The Kantian twelve categories and physical space and time are meant to account for Newtonian physics. Schiller ignores all of this as being of no concern to aesthetics. Interested in poetry and art, he interprets the imagination as the result of two forces meeting one another. The one (the *Sachtrieb*) produces ever more individuality-change-variety, the other (the *Formtrieb*) shapes and organizes all this material.[16] The first element is the perpetual gushing forth of novelty; the second is

---

15. Benedetto Croce, *Aesthetic* (2nd rev. ed.; London: Macmillan, 1922), 277; with corrections of the translation; hereinafter referred to in the text as "A." The reader is cautioned about the weaknesses of this English translation.

16. Friedrich Schiller, *Über die ästhetische Erziehung des Menschen* (München: Wilhelm Fink Verlag, 1967).

the synthesis achieved by the human mind in perception of reality and in aesthetic creation. In the choice of this terminology and in the conception of the two *Triebe* as complementary and cooperating functions of one identical human life, Schiller is influenced by Fichte (and Fichte by Schiller). Human life in the all-inclusive sense (not yours or mine, but everybody's) is the reality within which the *discordia concors* and *concordia discors* of the two *Triebe* are constantly enacted. Fichte's term for all-inclusive human life is the Self, which splits itself up into Self (= *Formtrieb*) and Not-Self (= *Sachtrieb*). The word Self is thus used in two senses: (1) all-inclusive life as a unity, and (2) this unity as split up into an immense number of individual selves located in nature, which is the great Not-Self. Schiller derives from this notion the idea of imagination as the product of two conflicting and yet cooperating forces—the idea which recurs in *Biographia Literaria.*

Coleridge not only eliminates rationalistic Kantian features from his doctrine of beauty, but he comes close to Babbitt in his insistence that intuitive wisdom forms part of truly great poetry. Coleridge supplies "the freedom and the synthetic elements that were absent from a philosophy like that of Hume." Unlike Kant, Coleridge does not supply them in an "abstract and rationalistic way." Some scholars who have set Coleridge down as an unsatisfactory, if not incompetent, interpreter of Kant have done so because he passes by much of Kant's thought in silence. But so does Schiller. The two men leave out of consideration the "abstract and rationalistic" elements in Kant. Yet it would be a mistake to attribute their selectivity to a lack of understanding. They seem guided rather by a secure sense of essentials.

Summarizing his objections to Kant, Babbitt writes, "Kant evidently raises in an acute form in all three of his Critiques the question of intuition. In *The Critique of Aesthetic Judgment* one is led to inquire whether one may not have a direct perception of the universal; in *The Critique of Practical Reason,* whether one must base one's conduct on a categorical imperative that remains a mere abstraction; in *The Critique of Pure Reason,* whether, craving as one does immediacy, one must be put

off with the 'unearthly ballet of bloodless categories.'" (OBC,
144) These criticisms do not apply to Coleridge. He does not
discuss the twelve categories; he is interested not in Newtonian physics, but in the imagination. The sense of duty, which
Coleridge calls "practical reason," is also far from a Kantian
abstraction. It is a supersensuous perception of noumenal reality. *Aids to Reflection* (1825) reveals that Coleridge's "practical
reason" is closer to a non-conceptual intuition of a higher will
similar to Babbitt's inner check than it is to Kant's practical reason: "Reason indeed is much nearer to Sense than to Understanding: for Reason (says our great Hooker) is a direct aspect
of truth, an inward beholding, having a similar relation to the
intelligible or spiritual, as sense has to the material or phaenom-
enal."[17] The lingering intellectualism in Coleridge's notion of
"practical reason" was on the verge of vanishing. Coleridge
might as well have spoken of "religious faith," for that is actually what the term signified for him.

In *Biographia Literaria* (1817) is seen at work not the practical
but the speculative reason.[18] This reason achieves a "transcendental deduction" of the imagination as a basis for poetics and
criticism. A "transcendental deduction" assumes the mind is
like a net; you cannot lift one knot in it without lifting the whole
net. The imagination is being "deduced" when it is shown to
be a necessary part of a categorial network: one cannot think
of the human consciousness without including the imagination. In other words, the imagination is one of the universals
constituting the human mind. In the area of philosophical
knowledge, definitions are not fabricated arbitrarily. Nor is it
an empirical fact, established by induction, that all human
minds have imagination. Induction assumes that exceptions
are possible, but in this case they are not. Our knowledge of
the categorial network is neither empirical in the empiricist
sense, nor *a priori* in the postulational sense. It is at once empirical and *a priori*—in the speculative sense. The speculative

17. Samuel Taylor Coleridge, *Aids to Reflection* (Port Washington, N.Y.: Kennikat
Press, 1971), 216-17.
18. Samuel Taylor Coleridge, *Biographia Literaria* (London: J.M. Dent and Sons,
1975).

method, or the method of transcendental deduction, is not that of empirical psychology; but in its own way it is just as empirical. Indeed, it is empirical in a deeper sense, as psychology deals mostly in the abstracted products of the Understanding (*Verstand*). The relation between empirical psychology and speculative reason is that the former tacitly presupposes the work done by the latter. The psychologist, as a human being, has a speculative philosopher within him, only he is not reflectively aware of this part of consciousness, and he believes that his method is simply and solely the study of "facts" in the ordinary empirical sense. The existence of the creative imagination is discovered by speculative inquiry; mere psychology, relying on the unreal but useful abstractions of the Understanding, is unable to see more than passive impressions passively associated. Coleridge tries to explain this as best he can to readers ill-prepared to understand.

Babbitt notes that the synthetic element is lacking in the philosophy of Hume. He applies to the latter the words of Mephistopheles, *"Fehlt leider! nur das geistige Band!"* (DL, 324) Coleridge's intuitive and synthetic imagination, by contrast, is a faculty that creates wholes, and wholes within wholes. Most fundamentally, it is the power that creates the symbols of that infinity in which everything existing has its being and from which it is separated only by abstraction from context. Coleridge is aware that some small part of a whole may be isolated by an act of the Understanding, be called an "impression" and treated as if it were an independent existent. Insofar as the Understanding is at work within men, they similarly tend to separate themselves from the context in which they have their real being. We pretend to be, and deal with one another as if we were, "self"-enclosed existents, divided from one another by hard and fast lines. Whatever the field, the Understanding cuts up wholes into atomic "facts" which are seen as only externally related to one another. This type of reason disregards the relations within the wholes, owing to which "facts" have whatever reality they can be said to have.

Coleridge is interested in imaginative wholes and not in the intellectualistic wholes accounted for in the Kantian categories of Newtonian science. Kant arrived at his idealism through study of mathematics and physics; but modern idealism is by no means dependent on this approach. In Croce's idealism, mathematical science is accounted for as a structure of pragmatically useful fictions. Kant's mathematical space and time and his twelve categories, corresponding to Newtonian physics, are likewise seen as pragmatic constructions. In Croce's view, the idealistic study of wholes got its start as a study of such pseudo-wholes, but it soon passed on to real wholes. Coleridge represents this passage from interest in fictional wholes to interest in concrete wholes of imagination. He does not attempt to prove the fictional and "unreal" nature of the Kantian categories, but in practice he reaches the same result as Croce by disregarding them.

Few better summaries of the essence of German idealism can be found than the ten "theses" in Ch. XII of *Biographia Literaria*. Coleridge expressly states as the aim of these theses "the deduction of the Imagination." But though he believes that another long and difficult chapter would be needed to complete the deduction, he holds back, feeling that he has tried the patience of his readers long enough. Describing Coleridge's treatment of the subject, Babbitt is ironical:

In the earlier chapters . . . he does indeed set out to define imagination . . . but tends to get lost in what he himself terms "the holy jungle of transcendental metaphysics." . . . After much preparation . . . he seems in chapter thirteen to be getting under way at last; but just at this point someone writes him a letter (the someone as we know now was Coleridge himself) warning him that he is getting beyond the depth of his public and advising him to reserve his more recondite considerations for his work on the Logos (which was of course never written). Whereupon Coleridge turns from Schelling and the Germans to Aristotle. The result of this escape from the "jungle" is a sudden increase in clarity. (OBC, 107-108)

Yes, clarity for the general reader. Babbitt does not do justice to Coleridge's skill in stating extremely difficult philosophical thoughts with the only kind of clarity they can have. Moreover, Coleridge felt that he had achieved his main purpose: explaining why the traditional account of the imagination (as impressions and associations) was simplistic, and why recognition of vitally coherent wholes was the proper basis of good aesthetics. In essentials, he had already succeeded in "the deduction of the imagination, and with it the principles of production and of genial criticism in the fine arts." The rest of *Biographia Literaria* extracts these principles from the new concept of the imagination and applies them in criticism. Hence the work has continuity. Many books with titles like "Principles of Literary Criticism" have been published in this century; but for the most part the principles are philosophically rather shallow, and often their application to the criticism of literature is jejune or missing. Coleridge goes to the philosophical depths in his search for principles, and his application of them in criticism is sometimes breathtakingly skillful.

As a result of his philosophical labor, Coleridge is in a position to present Aristotle's critical insights as consequences of his new concept of the imagination. There is in *Biographia Literaria* no such break as Babbitt implies: first the Germans, then Aristotle. Instead, Coleridge shows that from the principles of the Germans, as reelaborated by him, Aristotle's main insights can be deduced. Many in the England of Coleridge's time criticized Wordsworth rather mechanically on Aristotelian grounds. Babbitt might have inquired why only Coleridge was able to combine Aristotelian criticism with the concept of the creative imagination. With this combination, the understanding and use of Aristotle took a great step forward, which is easily seen when one remembers how the *Poetics* had been understood by Renaissance and neo-classical interpreters.

Babbitt's own understanding of the *Poetics* owes much to Coleridge, as does S. H. Butcher's classical exposition in *Aristotle's Theory of Poetics and Fine Art* (1895).[19] Since Coleridge's theory of poetry had everything to do with his passage through the "transcendental jungle," Babbitt was indirectly indebted to German philosophy. Still, Babbitt speaks caustically about Joubert as having "the advantage over Coleridge of not being

19. S.H. Butcher, *Aristotle's Theory of Poetry and Fine Art* (Corrected ed.; London: Macmillan, 1911).

addicted either to opium or German metaphysics," as if those inclinations were on the same level. (OBC, 122) Without Kant-Fichte-Schiller-Coleridge, would not the concept of "the creative imagination" have remained rather vacuous? It is on this very idea of imagination that Babbitt himself bases his main objection to Greek philosophy: "In its failure to bring out with sufficient explicitness this *creative* role of the imagination and in the stubborn intellectualism that this failure implies is to be found, if anywhere, the weak point in the cuirass of Greek philosophy." (RR, 308n.)

Neo-Thomist Louis J. A. Mercier misreads Babbitt when, in spite of passages like this one, he equates Babbitt's "higher imagination, used to reach universals, the permanent, the abiding," with the *intellectus* of Scholasticism.[20] It can of course be argued that *intellectus* has an intuitive component. But Mercier is reverting to the pre-modern, mimetic Aristotelian doctrine, which assumes that the only *active* function of the mind is an intellective power which abstracts universals from material offered by the senses. He believes he can attribute this doctrine to Babbitt, as the latter sometimes describes the imagination in the seemingly mimetic language of *perceiving* similitudes. However, Babbitt always has in mind a kind of perceiving that is not only imaginative, as distinguished from intellective, but *creative*. This "perceiving" is really a *conceiving*: "Now to 'conceive' is, in an almost etymological sense, to gather things together, to see likenesses and analogies and in so far to unify what were else mere heterogeneity. The imagination, says Coleridge somewhat pedantically, is the 'esemplastic' power—the power, that is, that fashions things into one." (DL, 13) The imagination institutes wholes which did not exist before. Babbitt insisted that a note be inserted in one of Mercier's books which contained an implicit criticism of the view foisted on him. The key sentence reads, "A chief source of ambiguity in the use of the word imagination is that, historically, it has been applied at times to the power that perceives and at times to the power

20. Louis Mercier, *American Humanism and the New Age* (Milwaukee: Bruce Publishing Co., 1948), 18 and Mercier, *The Challenge of Humanism* (New York: Oxford University Press, 1933), 163.

that conceives."[21] Babbitt stresses the latter, which he sees as creating non-conceptual wholes and universals.

A full examination of Babbitt's doctrine of the imagination as a distinct *organon* for the non-rational awareness of universals must await the discussion of related philosophical questions. Here another few comments may suggest the relationship between that subject and issues just treated. Awareness of a common human nature has been mentioned. What is that awareness, unless it be the intuitive and imaginative perception of the universal in man? According to Babbitt the consciousness of you, me, and others as human beings is first of all a pre-rational awareness. "The element in man's nature that he possesses in common with other men is . . . something that he *senses*, something that is in short intuitive and immediate." (RR, 80) No Kantian intellectual syntheses are needed to constitute the human community; this work is achieved most fundamentally through the same imaginative syntheses which make us aware of ourselves and others as really—not just numerically—individual. We have a direct, intuitive awareness of ourselves as "incomprehensibly like other men" and as "incomprehensibly different from them." (RR, 53) "Each man has his idiosyncrasy (literally his 'private mixture'). But in addition to his complexion, his temperamental or private self, every man has a self that he possesses in common with other men. Even the man who is most filled with his own uniqueness, or 'genius,' a Rousseau, for example, assumes this universal self in every word he utters. 'Jove nods to Jove behind us as we talk.'" (RR, 50)

The last sentence is a quotation from Emerson's essay on "The Over-Soul." It reveals an important parallel to and one likely source for Babbitt's idea of the higher self: the transcendental Self of German philosophy. Coleridge explains and affirms this notion by noting "the distinction between the conditional finite I (which as known in distinct consciousness by occasion of experience is called by Kant's followers the empirical I) and the absolute I AM, and likewise the dependence or

21. Mercier, *Challenge of Humanism*, 163-64.

rather the inherence of the former in the latter; in whom 'we live, and move and have our being,' as St. Paul divinely asserts . . . .''[22]

Babbitt complains that Kant affirms this doctrine in ''an abstract and rationalistic way.'' But just beneath the rationalistic surface there can be discerned philosophical impulses pointing to an intuitive Self, inherent in each of our intuitive selves. This Self is active not only in moral volition but also in that non-conceptual synthesis which gives us a common world and a common, yet always varying, humanity. If men were not first of all joined in an intuitive grasp of their universal humanity, they could not interact meaningfully, not form particular societies. Imagination can be described as the fundamental social bond. In the phraseology of Peter Viereck, the real bond of society is not the ''cash-nexus'' but the ''dream-nexus.'' ''Without the imagination's dream-nexus to hold [the] outer world together, its atoms would crack and scatter in an instant like blown sand.''[23] The atomism of ''impressions'' in eighteenth century philosophy corresponded to the atomism of isolated individuals in social thought. A ''synthetic element'' was needed also in social philosophy.

It has been left for later chapters to deal with Babbitt's often eminently justified and incisive criticism of romanticism. This chapter has drawn attention to what seems to be weaknesses and inconsistencies in his relationship to modern aesthetics. Babbitt has been shown to be insufficiently appreciative of various contributions to the notion of the creative imagination, an idea that is integral to his own position. His thought is far more compatible with some philosophical insights stemming largely from German sources than appears from his own explicit statements. This theme will be expanded upon in the remaining chapters of Part One, which analyze Babbitt's epistemologically relevant ideas with a view to supplementing them.

---

22. Coleridge, *Biographia Literaria*, Chap. XII, Thesis VI, 152n.
23. Peter Viereck, *The Unadjusted Man* (Westport, Conn.: Greenwood Press, 1973), 328.

Chapter 3
Scientific Reason and Experience

The discovery of the imagination as a synthetic, creative function constituting man's fundamental awareness of reality was certain to affect profoundly the way in which rational knowledge is understood. The subjects of will and imagination having been introduced, the emphasis will now be placed on the meaning of reason. A distinction will be developed between two kinds of rationality: pragmatic and philosophical. Almost unknown in contemporary thought, that distinction is necessary if philosophy is to become more fully aware of its own nature.

The notion of a distinctly philosophical reason is not familiar to Babbitt, but it can be shown to be a natural epistemological supplement to his position. The work of distinguishing philosophical from pragmatic reason may be begun conveniently by reviewing Babbitt's treatment of the thought-processes of natural science, an area where he possesses considerable insight. Babbitt argues, partly with the support of some leading contemporary thinkers, that although natural science is often regarded as the very model for the search for truth, it involves a deliberate distortion of experience for the sake of practical ends. The treatment of problems of reason in this and the following chapters will confirm and illustrate the continuous assumption that will, imagination and reason can be adequately understood only in relation to each other.

It is not known when Babbitt first became familiar with the modern pragmatic-economic-fictionalistic interpretation of natural science, but he must have been well-prepared to understand its message. Having graduated from high school, Babbitt returned to his school in the following fall and spent the 1884-85

academic year studying chemistry and civil engineering—
"oddly enough," says Lynn Harold Hough.[1] According to Babbitt's wife Dora, he did it "just to fill in his time."[2] One may
speculate that this young humanist, already deeply read in the
Greek and Roman classics and possessing strong views about
free will *versus* determinism, felt a need to understand physical science better.[3]

At a young age Babbitt became familiar with Emerson. Judging from Babbitt's early books, it seems that no matter what
he read, some passage from Emerson would come to mind. A
striking number of Babbitt's quotes from him are aimed at
breaking down scientific dogmatism. The young student of
chemistry and engineering seems to have extracted from Emerson an acute awareness of the *lacunae* and limitations of
mechanistic science. Thus whenever Babbitt discovered the
new pragmatic critics of scientific dogmatism, he was well prepared to understand them, having himself anticipated much
of their thought. At all events, he took a pragmatic view of natural science when, beginning about 1905, he had discussions
with the physicist Louis Trenchard More, Paul Elmer More's
brother. Yet he was strangely unable to make L. T. More understand his argument. More got the impression that Babbitt
rejected the mathematical method in science:

> His intense and stubborn individualism drew him to cham-
> pion the scientific method of Aristotle. He saw there Aristo-
> tle's marvelous success as a biologist and his equal failure as
> a physicist and mechanist. He had the same dread of
> mathematics as a logic as did Aristotle, seeing in it the chief

1. Lynn Harold Hough, *Great Humanists* (New York: Abingdon-Cokesbury Press, 1952), 134.

2. Dora Babbitt, "Biographical Sketch," in Frederick Manchester and Odell Shepard (eds.) *Irving Babbitt, Man and Teacher* (New York: Greenwood Press, 1969; reprint of the 1941 original), xi.

3. It is chronologically possible that Babbitt came across a magazine article, "The Dilemma of Determinism," by William James. This essay was first printed in 1884 and was subsequently included in *The Will to Believe* (1896). It contained some of those favorite ideas of Babbitt's that, as a freshman at Harvard, he would preach to W.F. Giese. See Giese's chapter in Manchester and Shepard (eds.), *Irving Babbitt*, 1-25. On the parallel between James and Babbitt, see Folke Leander, *The Philosophy of John Dewey* (Göteborg: Elanders boktryckeri, 1939), 137-40.

support to the mechanistic hypothesis and materialistic philosophy of Democritus. Babbitt would thus restrict science to observation and classification of phenomena alone; while I, as a physicist, was convinced that the geometrical theory of mechanics was the standard and ideal goal of the scientific method, since only by it can natural laws be expressed in quantitative terms.[4]

It cannot be true that Babbitt wanted to restrict science to observation and classification of phenomena; nobody familiar with modern science can have such a view. Babbitt must have meant something that L. T. More did not understand. And what he had in mind is formulated clearly in one of his books: "In a sense science becomes scientific only in proportion as it neglects the qualitative differences between phenomena, e.g. between light and sound, and treats them solely from the point of view of quantity. But the penalty that science pays for this quantitative method is a heavy one. The farther it gets away from the warm immediacy of perception the less real it becomes; for that only is real to a man that he immediately perceives. Perfectly pure science tends to become a series of abstract mathematical formulae without any real content." (RR, 138-139)[5] Babbitt wanted to explain to More that science is a structure of useful *fictions;* and More who, to judge from his books, believed all his life that physical nature is "out there," substantially real, just as Newton had described it, was quite unprepared to understand such a view. It was "the warm immediacy of perception" and not, as More believed, classificatory science, that Babbitt set up against mechanistic physics. Man has a direct perception of the flow of life, unmediated by any formulas or laws, which is more fundamental and real than the constructions of natural science. Henri Bergson, William James and the other pragmatists confirmed Babbitt's view that scientific classification maltreats experiential reality. Bergson speaks of more or less arbitrary *découpages* which cut phenomena out of their context in the whole. If Babbitt appealed to biol-

4. L.T. More, Chapter V in Manchester and Shepard (eds.), *Irving Babbitt*, 39.
5. Irving Babbitt, *Rousseau and Romanticism* (Austin: The University of Texas Press, 1977), 138-39; hereinafter referred to in the text as "RR."

ogy in his discussions with L. T. More, it was undoubtedly as part of his insistence on the legitimacy of concrete observation as distinguished from accounts adjusted to prefabricated abstract schemes. He may also have wanted to draw attention to the difficulties that organisms present to mechanistic science.

Babbitt may here be compared to Croce. The Italian philosopher, too, interprets natural science as being pragmatic. Having read *Estetica*, Babbitt writes of Croce in 1910: "His point of view is closely related to that special form of reaction against dogmatic and mechanical science of which I have . . . spoken. He shows himself one of the keenest of intellectualists in his attacks on scientific intellectualism. He makes many a trenchant distinction of just the kind that we need at present." (NL, 224)[6] Unfortunately, Babbitt seems never to have gone on to study Croce's *Logica* (1908). This book would have posed a problem to him: Is the "intellect" that criticizes scientific intellectualism itself the same sort of intellect, i.e., a pragmatic intellect? According to Croce, true reason (meaning philosophical thought) differs *toto coelo* from the type of reasoning which produces mathematical or classificatory fictions. It is the office of the former kind of reason to be critically aware of the nature of the latter, thus exposing the limitations of science. The relationship may be indicated by examining Babbitt's own distinction: (1) there is "the warm immediacy of perception" and (2) the "series of abstract mathematical formulae." Does Babbitt believe that this distinction is itself pragmatic—that is, a mere classificatory convenience? Or is it of some other kind? What is that concrete "perception" which is contrasted with "abstractions" and through which abstractions are seen to be such? Is this immediate experience an act of pure intuition, or is it something else? Babbitt gives an answer of sorts when he distinguishes between "imagination" and "perception," but he is content to draw this distinction in a loose, commonsensical way and offers little discussion of the problems involved. He might have reflected on the fact that in so far as concrete perception contains a judgment, namely, "This is real (i.e., perceived, not

6. Irving Babbitt, *The New Laokoon* (Boston: Houghton Mifflin, 1910), 224; hereinafter referred to in the text as "NL."

just imagined)," it is a kind of thought, but one that is different from both mathematical and classificatory rationality.

Perception is another term for concrete thought; it is an act in which immediate experience acquires conceptual self-awareness. Croce also calls perception historical thought, using "historical" in a wide sense. Historical thought and philosophical reflection are for Croce so closely related that they are ultimately indistinguishable. How can we know about an act of pragmatic *découpage*, unless we can observe it in some way, observe what was there before it took place, and observe its results? Similarly, we can observe our acts of mathematical construction. Three philosophical categories have thus been discerned: (1) classificatory activity, (2) mathematical activity, (3) historical-philosophical observation. They are called categories because a human consciousness cannot be conceived without each of these forms of activity being to some extent present, and because the distinctions between them are sharp in the sense that intermediaries on a sliding scale are inconceivable (a subject to be elaborated upon at the appropriate time). The notion of "reason" espoused by pragmatists includes the first and second categories but not the third, philosophical reason. For them, philosophizing is pragmatic rationality. Except for some sudden beams of light, which rapidly disappear, it is hard to see that Babbitt differs significantly from the pragmatists in his understanding of the nature of reason.

Primarily occupied with problems of ethics and imagination, Babbitt does not set himself the task of thinking through the subject of conceptual knowledge. Insufficiently aware of the nature of philosophical reason, he tends to misinterpret the history of its achievements. In particular, he is prevented from perceiving the element of continuity in the development of the epistemology of scientific knowledge—although, as has been seen, he assimilates some of its most important results in his own day. Babbitt does not appreciate the real significance of the *Critique of Pure Reason*. He points out that Kant introduces the "synthetic element" missing in Hume in "an abstract and rationalistic way." Babbitt's criticism is justified in that Kant is prone to press in *Begriffe* where they do not belong. Babbitt is right to insist that neither the moral will nor the creative imagination are conceptual. But he does not consider that in criticizing Hume's ideas about natural science, Kant has every justification to introduce the "synthetic element" in an abstract and rationalistic way. In natural science the synthetic element *is* abstract and rationalistic. Kant is defending the thought-processes of Newtonian science against Hume by disclosing their true synthetic function. Synthesis forms wholes. In Newtonian science the entire world of inanimate nature is constituted as one whole, of indefinite extension. Croce considers this notion a very important achievement, even though this particular whole is only a useful fiction, a creation of the understanding *(Verstand)*. The discovery of the "synthetic element," of wholes as products of the human mind, began as reflection about an unreal whole, the "nature" of physical science. But this breakthrough was followed by the study of concrete imaginative, moral and philsophical wholes and of whatever other "synthetic elements" could be discovered in human experience. In these fields, too, Kant made a beginning, even though his tendency everywhere to read conceptual rationality into what he studied is unfortunate. Once started, the study of wholes could be carried to greater perfection by others.

In Babbitt's day, Anglo-American philosophy was dominated by F. H. Bradley's monism and William James' pluralism. Babbitt contrasts them as a "metaphysics of the One" and a "metaphysics of the Many" (meaning by "metaphysical" doctrines that incorporate speculation divorced from concrete human experience). He thinks these two tendencies can be traced back to Parmenides and Heraclitus, respectively. Babbitt is at his worst when writing the following sentences: "The history of philosophy since the Greeks is to a great extent the history of the clashes of the metaphysicians of the One and the metaphysicians of the Many. In the eyes of the complete positivist [Babbitt's misleading name for his own view] this history therefore reduces itself largely to a monstrous logomachy." (RR, 7) It may be said in Babbitt's defense that his judgment is weakened by the words "to a great extent" in the first sentence and "largely" in the second. These qualifications imply that there have been some advances in philosophy, as distinct from vain metaphysical attempts. Even so, Babbitt is not very sensitive to what the mutual criticisms of various metaphysicians have meant for the progress of philosophy proper. Far from being just a "monstrous logomachy," the zigzagging between competing themes has borne fruit in some insights of high significance, many of them shared by Babbitt himself. This is the case although technical philosophers often do get lost in disquisitions remote from experience and the central problems of life. Stressing the need for ethical wisdom and effort, Babbitt is wont to brush aside modern technical philosophy as a meaningless indulgence of the *libido sciendi* and to look upon Western philosphy from the time of Locke as "a long debauch of epistemology." He adds, however, "This endless epistemological debate would be justified if it could be shown to have prepared the way for a more adequate reply to Kant's second question: What must I do?" (D, 85)[7] But even on Babbitt's own showing, isn't that in fact one of the results? For example, it has been noted that Babbitt finds the pragmatic interpretation of science highly useful for his own purposes. This theory did not suddenly fall out of the sky. It was the result of at least three centuries of inquiry, to say nothing of its indebtedness to earlier modes of thought. Babbitt makes little allowance for the predicament of the technical philosopher: trying to do his work properly, he will inevitably explore some by-paths and blind alleys in which thought may get lost. Babbitt seems to demand that philosophy should achieve tenable results without delay. This is an unreasonable demand ignoring the nature of thought.

It is possible to discern a continuous epistemological development from the Renaissance down to the *Critique of Pure Reason* and beyond, however much the metaphysical systems may have varied along the way. Ernst Cassirer's classical survey of scientific epistemology, beginning with Cusanus and the Renaissance thinkers and passing through Galileo, Descartes, Spinoza, Leibniz, Locke, Berkeley, Hume and numerous other

7. Irving Babbitt, "Buddha and the Occident," in *The Dhammapada*, translated and with an Essay on Buddha and the Occident by Irving Babbitt (New York: New Directions, 1965), 85; hereinafter referred to in the text as "D."

scientists and philosophers, discloses a step-by-step advance temporarily summed up in Kant's great work.[8] This example is sufficient to show that Babbitt's deprecating assertion about the history of philosophy is false to fact. Without Kant's *Critique* and the scientist-philosophers of the nineteenth century the pragmatic view of science would have been impossible.

As an example outside of the epistemology of natural science, Babbitt's own contributions illustrate how mankind is able to add to its knowledge of life. In the fields in which he is primarily interested he tries to improve upon his predecessors—and with much success. At the same time, his books bear witness to what he owes to an immense reading. Babbitt says about Rousseau that he asked the right questions but gave the wrong answers. Babbitt also observes that for a thinker to have asked the right questions is no small distinction. The point is that Babbitt's contribution would have been impossible but for the challenge of Rousseau, just as Socrates' would have been impossible without the Sophists. Philosophical thought is a continuous quest in which ever new thrusts of thought stimulate the rethinking of central problems. One of the purposes of this book is to show that Babbitt's work, in its turn, needs complements and corrections.

To anticipate briefly a later argument, it should be admitted that technical philosophy plays only a limited role in the acquisition of knowledge. A preeminent place belongs to the sages of the human race. They are the rare men of wisdom who are distinguished by their ability to see deeply into man's predicament rather than an ability to formulate concepts with precision. To a large extent, philosophy follows in the footsteps of such men. It tries to render conceptually systematic what great poets and other men of vision have already grasped. The point of view of the sages transcends mere technical philosophy, even when the sages do their part in developing it. Dr. Samuel Johnson was a very wise man, but his literary criticism and his *dicta* on a variety of topics are better described as *sagesse* than as philosophy. Similarly, Goethe, having left his Storm and Stress

8. See Vols. I-II of Ernst Cassirer, *Das Erkenntnisproblem in der Philosophie und Wissenschaft der neueren Zeit* (3 Vols.; Berlin: Bruno Cassirer, 1906-1920).

period behind, became perhaps the greatest sage that Germany has had. Historians of technical philosophy generally ignore him. Babbitt and More, in addition to being sages, produced not a little strictly philosophical thought. The latter is more open to criticism than is their remarkable *sagesse.* Their highest distinction, it is argued here, is that they were right, that they *saw* where most of their contemporaries, some of them better technical philosophers than they, were more or less *blind.* Yet the fact that philosophy in the stricter sense is largely dependent for its soundness on the insights of such men is no reason for discounting the conceptual work of the professional philosopher.

However, the epistemology of natural science needs to be discussed further. Attention should be turned to the rest of the passage summarizing Babbitt's view of science: "Perfectly pure science tends to become a series of abstract mathematical formulae without any real content. By his resort to such a method the man of science is in constant danger of becoming a mere rationalist. At the bottom he is ignorant of the reality that lies behind natural phenomena; he must ever be ignorant of it, for it lays hold upon the infinite, and so must elude a finite being like man." (RR, 138-39) It should be explained what is meant by a "mere rationalist" and by laying "hold upon the infinite." The latter is a problem to which Babbitt often returns. He quotes Pascal's famous words that man is shut in between two infinites, the infinitely great and the infinitely small. In his laboratory experiments the physicist cannot isolate his apparatus from the surrounding world. Everything in the universe exerts an influence on everything else. The attraction of the moon and sun, the warmth of the experimenters's body, etc., influence the result of the experiment. But no experiment can take account of *all* influences. To achieve practical purposes, the scientist must disregard factors which he deems to have a negligible bearing on his particular problem. When great precision is needed, he cannot abstract from some of the influences ordinarily ignored; they must be estimated and stated in figures. But an infinity of related factors remains, and estimating their influence would be an infinite task. The experimenter must always be satisfied with some approximation to exactitude, varying according to the particular investigation. Closed systems, isolated from the rest of the universe, are at best only useful fictions in the sense of "false assumptions made for practical purposes," as Vaihinger calls them. They are isolated by acts of will, the acts of *découpage* described by Bergson. There is thus a sense in which physical science proceeds by deliberately tearing phenomena out of context. The gap between physical science and the "infinitely small" can also be seen by asking what an exact measurement would be. Can a scale ever be read with mathematical precision or be constructed so as to be mathematically exact? There must always be a gap between physical formulae and concrete perception. Moreover, science cannot achieve a definitive system. As new experiences present themselves, the scientists must revise their conceptual system to accommodate those experiences. Their theories are provisional and hypothetical. As Babbitt points out, the physicist who attributes finality to his concepts is succumbing to an evil temptation. It is wrong for the scientist to "attach an independent value to the operations of the intellect that have only an instrumental value in the service of outer perception and to conceive that he has locked up physical nature in his formulae. The man of science thus falls victim to a special form of metaphysical illusion." (RR, 139) He becomes a "mere rationalist," putting rigid abstractions in the place of concrete reality.

Babbitt comments on the problem of the infinitely great and small: "Many of the speculations of science merely represent the desperate strainings of the human spirit to grasp in its essence and formulate what must forever elude it,—the final truth of the infinitely small,—just as a certain type of theology is an equally futile attempt to grasp in its essence and formulate the infinitely great." (NL, 210) According to Pascal, the universe is an infinite sphere, the center of which is everywhere, and the periphery of which is nowhere. There is for him no clearer sign of the omnipotence of God than the fact that our mind loses itself in this thought. We tend to despise whatever is small. The thought that the small can be forever divided into still smaller parts does not tend to elevate our minds to religion. But if it does not, it should, for these extremes meet in God, and in God alone. To Pascal, the infinitely great is more obviously relevant to religion than is the infinitely small. But they are both relevant to physics. Babbitt comments, "One suspects the more ambitious of the scientific theorists of attempting to do something that Pascal, himself an eminent man of science, declared to be impossible—namely, to grasp either one or both of the two 'infinites'—the infinite of largeness and that of smallness—by which man is encompassed." (OBC, xxvii)[9]

By drawing attention to the fictional element in the concepts of natural science one does not necessarily deny that they are grounded in reality in their own way. The natural scientist does interact with reality in its external aspect, and in a sense he tries to know it. He employs hypothetical constructs which are useful in *handling* his subject matter and which let him predict events. Mathematized general theories of nature or the universe are no less pragmatic because of their disembodied, highly abstract quality, for they offer strategies for the further experimental interaction with the outside world.

The constant gushing forth of concrete experiential material proves the provisional nature of the conceptual structures formulated by the natural scientist. While they contain truth of a kind, they never exhaust it. Put in a different way, the concepts have the only sort of truth that a symbolic language may have. That truth is never literal or definitive. To be sure, the symbols of natural science are systems of *signs* and thereby differ from the symbols of art, religion and humanistic inquiry which express interior meanings. Common to systems of signs and humanistic symbols is that their truth is never final and complete. Natural science is everywhere built on convenient approximations. Concrete and individual reality slips through the meshes of its conceptual nets. A net or a sieve cannot hold water. The inevitability of symbolism explains why there is something *illusory* about reality. What man catches in his net of concepts or "laws" is not necessarily unreal; by them he tries to lay hold on life's element of unity and permanence. But an integral part of reality is its inexhaustible manifoldness-

9. Irving Babbitt, *On Being Creative* (New York: Biblo and Tannen, 1968), xxvii; hereinafter referred to in the text as "OBC."

concreteness-individuality-change, which leaves knowledge provisional. Even philosophy, which looks for the universal in life as concretely experienced, is forever capable of improving upon its concepts; its search for truth never comes to rest in omniscience. Reality baffles our attempts to imprison it in concepts once and for all. That "illusion is an integral part of reality" furnishes the clue to Babbitt's meaning when he writes: "The fact is that we do not know and can never know what nature is in herself. The mysterious mother has shrouded herself from us in an impenetrable veil of illusion." (RR, 232) Babbitt is not expressing the Kantian doctrine of the thing-in-itself, as it is ordinarily interpreted. His meaning is that science has an infinite task. The element of manifoldness-individuality-variation will forever overflow the fixed and frozen finality of scientific laws and force their revision. What we know is certainly the thing-in-itself, but we know it only through "a veil of illusion," i.e., through a symbolism of scientific thought that is tentative and hypothetical. There is no absolute hiatus between a world of phenomena which can be known, and a thing-in-itself which cannot.

It must be added that Babbitt insists our "mysterious mother" can be approached not only through physical science but through biological science. Observation, he says, shows that there is a teleological element in nature. "At the same time it is well to remember that nature's ways are not man's ways and that the purpose that appears in her processes has little relation to the purpose that appears in some distinctively human creation." (OBC, 177) Babbitt does not explicitly address the subject whether in science the physical or biological approach brings us closer to the heart of nature. But in his last book, *On Being Creative*, he gives an important clue which seems to settle the matter. As the epigraph and "connecting theme" of his essays he quotes the Aristotelian dictum, "The first is not the seed but the perfect." The significance of this dictum is apparent when read in its context in the *Metaphysics* (1072^b). The context is a discussion of the "first mover," or God. Aristotle's physics cannot be separated from his metaphysics. As Sir David Ross points out, physics is distinct from a study which concentrates entirely on matter, which reduces a living body for instance, or an inanimate chemical compound, to its elements, and takes no thought of the structure which makes the living body or the compound what it is. Aristotle is in fact pronouncing in favour of teleology as against *mere* mechanism, in favour of studying the parts in the light of the whole instead of treating the whole as merely a sum of parts. Physics is the study not of form alone nor of matter alone but of informed matter or of inmattered form.[10]

Perhaps L. T. More did not get Babbitt entirely wrong; there *is* a chasm between More's purely Newtonian physics and Babbitt's view of nature, which is religious in the Aristotelian sense, a metaphysical physics—a view for which more can be said than L. T. More recognized.

It has become clear that while Babbitt recognizes the validity and importance of natural science, he views its thought-processes as inevitably taking liberties with the facts of actual experience. The reason of natural science puts abstractions in the place of concrete reality. Babbitt warns of the dangers of rationalistic doctrines that ignore the place of the part in the experiential whole. His stress on the limits of reason in grasping reality extends beyond its role in science. He is also prone to underestimate the accomplishments of technical philosophy as dealing too much in abstractions removed from the central problems of life. To understand the essence of his human nature, man must turn to immediate experience.

10. Sir David Ross, *Aristotle* (New York: University Paperback, 1974), 71.

Chapter 4
Philosophical Reason

Granted that the natural scientist must abstract from concrete observation, how would Babbitt describe the kind of work that is exemplified by his own books? He repeatedly points to the immediacy of experience as the proper frame of reference for inquiries into what is distinctively human; yet his books are not compilations of mere intuitions. They present *thought* about experience. Babbitt *argues* for his point of view, developing *concepts, distinctions* and *definitions*. As his books philosophize about man, they must employ reason of some kind.

Do we philosophize by means of classificatory, pragmatic concepts? Babbitt never concentrates on this problem of philosophical logic. He vaguely assumes an answer in the affirmative. This must be regarded as a weak part of his work. Here he could have learned much from Croce. Babbitt's relative inattention to the epistemological basis of his own ideas is not atypical of thinkers in this century who have been interested primarily in ethical wisdom and have sought to defend universal values. But until such theories become aware of and can defend their own epistemological foundation, they must lack confidence in philosophical debates and ultimately fail in the task of persuasion.

In analyzing this epistemological weakness as it appears in Babbitt, the following passage from *Democracy and Leadership* may serve as the starting point:

To determine the quality of our imaginings, we need to supplement the power in man that perceives and the power that conceives with a third power—that which discriminates. All divisions of man into powers or faculties are, I am aware, more or less arbitrary, but, though arbitrary, they are inevitable, if only as instruments of thought; and the threefold division I am here employing will, I believe, be found practically one of the most helpful.

In emphasizing the importance of the power in man that discriminates, I mean this power, working not abstractly, but on the actual material of experience. I may perhaps best sum up my whole point of view by saying that the only thing that finally counts in this world is a concentration, at once imaginative and discriminating, on the facts. Now the facts that one may perceive and on which one may concentrate are not only infinite in number, but of entirely different orders. (DL, 14-15)[1]

This threefold division is concerned only with what Croce calls the "theoretical" side of human nature. Babbitt does not here mention volition, which he divides into a higher and a lower will. One wonders whether he would call this latter division, too, "more or less arbitrary." The present quote suggests that he regards imagination ("the power that conceives"), perception ("the power that perceives") and reason ("the power that discriminates") as classificatory concepts sharing the defects of all classificatory concepts: vagueness and/or arbitrariness.

Concepts like "bald" or "red-haired" are inherently and inescapably vague. Any criteria invented to make their application precise are easily seen to be arbitrary; the boundaries between classes can always be drawn differently. Whatever the degree of precision achieved, borderline cases are always possible. Even seemingly "real" classifications, like "man" and "woman," permit of borderline cases, for example, a person changing sex. We cannot state precisely the meaning of classificatory concepts and how they should be applied to individual cases. The distinguishing characteristics of a flower are enumerated in a handbook of botany. They are in effect rules of action, certain observations to be made to ascertain whether a certain specimen belongs to a certain class. However elaborate the classificatory scheme, individual cases will baffle the observer. Pragmatic concepts are of two kinds, classificatory and mathematical. The

1. Irving Babbitt, *Democracy and Leadership* (Boston: Houghton Mifflin, 1952), 14-15; hereinafter referred to in the text as "DL."

latter are also operational but in a special manner.[2]

Babbitt admits he does not know *precisely* what he means by his terms "imagination," "perception," and "reason" or how to apply them in the analysis of experience. He is not unhappy about this, for he believes any set of classificatory terms would run up against the same difficulty. He would doubtless think the same about the distinction between the volitive-practical and the theoretical sides of human experience. But would he take a pragmatic view also of his distinctions between the higher and the lower will, the higher and the lower "immediacy," "super-rational" and "sub-rational"? If he did, the entire structure of his thought, whether he calls it his philosophy or not, would be threatened by collapse. It will soon be demonstrated that for the structure to remain standing at least one distinction must be definite and clear-cut, or "categorial," to use Croce's terminology.

Babbitt might admit this much and still argue that no one has gotten beyond vagueness in his definitions of "imagination," "perception" and "reason." Croce would answer that the aim of philosophy is to arrive at categorial distinctions. The advance of philosophy is the progressive elimination of mere pragmatic-psychological classifications. Even though this be an infinite task, which finds ever new challenges in fresh classifications forced upon our attention, what has already been achieved should not be underestimated. Thus the "imagination" in Coleridge's sense is no mere psychological classification: it is a clear-cut category, although keeping it clear-cut—by eliminating remaining traces of classification, preserving it from new intrusions of psychology and exploring its relation to other categories—is a never-ending task. Similarly, "pragmatic thought" has been well defined as a category, although work remains to be done, above all its clear-cut delimitation in every special case from "categorial thought." If "imagination," "perception" and "reason" are generally used vaguely as Babbitt says, the philosopher takes this fact as a challenge and attempts

---

2. The subject of pragmatic concepts has to be taken up in stages and will be expanded upon in later chapters.

to discern structural realities behind the terms. Unaware of this special task of philosophy, Babbitt suggests that if some psychological classifications other than his own are found more convenient, they should be adopted, as all definitions are "more or less arbitrary." Most of Babbitt's explicit comments about pragmatism are critical, but he is closer to its epistemology than perhaps he recognizes.

Pragmatism that has not been supplemented with a categorial logic, as in Croce's philosophy, is easily reduced to the absurd. It must finally become bogged down in a chaos of undefined concepts. Are all discriminations pragmatic fictions? Babbitt claims not to know very clearly what is meant by "discrimination" and says that what should be classified as "discrimination" is decided more or less arbitrarily. What is meant by "arbitrary"? Do we decide more or less arbitrarily what is arbitrary and what is not? By what standard do we measure "more or less"? Attempted pragmatic answers have to make use of some standard of reality and employ terms like "perception" and "facts." The trouble with pragmatism is that the standard, the perception of reality, by which degrees of arbitrariness are supposed to be measured, is itself defined more or less arbitrarily. Thus, the ideas of "arbitrary" and "more or less" turn out to be themselves more or less arbitrary. Epistemological pragmatism dissolves itself into a conceptual flux.

It would be ruinous for Babbitt's thought to treat his numerous dichotomies as more or less arbitrary fictions. It can be demonstrated that they are otherwise. Croce shows that there are discriminations of two types, those which are a matter of pragmatic convenience and those which are not. A merely classificatory logic excludes the idea of non-arbitrary dichotomies. The task of identifying categorial realities falls to philosophy proper.

In spite of the epistemological resemblance just described, Babbitt's general attitude towards the philosophical school of pragmatism is mostly negative. He is sharply critical of its failure to recognize the existence of a transcendent ethical principle. He also senses something wrong with its theory of knowledge. But Babbitt's stated criticism of pragmatism rests on little except intuition, because he does not—at least not explicitly—affirm the existence of real categories. He claims to reject "pragmatism which, instead of testing utility by truth, would test truth by utility; likewise for the closely allied theory of 'useful fiction' . . . ." (DL, 225) Yet his own "threefold division" of human faculties is recommended only as "the most helpful." Criticizing pragmatism, Babbitt sets up "perception" of the truth as the criterion by which to test utility; but if, in deciding what should be regarded as "perception," Babbitt falls back on the test of what is "most helpful," he himself is using some sort of utility as a test for truth.

Babbitt has been quoted as saying that "the facts that one may perceive and on which one may concentrate are not only infinite in number, but of entirely different orders." (DL, 14-15) The idea of perceiving and discriminating between these orders is highly problematic in view of the assumed arbitrariness of the definitions of "perception" and "discrimination." Threatened also is Babbitt's distinction between a "power in man that discriminates . . . working . . . abstractly" and one that works "on the actual material of experience." The former activity is presumably the metaphysical use of reason. The "actual material of experience" is what is directly perceived. If all these distinctions, including the very notion of "a distinction," are more or less arbitrary (in which case neither "arbitrary" nor "more or less" have a distinct meaning), Babbitt's entire structure of concepts breaks down. In actuality his insights are real indeed, and they have a firmer epistemological foundation than he assumes. By combining his thought with a categorial logic it is possible to extricate his concepts from the pragmatic morass.

Searching for the categorial realities behind the "psychological" classifications believed by Babbitt to be "the most helpful," one may first take note of his distinction, implicit rather than explicit, between the practical-volitive and the theoretical side of human nature. It will be explained later why this should be considered a categorial distinction. Babbitt introduces it, as it were, unawares. It has been suggested that even the empirical psychologist has an undiscovered speculative philosopher working within him. As regards Babbitt's distinctions within man's theoretical life, the imagination can be accepted as a categorial reality. Difficulties arise regarding "the power that perceives" and "the power that discriminates." It will be argued that the categorial realities are poorly covered by these classifications. The heart of the matter is that perception and discrimination are the same: we cannot perceive without distinguishing and categorizing. The power of perception is the reason of philosophy.

Philosophical reason underlies all intellectual activity, whether predominantly philosophical or not. This is the case even though the particular thinker may, as is the order of the day, be unaware of its role and peculiar nature. Philosophical reason is at work whenever Babbitt makes one of his numerous dichotomies. He introduces them one by one almost as if they were unrelated items. On closer inspection, they turn out to be so interrelated that each one implies all the others. Together they form a conceptual network, in the sense that already has been explained. To grasp, say, the distinction between constitutional and direct democracy, it is necessary to pass on to dichotomies of such terms as "popular will," "liberty," "equality" and "fraternity." These distinctions draw one into yet other dichotomies such as that of "will" in two senses (higher and lower); moral and utilitarian "good"; "comfort" in the religious and the utilitarian sense; "ideal," "soul" and "the infinite" in the classical and the romantic sense; "heart" as understood by Pascal and by Rousseau; "humanism" in Babbitt's sense and as a term for sentimental humanitarianism; and so on. The network of Babbittian dichotomies turns out to be a comprehensive philosophy.

Nevertheless, what has just been said about a synthetic Reason, about dichotomies forming a nexus, is not found in Babbitt's own books. He is incompletely aware of the nature of his own activity when establishing his dichotomies. He says he is practicing "the Socratic art of definition," but he sometimes leaves the impression of viewing the definitions as separate items and of being only vaguely conscious of their interconnection. He suggests that "we should make as many and as clear distinctions as possible and then project them like vivid sunbeams into the romantic twilight.'' (NL, 244)[3] But distinctions are partial definitions. Distinctions and definitions cannot be made quite clear unless they are explained within the categories of a systematic philosophy. Babbitt's success as a teacher depended on the willingness of his students to accept the terms in which his dichotomies were stated on a common-sense basis. The students did well to wait for the nexus to emerge as the end product of the particular course.

When a system of thought has been patiently apprehended, the time has come to inquire into the logic by which it was established. Teachers of philosophy usually begin at the other end. They may thus try to explicate theories of valuation before the students have attained even an elementary perception of the facts of the moral life. The result easily becomes a wild-goose chase in which not a single thought is caught and held firmly. Babbitt trained his students to perceive the role of morality and decadence in concrete historical currents. History and philosophy coalesced. If the question of valuation then arose, the alternatives were acceptance or rejection of an entire nexus of concepts and of the interpretation of history inseparably tied to this nexus. There was no room for will-o'-the-wisp acceptance and rejection of fragments of Babbitt's teaching. He told his students, ''Save your questions and objections until you can survey my moral theory as a whole!'' The students eventually found themselves up against a formidable mass of interpreted history which they had to re-interpret for themselves if they questioned Babbitt's interconnected criteria of interpretation.

Babbitt was strangely loath to attempt a consciously systematic philosophy. At the end of *The New Laokoon* he writes that he ''aspired at most to be a humble imitator of Lessing . . . not to achieve a complete and closed system, but to scatter the *fermenta cognitionis.*'' (NL, 252) A ''complete and closed system'' is clearly beyond the powers of man, but real philosophy is systematic as far as it goes. Babbitt's statement looks like a display of false humility. He possesses an imposing constel-

3. Irving Babbitt, *The New Laokoon* (Boston: Houghton Mifflin, 1910), 244; hereinafter referred to in the text as ''NL.''

lation of concepts based on effective philosophizing about many aspects of life. If he had gone on to philosophize about the epistemological status of his own thought, the result would have been an explicitly systematic approach and a logic of philosophy.

Philosophy as here understood corresponds to what Coleridge called the "speculative reason." But the idea of Coleridge and others is ambiguous in that it does not distinguish the speculative reason from some other spiritual activities. Like Kant and Fichte before him, Coleridge did not separate speculative reason from so-called "practical reason." The effort will here be made to show that in the final analysis the latter power is not a form of reason but is non-conceptual choice, or will. Another source of ambiguity, clearly noticeable in Coleridge and Schelling, was to confuse speculative reason with imaginative vision, and a sometimes questionable vision at that: the romantic God-Nature.

There are many comments on the nature of philosophy in Kant's various books, especially in the *Critique of Pure Reason*. But these comments are ideas scattered in passing. Kant is not sufficiently aware of the special nature of the topic to undertake a special inquiry. He asks and answers the questions, "How is mathematics possible?", "How is physics possible?", "How is biology possible?", etc., but he does not ask the question, "How is transcendental philosophy possible?" In other words, Kant pays close attention to the nature of what mathematicians, physicists, biologists, metaphysicians and artists are doing, but he does not probe very deeply into what he himself, the critical philosopher, is doing. The corpus of Kant's writings contains the three *Critiques* but not a *Critique of Critical Reason*. The absence of a volume on the logic of philosophy was the secret drive behind much post-Kantian philosophy. The gap was finally filled, however imperfectly, by Hegel's notion of philosophy as the self-knowledge of the Spirit. Fichte had moved towards the notion that the source of philosophical knowledge is what we *feel* in moments of ethical inspiration. In such moments we know that the world is the material on which to do our duty. The tendency of Schelling in the same matter was to say that when listening to a symphony we *feel* that natural history and human history together form one great, wonderfully perfect symphony. Art is *"zugleich Organon und Dokument der Philosophie."*[4] For Fichte and Schelling, something we "feel" is thus the source of truth about life and the world. Hegel, by contrast, emphatically states that philosophy is a special kind of *logical thought,* distinct from *Verstand.* This idea, involved as it is in clouds of obscurity like almost everything else in Hegel, was largely lost in nineteenth-century philosophy. It has been revived in the twentieth century by Benedetto Croce and Theodor Litt but has yet to be widely studied and understood.[5]

Most contemporary philosophers seem unaware of the logical problem in question. The following famous and representative ideas have put their mark on much of philosophy in this century:

There are no absolutely certain empirical propositions. It is only tautologies that are certain.[6]

The only knowledge a priori is purely analytic; all empirical knowledge is probable only.[7]

The principles of logic and mathematics represent the only domain in which certainty is attainable; but these principles are analytic and empty. Certainty is inseparable from emptiness: there is no synthetic a priori.[8]

But what about the alleged knowledge formulated in these sentences? Is it a priori? Is it empirical? Those who, appealing to Russell's theory of types, would opt for a third kind, have thereby admitted that the quoted sentences form an incomplete

4. F.W.J. Schelling, *System des transzendentalen Idealismus,* Sämtliche Werke, Vol. III, 612 ff.

5. The idea of a logic of philosophy is explained with great perspicacity in the first part of Theodor Litt, *Einleitung in die Philosophie* (Berlin: B.G. Teubner Verlag, 1933), esp. 33ff. Litt takes up this idea in all of his subsequent books. Of special importance is *Hegel; Versuch einer kritischen Erneuerung* (1953).

6. A.J. Ayer, *Language, Truth and Logic* (London: Victor Gollanez, 1936), 131.

7. C.I. Lewis, *Mind and the World Order* (New York: Charles Scribner's Sons, 1929), 309.

8. H. Reichenbach, *The Rise of Scientific Philosophy* (Berkeley: University of California Press, 1951), 304.

account of knowledge and that philosophy has an unexplored logic of its own. Reichenbach avoids the theory of types and contends that philosophy is empirical knowledge: "Scientific philosophy . . . insists that the question of truth must be raised within philosophy in the same sense as in the sciences. It does not claim to possess an absolute truth, the existence of which it denies for empirical knowledge. Inasmuch as it refers to the existent state of knowledge and develops the theory of this knowledge, the new philosophy is itself empirical and is satisfied with empirical truth."[9] But if this is so, hypothesis-verification is assumed to be the necessary logic of human knowledge. Affirming at least this one absolute truth, Reichenbach is inconsistent in his assertion that Scientific Philosophy "does not claim to possess an absolute truth."

In *Logic, the Theory of Inquiry* (1938) Dewey tries to show that pragmatic logic is self-applying, i.e., that we use pragmatic logic also when inquiring into the nature of thought.[10] He can uphold this thesis only by using terms vaguely. It can be admitted that all thought is a "trying out" of ideas to see whether they cover "the facts." This is a kind of "verification." This logic characterizes philosophy as well. But the facts of philosophical observation are not the kind of separate items which form the evidence for scientific hypotheses; rather, they are aspects of the permanent structure of experience. This structure is presupposed in the very formation of concepts like "hypothesis," "verification" and "facts" (in the scientific sense). That philosophy explores this permanent structure tentatively and step by step is misinterpreted by Dewey and others as evidence that the exploration is an application of pragmatic reason.

The weakness of Babbitt's vaguely pragmatic assumptions about the nature of reason may be further demonstrated by considering one of his favorite doctrines. According to Babbitt, one side of experience is what Bergson likes to dwell upon: "Life is a perpetual gushing forth of novelties." But there is in experience, Babbitt insists, also something recurring and permanent, which is also a matter of observation. This is Babbitt's

9. *Ibid.*, 325.
10. John Dewey, *Logic, the Theory of Inquiry* (New York: Henry Holt, 1938).

theme of dualism. What is the epistemological basis of the concepts in which he explains that dualism? Is "experience" (or "life," or any other synonymous term) a pragmatic concept? Pragmatic concepts are rules of action applied to materials of experience. But "experience" itself is the field to which rules of action are applied. In general, the concepts used to define "pragmatic concept" cannot themselves be pragmatic concepts. Thus, "rule," "action," "applying," "materials of experience" are not pragmatic. The same is true of "pragmatic concept." These are philosophical concepts expressing the permanent structure of human consciousness. "The perpetually ongoing formation and application of pragmatic concepts" also articulates a universal aspect of life. Pragmatic thought-action takes place within a larger whole; and the concepts used to describe the permanent elements of this larger whole are not pragmatic. Hence, "a perpetual gushing forth of novelties" is not an observation of experience in the empiricist sense, for it records no particular fact but an aspect of *all* experience. "The presence of something recurring and permanent" is also a philosophical concept. "Observation," "multiplicity," "change," "concreteness," "similarities," "analogies" and "elements of oneness" are other expressions of permanent traits of experience that are presupposed in any account of the nature of pragmatic thought-action; they are used in its very definition.

Babbitt has a strong sense of the limits of "reason" when it comes to grasping the essential facts of human life. He therefore says of the element of manifoldness and change and the element of oneness that they are "intuited." And so they are. But we also articulate what we intuit by forging a term for it. We give conceptual form to experience. The "what" may be a structural trait of experience, a category. According to Babbitt, the erroneous road leading towards a "metaphysic of the One" is attending exclusively to life's recurrent elements: Man allows himself to construct a prematurely closed system, blinding himself to or explaining away life's variety and change. "The metaphysicians of the Many," Bergson, for example, do not attend to what is permanent. How does Babbitt *know* all this? By what faculty is he able to explain the shortcomings of the two opposed types of metaphysics? He gives a rational account of the structure of experience and of the two ways of misinterpreting it. He expresses *conceptually* what he has also intuited. He does not argue his case by means of intuitions but by means of concepts. He is relying on philosophical reason.

If Babbitt's critique of the two opposed metaphysical errors is an example of *reason,* what status have the metaphysical errors? The deliberate neglect of variety and change in the metaphysics of the One and of permanence in the metaphysics of the Many can hardly be called love of truth. Disregard of the observable facts of experience must be considered a volitional interference with the functioning of the inquiring mind. Yet Babbitt believes that it is on account of *reason* that the unity is separated from the variety. In reality, the metaphysical system arises from an overpowering of immediate perception. A prejudiced will silences by *fiat* the doubts about the system that can never be quite subdued and that emanate from genuinely philosophical reason.

To his many dichotomies Babbitt should have added one of the word "reason." Sometimes he seems to feel a need for such a dichotomy. Consider, for instance, the inverted commas around "reason" when he writes, "The person who confides unduly in 'reason' is also prone to set up some static 'absolute'; while those who seek to get rid of the absolute in favor of flux and relativity tend at the same time to get rid of standards. Both absolutists and relativists are guilty of an intellectual sophistication of the facts, inasmuch as in life as it is actually experienced, unity and multiplicity are indissolubly blended." (DL, 169) The inverted commas around "reason" indicate the need for a distinction between the metaphysical speculation Babbitt is criticizing and philosophical reason. How could he know and criticize the shortcomings of "reason" except through a more fundamental, more truly reliable reason? The same need for a distinction is implied in Babbitt's remark that it is reasonable not to be a rationalist. (OBC, xxviii)[11] But as usual, he shows scant interest in questions of philosophical logic

11. Irving Babbitt, *On Being Creative* (New York: Biblo and Tannen, 1968), xxviii; hereinafter referred to in the text as "OBC."

and leaves the remark as a *bon mot*.

Dr. Johnson said, "All theory is against the freedom of the will, all experience for it." Babbitt quotes this dictum with approval. (DL, 228) But if Dr. Johnson were right, no rational reply could be given to a person who claimed the experience of freedom was illusory. The believer in free will could only entertain a rationally inarticulate feeling that the determinist arguments were somehow false. False? Even his own reason would tell him they were valid. Nor could he hope to find arguments for his inarticulate feeling. Attempting a *theory* of anti-intellectualism is not very promising, if *all* theory is against the freedom of the will.

Using a better terminology than Dr. Johnson's, one might say instead: All understanding *(Verstand)* is against the freedom of the will, while all reason *(Vernunft)* is for it. Mere "experience" or "intuition" is without voice in rational debate. *Philosophical accounts* of what we experience and intuit, on the other hand, can be opposed to deterministic theories which, when criticized philosophically, turn out to be abstract metaphysical decrees. Babbitt and P. E. More themselves actually theorize persistently in favor of the freedom of the will.

Speaking of Bergson and similar thinkers, Babbitt likes to say that they proved themselves the keenest of intellectuals when developing their philosophies of anti-intellectualism. To make more than *bons mots* of these remarks, Babbitt would have needed to distinguish between pragmatic and philosophic intellect. It is the latter that reveals the limitations of the former. The distinction between two kinds of reason is unknown also to Bergson, who never explains what within him performs the criticism of pragmatic rationality.

If Babbitt had achieved the dichotomy of "reason," he would not have termed his own point of view, which is sharply critical of positivism, "a more complete positivism." Positivism is the recording of individual facts. The human consciousness, to which Babbitt turns for reliable knowledge about man, is not a collection of atomic facts but a nexus of potentialities, of *potenze del fare*, to use Croce's phrase. Babbitt's higher will, for instance, is not a fact in the positivist sense but a *potentiality of action*.

Babbitt's thought would have been affected in still other ways by the dichotomy. He writes: "To suppose that one can transcend the element of impermanence, whether in oneself or the outer world, merely through reason in any sense of the word, is to forget that 'illusion is an integral part of reality.'" (DL, 168-169) Babbitt here claims to *know* something about the human predicament, to have access to a permanent and unchanging truth and reality. The sentence is thus self-contradictory. To put the criticism in a different way: Does Babbitt really *know* that "illusion is an integral part of reality," or is this idea, too, in part illusory? Babbitt says of Buddha, "The list of 'unthinkables' he drew up is almost equivalent to a denial that life can in any deep sense of the word be *known* at all." (DL, 168) But then Buddha had thought enough to know that life is "in any deep sense . . . unthinkable."

Man is certainly frighteningly ignorant; he has to act without knowing more than a fragment of the circumstances or consequences of his actions. The ever-remaining incompleteness of scientific knowledge involves this type of ignorance. Here it may be true, in Babbitt's words, that our knowledge "is destined always to remain a mere glimpse and infinitesimal fragment." (NL, 211) But our ignorance is not of the same kind in the area of philosophical self-knowledge. Here, too, there is room for infinite improvement of insight, but it is progress of a special kind: it is making clearer that which we somehow already know, although in an inarticulate manner. Man has, in a sense, always known his own nature. Sophocles, Homer and Shakespeare exemplify this knowledge. The never-to-be-completed task of philosophy is to raise the intuitive-imaginative insight represented by such writers into ever clearer conceptual knowledge. Progress in philosophy is not additive but qualitative.

Babbitt is exaggerating our ignorance partly because he is confusing the two types of reason. If pressed, would he actually maintain that Buddha's knowledge of the human predicament is "a mere glimpse and infinitesimal fragment"? It would then be difficult for Babbitt to justify his deep reverence for Buddha's wisdom and for that of other great sages and teachers of the race. Christ, Buddha, Confucius, Plato and Aristotle all understand human nature intuitively; some of them have also contributed greatly to the conceptual formulation of this knowledge. Inconsistently, Babbitt says about Buddha that he gives the impression of being a man who has thought out his ideas to the ultimate degree of clarity. (D, 72)[12] This, too, is of course an exaggeration, if there is no ultimate degree of clarity, but philosophy is forever striving to improve its grasp of reality.

Babbitt's own books contain insights about human nature as revealed in historical experience. He certainly claims more for them than that they represent "a mere glimpse and infinitesimal fragment." What meaning would there be in his oft-repeated term "the wisdom of the ages," if man does not have a greater capacity for knowledge. Babbitt would naturally recognize that his own understanding of various subjects will require complements, refinements or revisions, but the claim implicit in his treatment of some of these subjects is to have discerned their most essential traits. The assessment of this book is that this claim is largely justified but that his position can be strengthened by incorporating ideas of the type here being developed.

12. Irving Babbitt, "Buddha and the Occident," in *The Dhammapada*, translated and with an Essay on Buddha and the Occident by Irving Babbitt (New York: New Directions, 1965); hereinafter referred to in the text as "D."

Chapter 5
"The Scandal of Reason"

Irving Babbitt's first publication, which appeared in 1897, is an essay in defense of reason, "The Rational Study of the Classics." "Reason" here has a broad meaning: "Classical literature, at its best . . . appeals . . . to our higher reason and imagination—to those faculties which afford us an avenue of escape from ourselves, and enable us to become participants in the universal life . . . . The classical spirit, in its purest form, feels itself consecrated to the service of a high, impersonal reason." (LAC, 116-17)[1] Babbitt here tends to use "reason" as a term for all of the spiritual functions that define man's true humanity. This early, very broad meaning of the word is reminiscent of Eric Voegelin, who speaks of reason as "the source of order" and "the constituent of humanity at all times."[2] In his ensuing work Babbitt goes beyond Voegelin as he analyzes the "high, impersonal reason" into constituent elements: "I not only have more to say of will and less of reason than the humanist in the Graeco-Roman tradition, but I also grant a most important role to imagination." (DL, 10)[3]

In *The New Laokoon* (1910) Babbitt speculates that the contemporary process of dehumanization may continue indefinitely and produce "philosophy even more careless of rationality than that of the pragmatists." (NL, 238)[4] The rationality he implicitly

1. Irving Babbitt, *Literature and the American College* (Chicago: Henry Regnery, 1956; first published in 1908), 116-17; hereinafter referred to in the text as "LAC."

2. Eric Voegelin, "Reason: The Classic Experience," in *Anamnesis* (Notre Dame: University of Notre Dame Press, 1978), 89.

3. Irving Babbitt, *Democracy and Leadership* (Boston: Houghton Mifflin, 1952), 10; hereinafter referred to in the text as "DL."

4. Irving Babbitt, *The New Laokoon* (Boston: Houghton Mifflin, 1910), 238; hereinafter referred to in the text as "NL."

defends does not coincide, except in part, with that of the Anglo-Hegelians. He is even more unsympathetic to them than to the pragmatists. "It is doubtless better to be a pragmatist than to devote one's self to embracing the cloud Junos of Hegelian metaphysics." (LAC, 18) Babbitt unquestionably agrees with P.E. More who writes: "I confess that to me monism has always been merely another word for monomania, and I have followed Mr. James's sallies into the madhouse with a kind of gay amusement."[5] In the Preface to *Masters of Modern French Criticism* (1912), Babbitt welcomes the reaction against "intellectualism" in philosophy. Henri Bergson and William James contribute to a recovery of "noetic" truth by criticizing "scientific positivism" and other kinds of abstract rationalism. Yet Babbitt also sees them as erring seriously, not only in their relativistic naturalism, but in "reducing the intellect to a purely utilitarian role." (MFC, xxvi-xxviii)[6] The ambiguity of Babbitt's understanding of reason is again apparent. He vaguely recognizes a non-pragmatic role for the intellect, but the nature of that higher form of rationality is never adequately defined.

Babbitt is hampered by his habit of seeing a tension between experience and the operations of the intellect. Immediate consciousness presents man with the dualism of the One and the Many, but reason as Babbitt ordinarily understands it has to deny this primordial fact. A look at F. H. Bradley's logical system is here appropriate, for his philosophy forms an important part of Babbitt's, and More's, frame of reference in matters pertaining to reason. The following examination of Bradley's logic will help to explain why Babbitt calls the duality of experience "the scandal of reason." It will also formulate an alternative to Bradley's, and Babbitt's, logical position. It has been suggested that Babbitt's appeals to experience can have intellectual power only if they are simultaneously conceptual propositions. The Crocean idea of dialectic is precisely the logical recognition of the duality of human existence. Permitting conceptual accounts of life that are faithful to actual experience,

5. P.E. More, *Shelburne Essays* (11 Vols.; Phaeton Press, 1967), VII, 200.
6. Irving Babbitt, *Masters of Modern French Criticism* (New York: Noonday Press, 1963); hereinafter referred to in the text as "MFC."

dialectical logic provides an epistemological supplement of which Babbitt's doctrine of dualism stands in need. As the term "dialectic" has been used in many different ways since Plato, care has to be taken in explicating its meaning. The following summary of Bradley's position forms a convenient starting point:

His doctrine is all instinct with a vigorous effort towards the affirmations of a transcendental faith; but the paths which it follows are singularly like those of scepticism. The idea of relation is predominant in the life of the mind; and this idea, involving a contradiction, disappears when analyzed; there remains nothing but the one and indivisible reality which is revealed to us by concrete experience, and over which the necessities of action weave the artificial network of our concepts. Thus, while Bradley is a metaphysician, and an almost mystic one, he yet finds the justification of knowledge in the privileged needs of life. He is in agreement with the disciples of William James.[7]

This competent summary is in one respect misleading. Bradley is said to view reality as "revealed to us by concrete experience." As will be shown, he really says both yes and no to this proposition, stressing the "no." He argues that perception gives unreal appearances. We know reality by what might be called an "unearthly" use of reason. The law of this reason is "A = A, and not non-A." Any "earthly" use of reason is in conflict with this law. The quoted summary points out correctly that Bradley's idea of the "earthly" use of reason is similar to that of the pragmatists. Babbitt and More are influenced by this aspect of his teaching as well as by his idea that the "earthly" use of reason is riddled with self-contradictions. Although they reject the "unearthly" use of reason—that is, his metaphysics of the One—they assimilate his skepticism as regards the lower forms of knowledge. Those unfamiliar with Anglo-American academic philosophy around the turn of the century may be puzzled by the role played by Plato's *Parmenides* in the work of Babbitt and More. The clue to its role is found

7. Émile Legouis and Louis Cazamian, *A History of English Literature* (Rev. ed.; London: J.M. Dent and Sons, 1945), 1226-27.

in Bradley's *Appearance and Reality* (1893), which explains the self-contradictions of reason. Bradley presents a modern version of the old Eleatic logic: synthesis is impossible and inconceivable (although it is a fact), for synthesis involves seeing things in relation to one another, and "relation" is a self-contradictory idea. Since "earthly" thought is in fact synthetic, earthly experience must be mere appearance. "Reality" must be a Parmenidean unity.[8]

This unity seems vacuous to Babbitt and More. But in his *Principles of Logic* (1883) Bradley had taken pains to define "A = A" in such a way that the idea of a "system" could be included in it.[9] "Somehow," to use Bradley's favorite word, appearances form part of the Absolute, although not as appearances. In his notion of Absolute Experience, Bradley rises beyond the reach of any earthly telescope. The following sentence is illustrative: "Appearance . . . must be other than it seems." (AR, 140) As "appearance" means precisely "what seems," it is hardly meaningful to say that in the Absolute it is transformed into something "other than it seems." "Taken together" in the Whole, "appearances, as such, cease." (AR, 511) In the Absolute the objects of finite experience are "transmuted," "transformed," "dissolved in a higher unity," "suppressed," "destroyed," "lost." Bradley says repeatedly he does not understand "how" this can be so, but he has an inextinguishable faith that "somehow" the Absolute must be "a rich harmony" embracing "every special discord." (AR, 192) We have no direct knowledge of such an experience, but neither do we have any "basis on which to doubt that all content comes together harmoniously in the Absolute." (AR, 239)

Later philosophers who have charged inconsistencies in Bradley's concept of an Absolute Experience have often made their task too easy. John Dewey, on the other hand, believes there *is* an experiential basis for this concept. Bradley's theory, Dewey maintains, "rests upon one-sided selection of what actually

---

8. F.H. Bradley, *Appearance and Reality* (Oxford: Clarendon Press, 1946); hereinafter referred to in the text as "AR." The self- contradictions of reason are discussed in Book I, "reality" in Book II.

9. F.H. Bradley, *The Principles of Logic* (New York: G.E. Stechert, 1920), 131ff.

takes place in controlled inquiry. For every resolved situation which is the terminal state of inquiry exists directly as it is experienced. It is a qualitative individual situation in which are directly incorporated and absorbed the results of the mediating processes of inquiry."[10] This comment gives an inkling of the meaning of Croce's idea that absolute experience is what we have here and now. Even while rejecting Bradley's unearthly logic, Dewey admits the reality of an *intuition* of the Whole. "Even in the midst of conflict, struggle and defeat a consciousness is possible of the enduring and comprehending whole." For "every act may carry within itself a consoling and supporting consciousness of the whole to which it belongs and which in some sense belongs to it. . . . Within the flickering inconsequential acts of separate selves dwells a sense of the whole which claims and dignifies them. In its presence we put off mortality and live in the universal."[11] This is one element in Dewey that is neglected by those who judge him summarily by his attacks on "the classical tradition" and his naturalistic-behavioristic tendency (which is also more subtle and complicated than assumed by many of his critics). Dewey does not make enough of this sense of the whole, but it points to real similarities between his thought and Babbitt's, as well as that of the early More. Rejecting the logical scaffolding erected by Bradley around his monistic intuition, Babbitt and More nevertheless accept the intuition as a fact. Babbitt speaks of a "deep need of human nature—the need to lose itself in a larger whole." (RR, 136)[12]

10. John Dewey, *Logic, the Theory of Inquiry* (New York: Henry Holt, 1938), 533.

11. John Dewey, *Human Nature and Conduct* (New York: Henry Holt, 1922), 330-31.

12. Irving Babbitt, *Rousseau and Romanticism* (Austin: The University of Texas Press, 1977), 136; hereinafter referred to in the text as "RR." On the similarity between Dewey and Babbitt-More, see Folke Leander, *The Philosophy of John Dewey* (Göteborg: Elanders boktryckeri, 1939), Chapters VII-VIII. P.E. More has some critical remarks on "idealism," meaning in practice Bradley's philosophy, in his "Definitions of Dualism," *Shelburne Essays*, VIII, 268, 289. More insists on a sharp distinction between "the One" (which is supposed to be intuited) and "the Whole" (which is supposed to be a rational construct). But he is himself making use of Bradley's unearthly Eleatic logic. More's "the One" is just as much a rationalistic construct as is (on More's showing) Bradley's "the Whole." Both men rely on reifying logic. On More's critique of Bradley, see Folke Leander, *The Inner Check* (London: Edward Wright, 1974), 57-58.

A summary of why Bradley, and with him Babbitt and More, thinks relations are logical monstrosities is called for. "A is related to B" may be symbolized, A R B. The question arises, how is R related to A and how is it related to B? Still another sign has to be introduced, A r R r B. In Bradley's phraseology, "The links are united by a link, and this bond of union is a link which also has two ends; and these require each a fresh link to connect them with the old. The problem is to find how the relation can stand to its qualities; and this problem is insoluble. If you take the connection as a solid thing, you have got to show, and you cannot show, how the other solids are joined to it." (AR, 33)

Another way of explaining relations is as follows. There is no independent R, but the relation inheres in the two terms, A and B. But then a distinction has to be made within A between A in so far as it is a term of a relation (symbolized as *a*) and A in so far as it has an existence independently of the relation (symbolized as a). Then the question arises: how, within A, is *a* related to a? Related—here we are again! A distinction must be made within *a* and of course also within a; and so on forever. In Bradley's words:

A is both made, and is not made, what it is by relation; and these different aspects are not each the other, nor again is either A. If we call its diverse aspects *a* and a, the A is partly each of these. As a it is the difference on which distinction is based, while as *a* it is the distinctness that results from connection. A is really both somehow together as A (a-*a*). But *without* the use of a relation it is impossible to predicate this variety of A. And, on the other hand, *with* an internal relation A's unity disappears and its contents are dissipated in an endless process of distinction. A at first becomes *a* in relation with a, but these terms themselves fall hopelessly asunder. (AR, 31)

Let it be noted that the first alternative depends on a reification of R (as well as of A and B): R and A and B are explicitly taken to be "solids." The second alternative is also easily seen to be built on reification.

Dialectical logic, by contrast, solves these logical problems by radically rejecting reification in all its forms. The decisive step in this direction was taken by Hegel—the real Hegel and not the Hegel of the Anglo-Hegelians. The true import of Hegel's jettisoning of the law of contradiction ("A is not non-A") was getting rid of reifications. *Only* in this context can the law of contradiction be questioned. Croce and Giovanni Gentile understood this to be the basic idea of dialectics. This explains why "Hegelianism" has been entirely different in Italy than among the English-speaking. The act of synthesis is seeing things in relation to one another. According to Gentile, the logic of the reified *pensiero pensato* (thought completed) distorts the "spirituality" of the actual *pensiero pensante* (thought being thought). Croce explains reification as the illegitimate interference by the pragmatic understanding with the work of true reason.

In technical philosophy Babbitt and More were decisively affected when, under Bradley's influence, they accepted the notion of reason as inherently self-contradictory. They were essentially right in viewing Bradley's argument as Plato's *Parmenides* over again and in regarding Bradley's monism as one of the hypotheses overthrown in this dialogue. Unfamiliar with a non-Eleatic, non-reifying reason, Babbitt and More assume themselves to be dependent for true insight into the human condition on sheer intuition, superrational or subrational. Babbitt's Bradleyan, Eleatic assumptions are particularly evident in a passage from *Democracy and Leadership*. There is truth in the saying that history never repeats itself, Babbitt writes. But "it is about equally true that history is always repeating itself; and this is a part of the paradox of life itself which does not give us here an element of oneness, and there an element of change, but a oneness that is always changing. This implication of unity in diversity is the scandal of reason, and philosophers have, for the most part, ever since the Greeks, been seeking with the aid of reason to abstract the unity from the diversity, or else, by similar rationalizing processes, to stress the diversity at the expense of the unity." (DL, 146) We can intuit unity in diversity, but as soon as we try to formulate some case of it conceptually, we formulate a relation, and relations are illogical monsters. Participation, synthesis, the *methexis* of the Many in the One is the scandal of reason.

Dialectical logic accepts the mutual implication of unity and diversity. Croce agrees that the abstract unities set up by the pragmatic understanding are fictional and unreal. But the categorial structures of experience do not lose their reality when they are formulated in philosophical concepts, for such concepts do not emanate from reifying reason. A philosophical perception of a category of experience can always become richer, but from the first it is a perception of reality. The philosophical expansion and elaboration of the first glimpse of reality consists in the progressive elimination of whatever remnants of old pragmatic *découpages* may still interfere with perception.

The categorial unities are implicated in diversity in a different manner than the unities of pragmatic thought. Babbitt's inner check may serve as an example. As an ethical imperative demanding a certain quality of action the higher will is the same in all men, but because of the uniqueness of particular circumstances its specific content is never twice the same. The linguistic function illustrates the same point. As a symbolic function distinctive to human consciousness language is always the same, yet it is constantly changing, even within the same individual. It is hard to see why this kind of implication of unity in diversity should have to be the "scandal of reason." Only if one arbitrarily reifies relations and says, here is the One (the linguistic function) as one static "solid" and there are the Many (various languages) as other "solids," does it become impossible to understand how the One can participate in the Many.

The difference between Croce's logic and that of Bradley can be further indicated by quoting a passage from the latter's *Principles of Logic* and interpolating brief Crocean comments on it.[13] Most of these comments will receive elaboration later in the book. Bradley writes:

13. The passage to be commented upon is taken from Bradley, *Principles of Logic*, 94. While the following rather technical comments are intended to go to the heart of the logical problem at issue, continuity will not be broken if the reader should prefer to proceed directly to the end of the chapter.

The fact, which is given us, is the total complex of qualities and relations which appear to sense.

Croce would add that we are also aware of this complex as originating either in an act of perception or an act of pure imagination *(Dichtung)*. An example of an act of perception would be: I turn my head and accommodate the visual apparatus to perceive something. The sensory experience is immediately, without temporal lag, the receptacle of all my past experience which streams into it and interprets it. Though starting without delay, this may continue for some time. As the will-action (turning the head and adapting the eye) is taking place, I have only intuitive awareness of it, but I may then reflect on it and raise it to conceptual awareness. Knowledge that the visual experience belongs to the real world is the awareness that it issued forth from will-action (a subject to be explored in Chapter 8). No "mirroring" of external reality takes place. Both elements in the visual process, the will-action and the resulting visual experience, are created in the process of vision. Because they form the knowledge together, *the object of knowledge is created in the very process of knowing.* The aim of the process is not knowing "antecedent reality," in Dewey's phrase. Questions about what was antecedently real arise in the interpretation of what is now perceived.

"Epistemological realism" in the sense of the mirroring theory of knowledge, or "the spectator view of knowledge," common to Thomism and Marxism, should be discarded. Within his own areas of concern, Voegelin seems to be moving in that direction. The truth of existence (the "Metaxy") is not "an information about reality," he says. "The subject-object dichotomy . . . does not apply to the event of an 'experience-articulating-itself.'"[14]

Most theories termed "epistemological idealism" are equally questionable. The theory presented in this book regards the process of knowledge as creating the object of knowledge out of the "given." Whether or not this theory is termed "epistemo-

14. Eric Voegelin, *The Ecumenic Age* (Baton Rouge: Louisiana State University Press, 1974), 186.

logical idealism," it simply seeks to describe the phenomenal facts. (As an idealist, Croce does not recognize any extra-mental "given.")

But what we assert of this given fact is, and can be, nothing but an ideal content.

Bradley means by ideal content classificatory concepts like "tree" or "wolf." Croce would call attention to categorial predicates, like "something imagined" or "something perceived."

And it is evident at once that the idea we use can not possibly exhaust the full particulars of what we have before us. A description, we all know, can not ever reach to a complete account of the manifold shades, and the sensuous wealth of one entire moment of direct presentation.

But the logical subject, being *what* is perceived or imagined, *is* exhaustive; the logical predicate is either "something imagined" or "something perceived." Can we have no knowledge about what is not verbalized? If Bradley can speak about the "manifold shades" and the "sensuous wealth," he must have some knowledge of them. He does know those "full particulars" of which he is somehow aware, only not in the sense of having a stock of classificatory concepts applicable to every single particular. To know is to name, according to the rather arbitrary assumption of verbalism, which has had an unfortunate hold on logic since Aristotle. If verbalism were correct in this assumption, we could never know a piece of music, not even the simplest melody known to a child. All that would be knowable about the essential meaning of a poem or painting is what could be formulated in classificatory language. Knowledge certainly rests upon symbolism; but the melody, the poem, the painting are themselves the symbols. The proper basis for logic is a broad theory of language, or an aesthetic, in Croce's sense.

As soon as we judge, we are forced to analyze, and forced to distinguish. We must separate some elements of the given from others. We sunder and divide what appears to us as a sensible whole. It is never more than an arbitrary selection which goes into the judgment.

Bradley does not recognize the possibility of a non-arbitrary reason. What he means is that traits selected for *naming* are in some sense arbitrarily chosen. The basis of thought is for him attaching classificatory words to phenomena.

> We say "There is a wolf," or "This tree is green;" but such poor abstractions, such mere bare meanings, are much less than the wolf and the tree which we see; and they fall even more short of the full particulars, the mass of inward and outward setting, from which we separate the wolf and the tree. If the real as it appears is X = *a b c d e f g h*, then our judgment is nothing but X = *a,* or X = *a − b.*

If our *verbal* judgment is no more than what Bradley says, we nevertheless have in mind, that is, *think,* also *c d e f g h.* If Bradley himself did not, how could he be so sure he is leaving them out?

> But *a-b* by itself has never been given, and is not what appears. It was *in* the fact and we have taken it out. It was *of* the fact and we have given it independence.

How can Bradley be so certain, if he knows nothing about *c d e f g h?* What he calls "the fact" must fall inside his knowledge.

> We have separated, divided, abridged, dissected, we have mutilated the given.

But this cannot be asserted, if "the given" is non-existent *in so far as thought is concerned.* Further, Bradley has said that we "separate," "divide," etc., by "arbitrary selection." What about this theory itself? If it is self-applying, Bradley has arbitrarily selected his own analysis of the process of knowing.

> But, if this is so, and if every analytic judgment must inevitably so alter the fact, how can it any longer lay claim to truth?

> A later chapter will discuss the fact that instead of being classificatory concepts the *a b c d e f g h* may be qualia, qualifying traits individualized to the utmost limit, so that *a* or *b* are inconceivable in separation, which means that the thought of either of them involves the entire situation.

> Bradley did not need to be taught the elements of pragmatism. He did need a better understanding of Hegel, the philosopher of "concrete thought" and the "concrete universal." Dealing with the subject in question, Hegel himself unfortunately fails to draw the consequences of the idea of a con-

crete reason;[15] in this respect, Hegelianism, which affected the nineteenth century in an imperfect form, had to wait for Croce. But, unlike Bradley, Hegel did not separate concrete thought from man to make it the monopoly of an Absolute Experience, corresponding to Kant's *intellectus archetypus* (divine knowledge), leaving men with the *intellectus ectypus*. Hegel was groping his way towards the conclusion, later expressed more lucidly by Croce, that human thought—yours and mine and at every moment—is absolute thought and absolute experience. This idea brings obvious dangers, but as will be shown here it is quite compatible with humility in the religious sense, provided certain qualifications concerning the fallibility of human thought are insisted upon.

According to Bradley, "Nothing perfect, nothing genuinely real can move." (AR, 500) Bergson teaches the opposite—that time is "the very stuff of reality." Babbitt and More prefer the "both-and" of dualism. Bradley says, "Ultimate reality is such that it does not contradict itself." (AR, 136) Yet it seems this reality contains something irrational: "We do not know why or how the Absolute divides itself into centres, or the way in which, so divided, it still remains one." (AR, 527) If, on Bradley's own showing, his "A = A" as a formula for the universe does not fit the facts, it seems he should consider giving it up. This Eleatic formula is certainly as non-Hegelian as possible, and Bradley knows that it is. In the Preface to the *Principles of Logic* he writes, "I never could have called myself an Hegelian, partly because I cannot say that I have mastered his system, and partly because I could not accept what seems his main principle. . . ."[16] Hegel's "main principle" is dialectical self-con-

---

15. See the section on "Die sinnliche Gewissheit oder das Dieses und das Meinen" in G.F.W. Hegel, *Phänomenologie des Geistes* (Jubiläumsausgabe, 1927), Vol. II, 81-92. Here Hegel still retains the old doctrine of *individuum est ineffabile* which inexorably forces upon us as a consequence *de individuis nulla scientia*. Cf. Bradley, *Principles of Logic*, 48: "Ideas are universal, and, no matter what it is that we try to say and dimly mean, what we really express and succeed in asserting, is nothing individual." The world had to wait for Croce to overthrow the two mentioned maxims, and the *Weltgeist* appears to be in no hurry. Even today, Croce's insights have not been absorbed by the philosophers.

16. Bradley, *Principles of Logic*, vi.

tradiction. P.E. More, comparing Bradley's monism to James's pluralism, asks: "If any assumption is to be made, why not assume that the universe is, like our own inner experience, an illogical selfcontradiction?"[17] But if this seems preferable to More and self-contradiction happens to be Hegel's principle, More might have made a better effort to find out what Hegel was really trying to say. Little more is to be found on this subject in Josiah Royce than in Bradley, Bosanquet and other related thinkers. It is not hard to understand James's famous distinction between thick and thin and his feeling that Hegelianism, such as he met it in the English-speaking countries, suffered from thinness. The fertilizing stream coming largely from Coleridge had done whatever irrigation it could and disappeared at last in a desert. Anglo-Saxony reverted to its native empiricism. Hegelian philosophy met a better fate in Italy. Whatever Croce could be accused of, it is hardly thinness. Rather than study Hegel's own difficult and obscure writings, one does well to study Croce's statement of the new logic. Croce's logic is still combined with the old *Weltgeist*, the *spirito assoluto*, but his logical insights can be separated from this particular setting and made acceptable to dualism in Babbitt's and More's sense of the word. In Croce as in Hegel dualism is absorbed, as an inferior truth, into an ultimate monism. Babbitt and More object to giving ultimate priority to the One. This dissent need not preclude acceptance of the distinction between Reason and Understanding, philosophical and pragmatic thought. The self-contradiction at the heart of the dualism of Babbitt and More is "illogical" only to the reifying Bradleyan logic of the Understanding, which is permitted to make "solids" of what is not such in experience. Philosophical reason is precisely that *perception* of the duality of human nature to which Babbitt and More are constantly appealing. They call it an "intuition," but mere intuitionism can be left behind once it is understood that the *organon* for observing immediate, intuitive experience is a kind of reason.

17. P.E. More, *Shelburne Essays*, VII, 211.

Chapter 6
Historical Knowledge

The central purpose of criticizing and supplementing Babbitt's epistemological ideas is to demonstrate that experience has a conceptual ally in genuinely philosophical reason. After the critique of Bradley's and Babbitt's notion of a reifying reason abstracting concepts from the whole, more needs to be said about the sense in which philosophy is knowledge of experience and about the coexistence of universality and individuality in its concepts.

The indissoluble unity of philosophical self-knowledge and concrete experience can be illustrated by examples relevant to humanists of Babbitt's persuasion. A teacher of that orientation wants to help his students identify their romantic self. In one respect, the task does not require introducing anything new into the students; the romantic tendency was there long before they came under the influence of the teaching. What will be new for them, if the teacher succeeds, is the power of labeling these states of mind, relating them to one another and seeing them as variations on the same theme. The students are helped to recognize these states in the literature of the past two centuries. Through these literary experiences their original dumb and inarticulate nuclei of romantic feeling deepen and expand into richly orchestrated themes. The students experience the intimately related moods of pessimism, cynicism and disillusion which form, as it were, the reverse side of the romantic states of mind. They learn to group these together under some term like "realism" or *naturalisme*.

Nobody in the Western world can be wholly unfamiliar with Christian attitudes or with the moods of doubt and skepticism that are associated with a scientific metaphysic and form the

essence of the Enlightenment. The heritage from classical antiquity is also present in the souls of young people even before
historical studies make them aware of its origin. We are born
into a mighty stream of life affecting us in countless known
and unknown ways. This "living past" both expresses and
shapes our humanity. The study of history becomes therefore
a study in self-knowledge, a discovery of one's own self running parallel with the discovery of epochs in history. There is
a potential "liberal" and a potential "conservative" within a
young man long before he has developed an articulate interest
in politics. "Nationalistic," "democratic," and "aristocratic"
states of mind have somehow insinuated themselves into him
long before he could locate referents in historical contexts. This
material in however inarticulate form can be taken for granted
in the souls of young Westerners when they are first introduced
to the serious study of history. To the child, "history" is
primarily a collection of more less thrilling stories. The first
glimmerings of historical reflection in the teenager mark the
first step towards intellectual maturity.

The γνωθι σαυτόν (know yourself) has received a new dimension with the rise of historicism. The change has been so pervasive and revolutionary that it is difficult to recapture the state
of mind of earlier periods in the life of the race when consciousness of the historical dimension of self-knowledge was so
undeveloped as to be almost absent. The first book in which
a thinker formulates his self-knowledge systematically as a
structure of historical forces related to one another in intrinsically necessary oppositions and sequences, so as to be aware
of himself as a summary and conspectus of the past, is Hegel's
Phänomenologie des Geistes (1807).[1] Hegel did not create modern
historicism single-handedly, but his work is the first highly
developed expression of it. Hegel's book is characteristically
modern in that it joins history and philosophy so intimately
that the difference between them disappears.

1. Hegel's *Phänomenologie des Geistes* is known as one of the formidable works of
philosophy and should be approached by way of a good summary. The best may
still be in Kuno Fischer, *Hegels Leben, Werke und Lehre* (2 Vols.; Darmstadt: Wissen-
schaftliche Buchgesellschaft, 1963).

Babbitt's collected works can be described as a twentieth century phenomenology of the mind, offering self-knowledge, history and philosophy in one. Babbitt considers himself in essential respects a disciple of Buddha, but the difference between their types of thinking is in at least one way immense. Buddha traces a non-historic "chain of dependent origination." He looks back into earlier lives which he thinks he remembers. Babbitt traces the origin and growth of civilization and the noetic pathology of modern man. Without making it explicit, actually rather obscuring it as if on purpose, Babbitt is as much a disciple of German historicism as of Buddha and Aristotle. That he obscures this fact points to a defect in his own self-knowledge, that is, in his version of the historico-philosophical phenomenology of the mind. The author of *Literature and the American College* had reason, not indeed to "embrace the cloud Junos of Hegelianism," but to investigate more fully the historical roots of his own thinking. Once more, Emerson—the author of a splendid essay on "History" which summarizes the attainments of German historical culture—might have directed him backwards to Coleridge and the most creative period in German philosophy.[2] After the fall of Hegelianism in the middle of the nineteenth century, due to its considerable shortcomings and excesses, followed that decline of German philosophical culture which was much in evidence in Babbitt's and More's younger days. A rather crude substitute for philosophy, the positivism of Comte, the Mills and Spencer, had been imported. Paradoxically, Babbitt came to associate German intellectual culture primarily with the dehumanizing *strengwissenschaftliche Methode.* More reflection would have revealed that this method was not really an expression of authentically German philosophy but a sign of its temporary subjection to Anglo-French influences.

Paul Elmer More is no more attentive than Babbitt to the philosophical bases and affiliations of historical culture. In his essay on "The Pragmatism of William James," the source of

---

2. Ralph Waldo Emerson, "History," *The Selected Writings of Ralph Waldo Emerson* (New York: Modern Library, 1940).

his omission is perhaps more clearly visible than anywhere else. More quotes James: "The English mind, thank heaven, and the French mind, are still kept, by their aversion to crude technique and barbarism, closer to truth's natural probabilities. Their literatures show fewer obvious falsities and monstrosities than that of Germany. Think of the German literature of aesthetics, with the preposterousness of such an unaesthetic personage as Immanuel Kant enthroned in its centre! Think of German books on *Religionsphilosophie,* with the heart's battles translated into conceptual jargon and made dialectic." More comments, *"Macte virtute!* we cry, and toss hats into the air. There is no hope in Kant, neither in his followers nor in his metaphysical enemies. . . . I, for one, am ready to follow any leader out of the Egypt of Kantian metaphysics, and I would not belittle the honour due to M. Bergson and to Mr. James as the Moses and the Aaron of this exodus." At the same time, More does not like James's unhistorical contemporaneity: "Mr. James, who has pondered so well Bergson's analysis of the individual consciousness as a summing up of all the past, should have seen the application of the same definition to the general consciousness of mankind." It is ironical that had More inquired systematically into the origin of Bergson's notion, he would have been led straight back into that German philosophy against which he thinks he is reacting. Instead, his next sentence takes him in a different direction. James "should have seen that Bergson's rejection of reason as the arbiter of reality was no new thing, but the old insight re-defined in the terms of modern psychology."[3] More then takes up his favorite theme of a supra-rational intuitionism as old as the forest philosophies of India. He seems wholly unaware that Bergson's philosophy is also an offshoot of post-Kantian German philosophy. Paradoxical though it may seem, Kant's most important achievement may be to have initiated a *liberation* from the rationalism which More attributes to him. This rationalism can be seen as a cocoon to be sloughed off as the "synthesis a priori" works its way towards self-liberation and self-knowledge.

3. P.E. More, *Shelburne Essays* (11 Vols.; New York: Phaeton Press, 1967), VII, 200-202.

The real synthesis a priori is at once concreteness and universality, freedom and form. It expels rationalistic, formalistic and pseudo-classic wholes, placing them in proper subordination as pragmatic instrumentalities. The synthesis a priori is the process of creativity. It is the universals of life realizing themselves as they shape the incessant gushing forth of novelty. These universals are our Self, or selves, seeking to become more fully themselves. In that sense the synthesis a priori both "is" and "is not." In one manifestation it is the process of volition: the decision is the completion of "the practical synthesis a priori." It is also the process of imaginative and philosophico-historical perception of reality-in-the-making. Philosophico-historical perception is that ever-growing "phenomenology of the mind" which is human self-knowledge. For a brief and narrow segment of space-time, it was the perception of a man who wrote a book with that title.

The same perception was at work in the author of *The Republic*. The book temporarily summarizes Plato's philosophico-historical grasp of the world in which he lived. The microcosmos and the macrocosmos being identical in this case, *The Republic* can be said also to contain Plato's self-knowledge. His account of aristocracy, timocracy, oligarchy, democracy and tyranny is the dialectic of Plato's own human consciousness. He is aware of these modes of life as potentialities within himself and all human beings. This account is also a conspectus of the history of the Greek *poleis* where he saw these potentialities externalized. This dialectic of the soul, Plato feels, contains something of the timeless and universal. The modern reader is more keenly aware of the Greek setting as provincial in time and space and of the element of arbitrariness in Plato's sociological and psychological classifications. Still, the modern thinker perceives something of true universality in this phenomenology of the spirit. In Babbitt's language, it is reality glimpsed through a veil of illusion.

If *The Republic* can be said to be Plato's phenomenology of the spirit, why should unique significance be attached to Hegel? The answer is that even if Plato is superior to Hegel in some respects, Plato is only imperfectly aware of the nature of his own reasoning. To philosophize is not yet to be reflectively aware of the logic of one's own philosophizing. Plato has only limited critical awareness of the close involvement of his social philosophy in specifically Greek circumstances and historical events. He thinks it possible to reach timeless and ahistorical truth on a very slender basis of concrete experience: the basis needs to be just large enough to start the process of anamnesis. Moreover, his own logic forbids him to believe that historical experience could be called knowledge; it is mere *doxa*. History and geography have no place in Plato's notion of scientific knowledge, for there can be no knowledge of what is individual, changing, concrete. Plato could not have written a history of the Greek *poleis* or even have wanted to write one, if he had had access to the necessary materials. In his view, the result would not have been *episteme*. Scientific knowledge must take the form of typology.

Aristotle retains this notion of scientific knowledge, but he also believes that the empirical basis must be expanded in order to reach the εἰδη, the "forms" of things. We do not know εἰδη by anamnesis, as is the belief of the mathematically minded Plato. We "abstract" them from concrete materials; and if typologies are to be true, plenty of materials must be obtained from which to abstract them. Thus, Aristotle begins his science of politics by studying empirically a great number of concrete regimes. But concrete material by itself, whether in politics or biology, has no scientific status. *De individuis nulla scientia.* History does not have the dignity of scientific knowledge.

The neglect of history is but an aspect of the Platonic and Aristotelian understanding of the nature and function of the intellect. What is not touched by the intellect cannot be an object of knowledge. According to Plato, only the Ideas in their transcendent majesty can be known. Aristotle denies the existence of transcendent Ideas; he regards the εἰδη as immanent in the τόδε τι, in the existential object. But while Aristotle rejects the association of form with number among some of the disciples of Plato, he retains the notion that the mind can know only form. "It was a good idea to call the soul 'the place of forms' . . . ." (*De anima*, 429a). Many ambiguities are left in Aristotle's logic, as the genus is supposed to be more real than the individual. A crucial question is never faced: if the intellect cannot in any way touch the υλη, the "matter" of things, how do we know that this matter exists? The answer, "by perception," cannot be accepted, for perception is supposed to give knowledge only insofar as it perceives the "forms" of things. Paul Elmer More believes that Aristotle's dictum εν τη αισθησει η κϱίσις, "in perception lies the judgment" *(Eth.nic.*, 1109b), contains the essence of his philosophy. But κϱίσις (judgment) becomes impossible if by definition the intellect cannot touch "matter" but is restricted to awareness of "forms." Paradoxically, this very dictum strikes at the heart of Aristotle's logical system and potentially constitutes its refutation.

The contrast between the classical and modern notions of science has been well stated by John Dewey, though only with reference to pragmatic concepts. Consider medical science as an example. At medical school the physician acquires a great number of classificatory concepts of various diseases, their symptoms, and so on. According to the classical notion criticized by Dewey, "science" is something that the physician carries in his head when he approaches the patient. According to Dewey, science is concrete action, the application of general methods to the case at hand. "The *ultimate* objects of science are *guided* processes of change."[4] The healing processes promoted by the physician are guided processes of change. They are what medical science is for. If we reflect only on what the physician has in his head before dealing with particular patients and baptize that something "science," we isolate and hypostatize a preparatory stage in a larger process which is fully revealed only when it reaches its end. The classical idea of scientific knowledge stops at the penultimate stage. Dewey's perspective on science brings us close in some respects to the notion of knowledge developed in these pages, but an important element is missing in that Dewey cannot satisfactorily explain our knowledge of the individual case, for example, the particular patient. Do we know him by perception? Coming

4. John Dewey, *Experience and Nature* (New York: Dover, 1958; reprint of 2nd rev. ed.), 160.

from a pragmatist, that answer is clearly unpersuasive. If reason is only pragmatic, consisting of abstract rules of action, knowledge of the particular case and the application of science to it become inexplicable. For knowledge of the individual case to be possible, there must be a non-pragmatic type of reason coinciding with perception, which means that pragmatic logic is an incomplete account of knowledge. The physician's treatment of the patient comprises *res gestae,* things done; his (and the patient's) awareness of these acts are *historia rerum gestarum.* This historiographic awareness of things done is a knowledge of concrete existential processes. *De individuis omnis scientia:* the philosophical categorizing of modes of activity accompanies and makes possible the pragmatic application of the methods of medical science. The perception of the concrete situation with the fullness needed for a decision on medical action is an example of *knowledge.* It is the theoretical basis for the physician's decision to act thus-and-so. The *intellectus* of the classical tradition needs to have its rational element broken up into its constituents, the philosophico-historical reason of modern historicism and abstract pragmatic rules of action.

Reading Dewey's books, the Crocean philosopher moves for long stretches within the Crocean thought-world and explores it better by means of some of Dewey's concepts. In Bertrand Russell, on the other hand, the Crocean philosopher finds little that he can accept as good philosophy. According to Russell, the particular is constituted by "qualities" considered to be universals. A "certain shade of red" is a universal which may appear in many different spatio-temporal contexts. This theory explains away individuality in the historicist sense. The entire universe, Russell argues, is a combination of universals. The need for proper names would disappear, if our knowledge of the universals constituting an individual were complete.[5] And how does Russell know that this metaphysic is true? By assuming something he doesn't know. We would know this is so, "*if* our knowledge were complete." The Neo-Kantians of the Marburg school (Cohen, Natorp, Cassirer) had a simi-

---

5. See Bertrand Russell, *Human Knowledge* (London: Allen and Unwin, 1948), esp. the chapter, "The Principle of Individuation."

lar theory. According to them we cannot know the thing-in-itself, but the aim of science is getting ever closer to the goal of exhaustive knowledge, dissolving individuality into universals. If this goal can never be reached, as the Neo-Kantians contend (presumably with Russell's consent), Leibniz' metaphysic—that every particular is constituted by universal "qualities"—was rightly rejected by Kant. Clearly, Russell's theory, though different from Platonic and Aristotelian philosophy in so many other ways, is connected to the old view that the intellect deals only in ειδη and cannot touch "matter."

The scholars of the Marburg school rejected the Leibnizian view insofar as it was a metaphysic but retained it as a Kantian Regulative Idea, an unattainable ideal which human knowledge is forever straining to approximate more closely. Thus, individuality was as problematic to them as to Russell. A rival Neo-Kantian school at the beginning of the century, the *badische Schule* of Windelband and Rickert, insisted on the irreducible individuality of whatever is historical. Scientism thus stood opposed to a more humanistic historicist philosophy. Placing Ernst Cassirer with a scientistic- minded school may surprise some who are familiar with his later work. They may point out, for instance, that Cassirer's *An Essay on Man* (1944) has an interesting chapter on "History." But this chapter seeks to eliminate the idea of history as "idiographic," as dealing with *das Einmalige*, to use Windelband's and Rickert's terms. Having these rival Neo-Kantians in mind, Cassirer maintains that theorists of historical knowledge have been mistaken in looking for a special logic of historical knowledge: "They took the greatest pains to construct a new logic of history. But all these attempts were doomed to failure. For logic is, after all, a very simple and uniform thing. It is one because truth is one. In his quest of truth the historian is bound to the same formal rules as the scientist. In his modes of reasoning and arguing, in his inductive inferences, in his investigation of causes, he obeys the same general laws of thought as a physicist or biologist."[6]

Croce agrees that truth is one, but he denies that logic is "a

6. Ernst Cassirer, *An Essay on Man* (New Haven: Yale University Press, 1962), 176.

very simple and uniform thing" and that science gives truth. Science gives fictions which are useful for many purposes, among them the purpose of extending historical knowledge. The function of science is to *work*. Its "truth" is in the working, whereas knowledge of reality (a reality which includes the working of science) is strictly philosophico-historical. In the end, Cassirer's theory of history is a variation on the old maxim *de individuis nulla scientia*. The idea that the mind can touch only what is "formal" is the limitation also of his aesthetics. The chapter on "Art" in *An Essay on Man* contains the following sentence, "*Rerum videre formas* [to see the form of things] is a no less important and indispensable task than *rerum cognoscere causas* [to know the causes of things]." Croce, by contrast, defines art as *res videre*. To single out the *formas* as alone within the grasp of the mind is as complete a denial of art as Cassirer's theory of history is a denial of history. Cassirer's theory of language similarly includes the assertion that we can only speak in universals. In other words, he retains the old view of *individuum est ineffabile*, as does Dewey's theory of language. Croce rejects this maxim. Cassirer's "pre-scientific symbolic forms" turn out to be window-dressing masking the stark scientism of the Marburg school. Cassirer expresses his own view when he notes that science "is held to be the summit and consummation of all our human activities, the last chapter in the history of mankind and the most important subject of a philosophy of man."[7] But what about the epistemological status of the philosophy of man itself? What about the claims of Cassirer's own subject? As a Kantian, he never gives a very satisfactory answer. If he had raised and tried to answer the question, he would have passed beyond Kant to Hegel. There is certainly much truth in Eric Voegelin's picture of Hegel as an "egophanic" thinker, a modern "gnostic." But even such a man can perceive important philosophical truths. The best guide in disengaging the valid elements of Hegel's philosophy is probably Croce, although in some respects he may have initiated rather than completed the task.

7. *Ibid.*, 170, 207.

Chapter 7
The Logic
of Knowledge

The preceding critique of Babbitt's understanding of reason and of various doctrines separating reason from the experiential facts has suggested that experience acquires conceptual self-awareness in philosophical perception. If, as Babbitt contends, human existence is dualistic, a "oneness that is always changing," there can be no genuine knowledge of life unless thought is attuned to the unity of the universal and the particular. The epistemological basis for Babbitt's theory of dualism or for Plato's notion of *methexis*, to mention a closely related concept, cannot be an abstract, ahistorical reason. Philosophy must be able to grasp the universal *in* the concrete. The "paradox of dualism" presents no logical problem to the reason that shuns reification. To complete the proposed epistemological supplement to Babbitt and more generally to advance the general theory of knowledge being developed, the idea of dialectical logic needs to be elaborated upon. The sense in which reason is inescapably historical has to be further explained.

Reason is itself constituted by the dualism of life. It is one of the universals of human consciousness seeking self-realization. Human thought does not conform to the formula "A = A, and not non-A," which assumes a static, tensionless conceptual self-identity. Actual thought is a straining towards truth, a conceptual self-identity in search of itself. Further criticism of the old *principium identitatis* is the more appropriate, because the ancient habit of reifying ideas is still the wholly dominant disposition in logic. It seems equally common among those who reject and those who admire the classical and Judaeo-Christian traditions.

The term "dialectical" is today commonly associated with

extravagant metaphysical theories of history. In this chapter, the term refers to something quite different: the logic of the thought-processes whereby man acquires a knowledge of reality. The thesis to be developed here will counter the belief that dialectical logic must carry some assumption of omniscience. The thesis may be stated briefly as follows: Thought, like all human life, is continuous activity. Although it contains an element of oneness or identity, namely, that it aims at truth, thought never comes to rest in static ideas divorced from the flow of history. Knowledge is carried by concepts that can be forever improved. Cognition is a dialectical straining towards, never the achievement of, perfect clarity. There is indeed lasting truth about life, but it is truth apprehended in the midst of history.

The dialectical and historical nature of thought may be brought out through an examination of the following proposed rule for the interpretation of philosophical texts: "An adequate interpretation is such an interpretation as understands the thought of a philosopher exactly as he understood it himself."[1] Formulated by an influential student of the history of political ideas, this well-known principle exemplifies a certain epistemological disposition. The question of what is philosophical interpretation is but an aspect of the problem of knowledge. Perhaps it should be made explicit that the purpose of considering the mentioned principle of interpretation is not to give a general assessment of the epistemology of a particular thinker but merely to provide a specific point of reference.[2]

How does a philosopher understand his own thought? One problem with the question is that there is no static *now* in the flow of thought which can be selected as the definitive position of the author. An interpeter may rely on a written work, but a text is never an unambiguous final word. It is rather the incomplete and fragmentary record of a process of inquiry that overflows the merely apparent finality of particular formula-

---

1. Leo Strauss, *What is Political Philosophy?* (Glencoe, Ill.: The Free Press, 1959), 66.

2. In the work of Leo Strauss the tendency of thought represented by the quoted principle of interpretation coexists with other elements closer in some respects to the epistemological theme of this book. See note 9 below.

tions. Even as a philosopher finishes a manuscript, new thoughts are occurring to him and modifying the meaning of what has been written. While still writing he is aware of many possibilities for developing his thoughts which he decides not to delve into. Some of his ideas are left vague. The reason may be lack of space, lack of interest, or that his thought has not yet matured to such an extent that a clearer statement is possible. Perhaps he wants to conceal an inopportune notion, or perhaps ideas are excluded for possible separate treatment. The implications of what is written for related subjects are beginning to emerge already at the time of writing, and after completion of the manuscript they come to mind increasingly. Some things which appeared clear when first formulated begin to appear problematical. A written work is, strictly speaking, always unfinished. The text could have been rewritten and expanded indefinitely. A limited number of words cannot contain all of what would be necessary to clear away every obscurity; the latter is in fact a never-ending task. A given treatise is a report on a continuing process of inquiry and is out of date even before it is finished.

A philosophical work is loaded with intellectual connections which are not all explicitly stated. Every concept is a dynamic center in which are interwoven innumerable threads of thought. Each thread is connected with a complex of other thoughts which are, as it were, represented by it. If one thread is picked up, the entire complex is brought to awareness, and it in turn draws attention to related complexes. There is truth in Hegel's teaching that whenever we think, we are thinking *das Ganze*, the Whole.

To illustrate further the complexity and continuous movement of thought, different ideas also carry with them different emotional qualities. To a classical humanist beginning a work on the theory of politics, the thought of Machiavelli may create feelings of distaste. This colors his way of thinking and writing about Machiavelli's ideas. The author may be more sympathetic and receptive to ideas formulated by Christians, because in the past he has found many of their theories compatible with or complementary to his own. But such reactions of antipathy or sympathy are not constants, just as ideas are not static and simple. While writing his manuscript, the classical humanist may be surprised to discover connections between his own ideas and those of Machiavelli which trigger revisions in his perception of life. His general frame of mind undergoes a subtle change. Not only does the work of Machiavelli start to acquire a more ambiguous emotional coloring, but simultaneously, in the light of his new insight, his view of Christianity and also of his beloved Greek masters begins to change.

All of the above considerations are but examples of the influences constantly at work in the mind of an author. Is all this movement and ambiguity in his written work? Only a naively literalistic conception of a text could conceal that it is. The knowledgeable and intelligent reader knows or senses the presence of much between the lines. The author has his ways of helping the reader to do so. Between individuals who are more or less attuned to a certain sphere of ideas there is an unspoken common understanding, because of which many things can be left unsaid. This assumed common ground is part of what gives the written work its real meaning.

Thought is never static. It is an ongoing quest for a deeper, more comprehensive truth. Even the greatest philosophers are constantly developing, and with them their readers. In the same work one may notice changes in the meaning of words reflecting a new insight in the making. The author may not even be aware that sometimes he uses a certain term crudely, sometimes in a more sophisticated manner. Ideas are given new emphases, until a virtual transformation has been effected. It has been said that one cannot enter *The Critique of Pure Reason* without *das Ding an sich* and cannot come out of it with *das Ding an sich*. If the written text of a treatise can be said to have something static about it, the words have meaning only as symbols for this continuous process of thought in which truth is being articulated, and, of course, sometimes eclipsed.

Questioning an author about his exact meaning in a book is to invite a continuation of thought. Responding to queries, the author may say: ''Yes, what I had in mind was something close to what you suggest. But I am not sure you are entirely correct. Perhaps you could explain yourself better.'' ''Of course, today I would put more emphasis on this issue than I did then. Come to think of it, I may have started to do so even then.'' ''I can see now that this idea was still rather poorly developed. How could I have overlooked those connections?'' ''I am not sure you are right about this matter. To tell the truth, I have gone back and forth a great deal on this issue.'' And so on. In the very act of interpretation thought continues. Whatever conclusions are reached are not mere repetitions of previous thoughts. They are attempts to formulate anew what the author was trying to express in the original work. Weaknesses and strengths are discovered in the old formulations. Looking back on his own book, the philosopher can see that some interpretations of it are clearly false. Other interpretations may at first seem highly questionable, but at second thought they are discovered to capture some facet or implication of the work which the author had not previously noticed or grasped with sufficient clarity. He was grappling with large and difficult problems then, and he is grappling with them still.

If the writing of the treatise was itself an attempt to articulate partly elusive truths, how could the author return to the work ''exactly as he understood it''? The text at its best reflects truths-in-the-making. The author's particular formulations and emphases were occasioned by his intellectual circumstances at the time. These pushed certain problems or parts of problems into the forefront and made possible certain solutions. Having acquired new insights and experiences, he has of course not entirely forgotten his older meaning, but it is no longer possible, even if he wanted, to return to his previous state of mind. Neither would he want to. The philosopher is not an antiquarian. Only that has real interest to him which promises a solution to still unsolved intellectual problems. Plato as an older man is different than Plato as a young man. This in no way denies the continuity of his intellectual life's work which makes it possible to speak of Platonic philosophy. But the latter is not some uniform, static theme of thought excluding elements of ambiguity, confusion or even contradiction. Platonism is a powerful approach to fundamental questions which is more or less successful in different texts or parts of texts. To decide what is most truly Platonic, or, rather, what is closest to the truth, was the unfinished work of Plato himself. This work will continue among those who are his disciples and critics. What *exactly* Plato meant is not the right question to ask inasmuch as his thought never came to an end in petrified ideas. The notion of a philosophical treatise elevated above the stream of history and containing the definitive position of a thinker is an unreal abstraction, a literalistic reification of what is actually a continuous, forward-looking activity. The real question faced by the philosophical interpreter of Plato is not what "exactly" did Plato mean, but what in his ideas has lasting validity. It goes without saying that an answer presupposes intimate familiarity with the works of Plato. Equally elementary is the observation that interpreters from other historical periods must try as best they can to open themselves up to meanings to which they may be blinding themselves by unfounded prejudice.

The idea that the originator of a doctrine "understood it in one way only, provided he was not confused," hardly reflects a well-developed epistemological position.[3] Upon reflection, no thinker could deny that his work has many layers and facets and that on most questions he has wavered somewhat. Whether fully conscious of it or not, every thinker always assumes, not only that he can understand himself better and express himself more precisely, but that others may be able to improve upon his very best insights. Intellectual humility was certainly not lacking in the man who believed that wisdom is knowing how little we know. Not even the truly great philosophical treatises contain any unequivocal, precisely clear lines of thought subject to no further clarification and improvement. Besides possible mistakes, they contain a multitude of more or less developed philosophical potentialities, some of which were not even known to the author at the time of literary composition.

If Plato himself would have been hard put to explain *exactly*

---

3. Strauss, *What is Political Philosophy?*, 67.

what he originally meant in the *Republic*, what about modern readers of Plato? Using the mentioned principle of interpretation, how could they qualify as interpreters? Trying to understand, say, the meaning of Plato's "timarchic man" or "tyrannical man," could they rid their minds of any associations to what Augustine, Machiavelli, Hobbes or Nietzsche have said about such subjects as the pursuit of honor or power? Or, in the attempt to understand Plato's conception of justice, could they help but be influenced by everything else they have read about the subject of justice, including defenses and critiques of Plato? To ask these questions is to answer them. It is not possible to empty one's head of the past. Every reader must of necessity interpret in the light of his own experience and knowledge, broad or limited as these may be. Our own experience and knowledge stream into our effort to understand a certain thinker, and they are expanded in turn by the activity of interpretation. Nothing can ever be read in the same way twice, not even a theorem and proof in Euclid. Our consciousness is changed, however imperceptibly, by each new moment.

It is not possible, then, for the philosophical interpreter to "isolate" himself with a particular text. Such isolation would destroy his power of interpretation. There is no such thing as first understanding a text and then passing judgment on it. To understand is to assess.

Any implicit claim that some particular philosopher or school of philosophy has *the* answer to every significant question and that succeeding history has only obscured the truth, would of course assume such exceptional extrahistorical knowledge also on the part of the interpreter who is making the claim. For lesser interpreters working in a state of merely human illumination, being able to draw on a broad range of historical experience and reflection is rather an indispensable advantage. While the great philosopher may have seen better than others in certain areas, he cannot be assumed to have seen perfectly, and he may have seen only dimly or not at all in some areas. Even thinkers who have regressed in some essential respects may be of help in revealing weak spots and mistakes in the great philosopher and also in directing attention to undeveloped potentialities.

Contemporary critiques of "historicism," as exemplified by Leo Strauss, do not delve very deeply into German philosophy and typically do not address the kinds of issues that are discussed in this book. The problem of history is brought up in rather general terms that bypass the heart of the epistemological matter. What is criticized as "historicism"—an emphasis on history that tends to undermine universality—is only one possible off-shoot of German historicist philosophy and a tendency only tangentially related to historicism as here understood. To those arbitrarily assuming that historicism must destroy universality, talk of the historical nature of thought, or of human life more generally, seems a threat to the idea of truth (and the idea of moral right). But to insist that we are forever trying to clarify our insights into reality and that we must do so within the more or less favorable intellectual and other circumstances which are our own life is most certainly *not* the same as to dissolve philosophy into a sea of historical relativity. One may acknowledge the historical and provisional nature of human knowledge and still transcend, for example, the doctrine of pragmatism.

The present criticism of a belief in ahistoric, "exact" ideas does not in any way contradict the argument in earlier chapters that philosophy looks for categorial distinctions between permanent structures of consciousness that do not blur into each other. The discovery of such sharp boundaries within experience does not put an end to thought, but, on the contrary, challenges the philosopher to make the distinctions conceptually clearer by weeding out remaining pragmatic interpretations and by understanding better the relationships between the permanent structures as they shape the continuing flow of life. Man is not afforded an uninhibited spectator view of an independently existing reality, but perceives structural reality *through* a more or less limited historical perspective. The philosophical truth at his disposal both is and is not sharply defined.

Philosophy is unity in diversity, a "oneness that is always changing." Even when our insights about life are just vague and fragmentary, we do know the truth—only in a vague and fragmentary manner. If it is not within man's capacity to answer the fundamental questions once and for all, so as to make further thought superfluous, good philosophy has weeded out a great many mistakes and confusions. And it can forever deepen and expand whatever insights it has acquired. Trying to uncover more of the truth amidst a life that never stands still, philosophy is constantly renewing itself. Of course, real thought does not lurch back and forth idiosyncratically and erratically. It maintains a basic continuity. This it does through an absorption of old insights which is at the same time adjustment to the challenges brought by new circumstances. Philosophy is indistinguishably old and new. Its concepts are sharpened and deepened in a process of reformulation which is inspired in large measure by the need to overcome the seemingly inevitable lapses into confusion or downright intellectual decadence. Different historical circumstances bring to the fore different aspects of the eternal questions and make possible, although they do not guarantee, an ever richer understanding of life's potential. Perception of reality has not been absent in any previous philosophical effort worthy of the name. If we keep returning to Plato and Aristotle, it is because they have seen deeper than most, and because so much in their work transcends their own historical circumstances. But the oneness of truth-in-the-making that permeates all great works of philosophy maintains and expands itself only by means of a rearticulation which is at the same time development.

There is obviously nothing automatic about philosophical progress, so that each century would bring not only better but more widely shared ideas. Periods of new insight can give way to periods of general intellectual decline. Or perhaps creativity in the field of aesthetics is accompanied by regress in the field of ethics. Or advances in the understanding of some parts of a problem take place at the same time that there is contraction of the understanding of other parts. But in the largely unpredictable ebb and flow and currents and crosscurrents of history is contained the potential for intellectual progress. Learned and creative minds, spanning the centuries and capable of unexpected syntheses of the groping philosophical attempts of earlier thinkers, sometimes manage to advance philosophy permanently—permanently, that is, for those who are able to absorb their insight. This process of absorption is of course at the same time always rearticulation in new intellectual circumstances.

The notion that we should "understand the thinkers of the past exactly as they understood themselves" assumes that human ideas can have an unequivocal, timeless self-identity and that interpreters can recapture them in this static, ahistoric form.[4] According to the old *principium identitatis*, an idea must be itself and not something else. "A must be A and not non-A." But this principle in isolation does not recognize the continuous development of concepts. A few examples may be in order.

The development of the concept of beauty can be studied in the history of aesthetics. It once centered upon the notion of *mimesis* (imitation). The expansion, revision and transformation of this concept from the Greeks through the Scholastics and Baumgarten to the modern aestheticians and the modernized classicism of Irving Babbitt is unity in diversity. Is it still the same concept? Yes and no. When we entertain the concept of beauty today, we do, in a manner of speaking, have in mind the same as the Greeks: we hold before us a certain permanent aspect of reality, its moments of imaginative (intuitive) intensification. But we are now in a position to state that reality with greater conceptual clarity.[5] Has the concept changed? It has deepened. This deepening has taken place over the centuries, but to some extent it is also taking place in each living moment. Life is continually offering material for conceptual reflection. Every new experience of beauty enriches the concept for the individual. The reader should perhaps be reminded that this is a discussion of the logic of conceptual knowledge. The direct experience of beauty is of course not a concept; as will be discussed at greater length, beauty is a state of aesthetic enjoy-

4. *Ibid.*, 67.

5. Obviously, not every modern individual, regardless of intellectual preparation and facility, will in fact understand the reality of beauty with greater conceptual clarity than the best of the Greeks.

ment oblivious to cognitive purposes. The *concept* of beauty takes philosophical account of the nature of such enjoyment.

To further exemplify the dynamics of thought, take a concept like "democracy." Plato's understanding of democracy was influenced in large part by specifically Greek political circumstances and especially his own experience of decadent popular government. Since his time, the term has taken on a wealth of new meaning, at least some of it vaguely anticipated by him. Reflection occasioned by the experience of Rome, say, or of America and France in the eighteenth century and of democracies in our own century has added many dimensions and distinctions to the concept. Plato's meaning is in a sense still alive. There is no modern understanding of popular government of any depth and subtlety which does not owe immeasurably to Plato's insights into the lower potentialities of democracy and the human soul and to his understanding of politics generally. But Plato's concept of democracy has been absorbed in the modern world into concepts of greater comprehensiveness and precision.[6]

As reflection is a straining towards increased clarity, conceptual modification marks each moment of thought. In the process of trying to understand, for instance, a new book on popular government or some political development in the United States, our concept of democracy undergoes more or less significant change. Of course, an infinite number of possible considerations feed into our thinking about a particular problem. Reflection on seemingly distant subjects have implications, however indirect, for the problem in the center of attention, so that the continuous development of concepts involves, among other things, sometimes unexpected syntheses and shifts of emphasis and the constant crossing of the conventional boundaries between academic disciplines.

---

6. For some of the distinctions and implications which are contained in any well-informed modern concept of democracy, see Claes G. Ryn, *Democracy and the Ethical Life* (Baton Rouge: Louisiana State University Press, 1978). Lacking in Plato, among other things, is a distinction between plebiscitary, majoritarian democracy and constitutional, representative democracy. These notions of popular government use the same label but are essentially different and imply very different views of the nature of man and society.

Also in the abstract fields of mathematics and geometry concepts are always held dynamically. A long historical development is reflected in the process whereby modern students learn, for example, the concept of "number." The simple number known by a little child is progressively modified through instruction and reflection. The concept is transformed into something highly complex as the child is exposed to decimals, irrational numbers, infinitesimals, "0" as a number, and so on. As the mind dwells on the number "3," all of these meanings are potentially present, and others may be taking form; the particular number cannot be thought in isolation from some context which gives it meaning. The concept of "triangle" is similarly held dialectically. For us, triangle is not quite what it was for Euclid; for example, the concept now includes the possiblity of spheric triangles and saddle triangles. The modern concept both is and is not new.

The same dialectical tension marks every human thought as it actually takes place. The reading of a philosophical treatise may be used as a final illustration. The reader of the treatise must first feel his way. Guided by the author, he is oriented to the general subject and acquires a rough, provisional idea of a concept presented in the text. In the course of the reading, the concept emerges with greater clarity. In a sense it is still the same concept as when it was first introduced in the early pages; if it were not, continuity in the reading would have been impossible. But it is also *not* the same concept; it has grown, deepened.

And so with every single moment of thought. It both replaces and develops the past. The logical formula of "A is A and not non-A" expresses a belief, shared by formalistic logicians of many different types, that intellectual coherence requires "that" to be "that" and nothing else: A concept cannot simultaneously and indistinguishably both be and not be itself. But *principium identitatis* is a formula for the static and the reified. It can be the law of thought, never in fact, but only by decree. "A = A" simply *assumes* a tensionless intellectual identity which is nowhere to be found in human thought as it *actually* occurs. Real thought is a manifestation of dualistic life, and its logic is dialectical. This

argument is not so much a flat rejection of the *principium identitatis* as it is an insistence that this principle, by itself, does not
describe the pursuit of truth. In one sense, a philosopher's brilliant insight does have identity with itself; it is an attempt to
articulate a truth. "A = A" thus symbolizes *one* dimension of
the cognitive act.[7] But not even the concept of the most profound and brilliant philosopher is perfect or exhaustive; it is
deepening and growing into greater identity with itself as he
or his disciples discover new aspects of problems and clear away
obscurities, mistakes or partial mistakes. Does anyone ever
understand himself with perfect clarity? As he was dying, Hegel
is supposed to have uttered these words, *"Nur einer hat mich
verstanden."* (He was thinking of himself.) But then he added,
"Und auch der hat mich nicht verstanden."[8]

What is true of individual philosophers is true of all philosophy. Human knowledge is a perpetual straining towards
greater clarity and precision.[9] It both has and does not have
identity with itself. "A is A and not non-A" signifies an
assumed final culmination of thought. But in human life, Truth
with a capital T, which may be symbolized as "A," is only an
aim, and as such it is yet to be fully realized. Where there is
an increase in clarity, Truth *is being realized.* "A" is *becoming*

7. It should be noticed, however, that the formula "A = A" is itself dialectical in
that it assumes both the identity and the separation of what is on each side of the
equation mark.

8. "Only one person has understood me. — And even he has not understood me."

9. Needless to say, Leo Strauss is well aware that philosophy is a *quest* for truth.
Indeed, he stresses the fact. But his idea is not worked out systematically. It con-
tradicts the tendency of thought already discussed. Strauss writes, "Philosophy
is essentially not possession of the truth, but quest for the truth." This recognition of the provisional, dynamic nature of thought is difficult to reconcile with the
notion of static, "exact" ideas implied in the rule of interpretation also proposed
by Strauss. The idea that philosophy is essentially a *quest* for the truth might seem
more compatible with the argument presented here. But the quoted sentence raises
a key problem. How could there be a *quest* for the truth which is not to some extent
simultaneously and indistinguishably *possession* of the truth? The quest would otherwise lack direction, which is a contradiction in terms. Dialectical logic does away
with static, reified alternatives like Truth or non-Truth and explains the dynamic
reality of simultaneous possession and non-possession of the truth. If taken at their
face meaning, Strauss' words that philosophy is "essentially" *not* possession of
the truth and that perhaps the fundamental questions "cannot be answered" are
open to the type of objection that can be directed against pragmatism and other
relativistic notions of knowledge. (*What is Political Philosophy?*, 11.)

identical with itself. In as much as concepts never achieve complete self-identity by coming to rest in omniscience, "A" is simultaneously and indistinguishably "non-A." What strikes the merely formalistic and abstract logicians as a contradiction is a fact nevertheless. *Principium identitatis* does contain an element of truth. But that truth is distorted unless the principle receives the complement which lifts it out of the sphere of abstract reifications.

Chapter 1 demonstrated that, like Eric Voegelin and others, Babbitt resists literalistic hardening of theological dogmas as distorting and obscuring experiential religious and ethical reality. What has been criticized in this chapter, a reifying conception of philosophical truths or texts, analogously distorts and obscures the nature of human philosophical knowledge. The belief that a philosophical statement may contain wholly unambiguous meaning and is to be understood *exactly* can be described as the epistemological counterpart of religious fundamentalism.

The principle of logical dialectic here explained is never considered by Irving Babbitt, and yet it is fittingly described as the logical-conceptual aspect of that dualism which he regards as the fundamental fact of human existence. Philosophical reason is itself constituted by the dualism of human existence and is fully in tune with that reality. What Babbitt calls "the scandal of reason" is the creation of a very different, pragmatic rationality which pursues an abstract and illusory consistency. Far from threatening truth and intellectual coherence, dialectical logic—symbolized as "A is A *and* non-A"— is how we *actually* think and how we are able to know life as *it* really is, "a oneness that is always changing."

Chapter 8
Will and Knowledge

Weaknesses and omissions in Babbitt's view of reason have been examined with the aim of developing the idea of philosophical reason as a natural supplement to his thought. The stage has been reached at which a particularly difficult problem must be confronted. Dealing with that problem is a prerequisite for explicating the strengths of Babbitt's position in Part Two of this book and essential to the epistemological synthesis that is made possible by the respective strengths of Babbitt and Croce. It has been argued earlier that in philosophical perception experience and concept coincide. However, as dreams illustrate, what man experiences is not always reality. It must be explained what distinguishes the experience intrinsic to philosophical knowledge from other types of experience. Differently put, what is the philosophical criterion of reality? To answer that question, more attention must be given to the relationship between will and reason. This is a subject on which Croce has written extensively. In part, he makes explicit and clear what lies implicit in Babbitt, but he also adds significantly to the latter. The following analysis of Croce's understanding of the interaction of will and reason connects the earlier discussions of reason with Babbitt's notion of the practical criterion of reality, as presented in Chapter I. What Croce adds to Babbitt is the notion of philosophical reason and the idea of will-action as anchoring it in reality. Concluding Part One of the book, this chapter comes back full circle to Babbitt's stress on will as the key to reality. The assumption that will, imagination and reason can be properly understood only systematically, that is, together, will again be confirmed.

Babbitt and Croce agree that Kant's concept of "practical reason'' should be discarded and replaced by ''ethical will.'' The term ''practical reason'' is an invitation to misplaced intellectualism. Croce points out that as long as a sharp distinction is maintained between theoretical and practical reason, the danger of confusion is diminished, because then the terms may come close to meaning simply knowledge and moral will.[1] Even so, the term ''practical reason'' easily leads to a confusion of moral will with conceptual intellection of some specifically ''practical'' kind. In fact, Croce insists, there is no such thing as ''practical reason''; there is only theoretical reason giving a description of, among other things, the practical will. (''Practical reason'' in the sense of pragmatic rationality is a different subject.)

It will be shown in Part Two that Babbitt goes beyond Croce in his definition and criticism of ''rationalism'' in ethics. Applying Babbitt's definition of moral rationalism, one discovers a lingering rationalism in Croce himself. Croce is superior to Babbitt in explaining his views with philosophical clarity, but it can be argued that Babbitt reaches deeper.

The problem of the *moral* will in relation to knowledge will be treated in a later chapter. Here discussion will be limited to the relation of will in general to knowledge. In dealing with this particular topic there is no need to combine analysis of Croce's views with side glances at Babbitt's opinions. In these matters Babbitt thinks along the same lines as Croce, even though his thoughts are not worked out to the same degree of clarity.

The epistemological fulcrum of Croce's ''historicism'' is his interest in a kind of knowledge that is neglected by other philosophers: the autobiographical knowledge of what we have just been doing. Individuals have been known to suffer a loss of memory so that they no longer know who they are. They may go to another city, find lodgings there, begin a new life.

---

1. Cf. Croce's remarks on Kant's practical reason in *The Philosophy of the Practical* (New York: Biblo and Tannen, 1967; reprint of the 1913 Macmillan edition), 150-52; hereinafter referred to in the tex as ''PP.'' The English translation is sometimes inaccurate and misleading.

All the time they are in the dark about their identity. But even such a person must keep a running record of what he has just been doing. Without at least a short-range memory no human consciousness could exist. This consciousness is *historical knowledge,* even if it be reduced to the history of the immediate past. The "now" is a very difficult concept, but at least it can be said that as soon as we become reflectively aware of what is in the "now," the "now" is already history. We cannot be theoretically aware of what is now happening, only of what has just happened. Self-knowledge, as an awareness of our own acts as we go along, is historical knowledge in the sense of autobiography cut down to what is in the immediate past. The self conducting the autobiography is of course, as previously explained, a human consciousness transcending idiosyncratic individuality. More complex products of autobiography and general historiography are constructed on the ultimate basis of men's short-range awareness of their volitive responses to whatever "turns up." *What* it was that turned up is decided in the act of interpreting it. Thus the basis of knowledge is awareness of our own acts, an awareness which is historical knowledge.

The Crocean theory distinguishes between the act of valuing and the historical knowledge of this act. The historical recording of the act of valuing is the *value judgment.* This judgment is distinct from the *valuing* which is inherent in the act of choosing itself. Mere volition is theoretically mute: it is choosing, preferring, doing. As philosopher-historians we record these acts of acceptance and rejection in articulate and verbalized judgments: "This is good and that is bad," meaning "I preferred this and rejected that" or, since the historical judgment is almost contemporaneous with the act of volition, "I prefer this and reject that."

According to Croce, and Babbitt is obviously in agreement, there are two distinct modes of willing or valuing—ethical and non-ethical The non-ethical acts he calls "merely utilitarian," or "merely economic." (The word "merely" should be noticed. According to Croce moral action is always also economical, in the sense of being disciplined to a purpose. "Merely" economical means that the action is unaffected by a moral motive.) Observing what we have done, we say, "This action was morally good" or "This action was prudent, economically effective, politically clever" (other adjectives being possible depending on the circumstances). In these judgments we record historically the presence of a value in an action performed. *Valuing* is not the theoretical recording of values inherent in actions of the past; it is the *bestowing* of some sort of value on new actions in the very process of creating them. The judgment of value comes after the event; the valuing *is* the event. The inspiration of new, still unperformed actions may be ethical or non-ethical, but in either case value is conferred in the enactment itself.

In the case of a single simple desire, the notion of conferring, bestowing value on something by desiring it is familiar and easily understood. Desiring a cigarette is investing the act of smoking it with value. The non-smoker does not bestow value on this act. It is more difficult to hold on to the idea of bestowing value when there are competing desires and a need for deliberation. Yet presiding over the deliberation is a will, either moral or merely "economic," which prefers this and rejects that incipient action. Preferring is bestowing value on what is preferred in the very creation of the act. Rejecting is bestowing negative value, or anti-value, on an incipient action and thereby eliminating it from possible future existence. This element in the deliberation is not "making up one's mind" in the theoretical sense of the word "mind"; it is making up one's will. This is so even though an important part of the deliberation is the ongoing expansion of what Croce calls "the theoretical basis of action." The practical need dominant at the moment inspires a need to *know* the given situation as a necessary preliminary to continued volition. Depending on the circumstances, such as the time available and the importance of the decision to be made, the theoretical basis can be expanded indefinitely to bring the human past in the widest sense to bear on understanding the present situation. Various possibilities for volition are enacted in the imagination (which is the aesthetical mode of theoretical activity). This intuited practical experience becomes the object of a judgment of value in subsequent logical-theoretical acts in which the presence of a certain quality of will in the imagined enactments is recorded historically. Without theoretical moments, however short, new actions cannot take place. But the actual decision itself is a non-theoretical, practical act. The decision is *making up one's will*, *bestowing* value on the act which is being created and negative value on the suppressed possibilities. Yet we tend to intellectualize even the decision itself and conceive of it as the logical conclusion of a purely theoretical argument. We are led to do so because of the presence and prominence in the deliberation of the ongoing expansion of the theoretical basis. The decision emerges out of a complicated and intimate collaboration of mute volitions and theoretical acts, but when it comes, it is just as value-bestowing and creative of new reality as is the thoughtless, spontaneous action of taking a cigarette and lighting it. Aristotle's idea that a decision is preceded by a "practical syllogism" arises out of that confusion of cognition and volition which Croce seeks to disentangle. This confusion leads to the misinterpretation of will as practical reason.

Croce's theory is developed at length in *The Philosophy of the Practical* (PP, esp. 86-93), but a brief statement of it is found already in the *Aesthetic:*

Some psychologists . . . place before practical action an altogether special class of judgements, which they call *practical* judgements or *judgements of value.* They say that in order to resolve on performing an action there must have been a judgement to the effect: "this action is useful, this action is good." And at first sight this seems to have the testimony of consciousness on its side. But closer observation and analysis of greater subtlety reveal that such judgements follow instead of preceding the affirmation of the will, and are nothing but the expression of the volition already exercised. A good or useful action is an action willed. It will always be impossible to distil a single drop of usefulness or goodness from the objective study of things. We do not desire things because we know them to be good or useful; but we know them to be good and useful, because we desire them. Here

too, the rapidity with which the facts of consciousness follow one another has given rise to an illusion. Practical action
is preceded by knowledge, but not by practical knowledge,
or rather, knowledge of the practical: to obtain this, we must
first have practical action. The third moment, therefore, of
practical judgements, or judgements of value, is altogether
imaginary. It does not come between the two moments or
degrees of theory and practice. (A, 49-50)[2]

It might be asked, "Why would I desire something, if I have
not already judged it to be good?" The answer is that the
"why," the enticement, the valuation, is in the prevailing will
or desire itself. A certain prevailing volitive orientation affirms
or negates incipient potentialities as pleasing or abhorrent to
itself. It does of course make every difference to the individual's
well-being which type of practical urge he allows to be the principle of valuation. It has already been explained that there is
in man a special quality of will which defines the ethical good
and which draws the individual to itself by virtue of the promise
of happiness that is its own nature. Selfish will or desire, by
contrast, is destructive of that special volitive orientation and
satisfaction, but it too has power according to its own intrinsic
attraction of pleasure.

Does knowledge precede volition, or does volition precede
knowledge? According to Croce, the relation is circular. We cannot act without knowing our situation, including our where-
abouts. But we acquire the knowledge needed for action
because we want it. All the forms of human activity—practical,
aesthetical or logical—are but different manifestations or
emphases of will. Thus every act of cognition is at the same time
a volition. A man governed by a strong desire, whether moral
or immoral, acquires the information needed to satisfy his
desire. Even when cognitive processes are philosophical and
thus governed by the intrinsic requirement of truth rather than
utility, they are *ultimately* instrumental to practical needs, to live
well in some sense of that term. The "theoretical basis for

2. Benedetto Croce, *Aesthetic* (2nd rev. ed.; London: Macmillan, 1922), 49-50; hereinafter referred to in the text as "A."

action" is a function of what men desire and varies with the desires. The individual who is inspired by moral will attends to different matters and with less susceptibility to self-serving prejudice than the slave of some passion. He procures the knowledge he needs for transforming his moral inspiration into concrete good actions in the circumstances of his life and times.

Cognition and practical volition work together in every moment of conscious life. There are moments when we *will* cognition more than anything else; these are moments when we are confused and do not understand our situation. In other moments the situation is sufficiently clear in our mind for the will to proceed to practical, non-cognitive action. But this action is accompanied by awareness of what we are doing. If this awareness ceased, we would no longer have a human consciousness. All human activity is volition, and thinking is historical awareness of our volitions. As thought itself is at the same time volition, we record cognitive acts in subsequent cognitive acts. No acts occur, whether practical-volitive, cognitive-volitive or intuitive-volitive, that are not almost contemporaneously recorded historically. The knowing of something is certainly a knowing, but not a knowing of itself; the knowledge of this act of knowing is a subsequent act of knowing.

It is pertinent, in discussing the nature of historical self-knowledge, to recall Babbitt's contrast between "pure science," which tends to become "a series of abstract mathematical formulae without any real content," and "the warm immediacy of perception." (RR, 138- 39)[3] What is perception? The kinds of observations which are recorded in the "protocol statements" of physical science are in a way obviously far removed from human self-knowledge. Yet an individual cannot affirm that he "observes" something and record it in a protocol statement without having a knowledge of his act of observation and of his making a linguistic statement. He perceives his own acts and categorizes them; the perception of the acts is the categorizing and the categorizing is the perception. Such perceptions

3. Irving Babbitt, *Rousseau and Romanticism* (Austin: The University of Texas Press, 1977), 138-39; hereinafter referred to in the text "RR."

of self-knowledge are logically prior to all other types of knowledge. Discussions of "introspection" which fail to perceive their own logical foundations remain on the level of epistemological naiveté.

History, as Croce uses the word, includes human history and what used to be called "natural history." Autobiographical knowledge is logically prior to natural history. For example, assuming that I am a "natural historian," I may observe in myself a moment of hesitation when it comes to deciding whether an animal or plant should be referred to a certain *species* rather than some *genus;* perhaps I decide to invent a new *species* which would be more suitable. The task is finding a useful *découpage.* I cannot know about acts of *découpage* unless I can observe them, observe what was there before they took place and observe their results. I am an historian of my own activities at the same time that I am an historian of the things observed in nature.

The question arises whether Babbitt's term "warm immediacy" is appropriately applied to observation of our own activities. The term is appropriate insofar as these activities are concrete existential phenomena; it is inappropriate insofar as the observation of them is at the same time a categorizing judgment. My autobiographical judgments in the just mentioned example run something as follows: "This is observing a phenomenon (not imagining it); these are acts of defining classificatory concepts; this is trying out the concepts for classification on the phenomenon and observing discrepancies; this is an act of defining a new classificatory concept; and now I decided to make use of this possibility." In a series of historical judgments, judgments of self-knowledge, I register the ongoing existential process. These judgments are not quite so warmly immediate as Babbitt seems to assume. Any act of perception, no matter how uncomplicated its content, is a judgment, "This is something perceived, not imagined." For this reason perception can be called concrete thought. This union of immediacy and thought is especially obvious in the observations of self-knowledge. In perception, "warm" immediacy is married to "cold" categorizing.

If we want warm immediacy uncontaminated and unchilled by categorizing thought, Croce argues, we have to stop thinking in the sense of categorizing our activities. One such state is intense aesthetic experience. Listening to music we are concerned only with its internal musical coherence. If we are in a concert hall, we can perhaps be said to perceive the music in that tones reach our ears, yet, there seems to be general awareness that the word "perceive" does not fit musical experience. Insofar as we are interested in the music as such, we do not care whether we are "imagining" or "perceiving" it. This is what Croce means when he points out that in aesthetic experience we do not care about reality. The word "perceive" is appropriate only when there is an intention to know reality. In aesthetic experience we merely want to experience or (in Croce's terminology) "intuit" something, whatever its reality. "Willing suspension of disbelief" could equally well be called willing suspension of belief, because in these moments we do not care about believing or disbelieving. In the process of absorbing a novel, we care only that it should be aesthetically enthralling. Moments of critical discernment follow upon and presuppose these moments of logically mute, merely intuitive experience.

"Intuition" is thus immediacy uncontaminated by thought, whereas "perception" is at once immediacy and thought, or concrete thought. Readers of Croce's *Aesthetic* have often asked, how does Croce know that "this is an intuition" and that "that is a perception"? What is his criterion for distinguishing one from the other? The answer is implicit in what has already been explained: all depends on the intention issuing in the particular experience. Retrospective self-knowledge may tell me, "I had this experience because my intention was suspending belief and disbelief in order merely to intuit; now I have returned to perception and am reflectively aware that I have had an aesthetic experience." Alternatively, retrospective self-knowledge may tell me, "I had this experience because my intention was to know." In the latter case I call the materials experienced contents of perception.

Hallucinations and illusions are also contents of perception insofar as the intention behind them is knowing reality. They nevertheless become classified as hallucinations and illusions by application of the criterion of coherence. Epistemological treatises err, however, in assuming that aesthetic contents are known to be imaginary by application of the same criterion of coherence. They are known as not being real by going back to the intention out of which they were born. Many worlds can be imagined which are coherent. How do we know that one world is real? The real world is the one to which our decisions and actions belong. A man makes sure he is not dreaming: he performs a series of actions, pinches his skin, lifts objects and puts them down, walks a few steps, turns his head right and left, and so on. This series of actions is quite persuasive; in dreams we never perform them systematically and in full awareness of what we are doing. The ultimate criterion of reality is the anchorage of coherence in will-action. Coherence *per se* does not give reality.

Croce is aware that something should be added about will-action in order to make clear his distinction between the two intentions. The perceptive intention is to know reality; the aesthetic intention is to have an intuition, disregarding the question of reality. What is this ''reality'' which forms a part of the definitions? Croce answers the question in a section of his *Philosophy of the Practical.* (PP, 262ff.) He starts from a distinction between ''mere desires'' and ''acts of will.'' Acts of will realize desires, but many desires remain unrealized. Desires are ''such stuff as dreams are made on''; if unrealized in action, they may give rise to intuitive visions of ''possibilities,'' to use Croce's phrase. We suspend belief and disbelief and permit desires to be thus transfigured. In ordinary daydreams the visions are overlaid with sensual stimuli, for instance, stimuli to our will to power, but insofar as the visions are unencumbered by such elements, the transfiguration of the desires can become complete, in which case there is a purely aesthetic vision. Practical acts of will, or decisions, on the other hand, are such stuff as perceptions are ''made on.'' Decision-action as a doing is followed by an undergoing; perception is the reflective awareness of this doing and undergoing. ''This is real" means, "this is decision-action and subsequent under-going." "This is unreal" means, "this is a projection of mere desires."

According to Croce the criterion of reality is "nothing but the first reflection of the spirit upon the practical activity itself, giving rise to the duplication of reality that has happened and reality only desired, or of reality and irreality, of existing and inexisting." (PP, 264) *"For the determination of the relation between desire and action, and only for that, the criterion of existence is not necessary, because that relation is itself that criterion."* (PP, 265; emphasis added)

Perception proceeds by choice among products of intuition, some of which are judged to be fashioned out of material offered by actions, while others are seen to be mere fancies, that is, fashioned out of material offered by mere desires. Thus the judgment of reality supervenes upon a first moment of merely aesthetic, unreflective awareness, however brief in duration. Even when the predominant intention is to explore reality, there are fractions of seconds when first of all we want to be aware of *something* before deciding what that something is: fancy, or reality, or a mixture of both. Reflective awareness, or perception, is critical awareness; but the will to critical awareness demands procuring material to be critical about, demands in other words moments in which the imagination constitutes wholes of experience. Croce writes of this unleashing of intuition:

> Since to art is wanting the distinctive criterion between desires and actions . . . the real as possible, and the possible as real . . . it would be . . . correct to say that art is beyond the distinction between the possible and the real, it is pure of these distinctions, and is therefore pure imagination or *pure intuition*. Desires and actions are, we know, of the same stuff, and art assumes that stuff just as it is, careless of the new elaboration that it will receive in an ulterior grade of the spirit [i.e., logical judgment], which is indeed impossible without that first and merely fantastic elaboration. Likewise when art takes possession of historical material, it removes from it just the historical character, the critical elements, and by this very

fact reduces it once more to mere intuition. (PP, 266-67)[4]

Philosophical perception records in existential judgments what the will has wrought. The specifically philosophical criterion of reality is the direct perception of the difference between will realized in action and will remaining in the form of unrealized desire, more or less transfigured into imagination. Thinking and imagining are no less products of will than is practical action. Croce calls them "theoretical" activities. Not even dreaming is a suspension of action (as any physiologist would confirm in his own way). The events depicted in more or less poetic intuition are identified in philosophical perception as not belonging to the historical world of action, but philosophy also records the historical existence of the intuitive activity that creates images of that non-historical type.

Briefly to summarize the findings of this chapter and all of Part One of this book, philosophical reason gives conceptual self-awareness to the categorial structure of experience, experience having been constituted into a pre-cognitive whole by the imagination. Perceiving the unity of the universal and the particular through concrete thought, philosophical reason has as its criterion of reality the historical self-awareness of the will. In Part Two the interaction between will, imagination and reason will be explored further, now with special attention to the ethico-aesthetical issues emphasized by Babbitt.

4. The English translation is here quoted with a correction.

Part Two

Chapter 9
Will and
Imaginative Truth

Part One of this book has criticized and supplemented the work of Irving Babbitt in areas pertaining to the nature of reason and a categorial logic. More generally, it has prepared a philosophical framework for demonstrating the full epistemological significance of Babbitt's insights regarding the relationship of imagination and will and for incorporating those insights into a theory of knowledge. It is time to take up a subject which is treated at great length by Babbitt but which has only been mentioned in passing: the role of the imagination as a source of wisdom and as a source of more or less dangerous illusion. This is a decidedly non-Crocean theme distinctive to Babbitt. The subject has been postponed for separate treatment because fragmentary discussion of it in the context of the previous chapters would not have been very illuminating.

Babbitt attributes decisive importance to the imagination in the shaping of man's understanding of life. Certain types of imagination draw us into misleading views of the world, and indeed, may make us lose touch with reality. Other types tend to improve our hold on life. It is helpful, in trying to understand Babbitt's doctrine, to keep in mind the notion of will (ethical or unethical) as the energy which carries all human activity, whether practical, philosophical or aesthetical. Many words—desire, wish, aspiration, impulse, interest, inclination, passion, etc.—denote the fundamental impelling power of will without which the life of human society and culture would cease. Will is the generic, categorial name for that infinity and variety of impulse that orients the individual to particular tasks. Whatever the kind of activity taking hold of man, be it practical or contemplative, it must be sustained by some desire, by will.

To get to the heart of Babbitt's ethico-aesthetical doctrine, it is important to recognize that, in one sense, will and imagination are the same. A desire, in reaching the human consciousness, is no longer some blind practical urge. Even a seemingly simple impulse to quench one's thirst immediately translates itself into imagination. It becomes, for example, the intuition of clear, cool water passing down one's throat. Without articulating itself in concrete images, the desire to drink is unaware of itself, indefinite, and powerless to move the individual. The intuition is potentially highly complex, for the imagined act of drinking must include a sense of the larger situation of life in which it is taking place. Particular short-range impulses of desire emanate from a broader disposition of character. What is expressed in each intuitive transfiguration of desire is also a more comprehensive vision of life's possibilities. Different personalities will be attracted to different possibilities. Babbitt explains that men develop such imagination as is pleasing to their underlying orientations of character.

If will decides the direction of human activity, Babbitt also emphasizes that the human will is dualistic, forever torn between higher and lower potentialities. Both of these poles of man's being express themselves in imagination. Transfigured into more or less poetic intuition, the higher or lower desires acquire the power that comes with concreteness, sensual texture, immediacy. As intuitions they are not realized in practice; but, as living visions of what life could be, they stir the human self, inviting practical action consonant with themselves. It has often been noted in older Western philosophy that what is highest in man cannot by itself withstand strong contrary passions. Plato stresses the need for a power of "spiritedness" (*thymos*) to enforce the authority of reason. Babbitt finds the highest moral authority not in intellect but in will of a special quality. That will is never present to man in its fullness. It is a potentiality for Good to be progressively realized in continuous tension with an opposite quality of will. To become more fully realized, the ethical will needs the power of imagination to give it concreteness and to draw the human will more deeply into its own potentiality of goodness. In the perpetual struggle between higher and lower possibilities of existence, Babbitt argues, "the imagination holds the balance of power." In this sense he agrees with Napoleon that "imagination governs mankind." (DL, 10)[1] To prevail, the ethical will must express its purposes through the magnetic imagery of intuition.

Corresponding qualities of character and imagination tend to beget and reinforce each other. An individual caught up in a life of hedonistic pleasure-seeking is predisposed to be responsive to works of poetry which are carried by a similar sense of life's possibilities. As his personality is absorbed into poetic vision of new hedonistic thrills, his will finds satisfaction in it and deepens in its commitment. Moments of aesthetic enjoyment tend to call forth corresponding attempts at practical realization of desire. Such transition to practical action is never automatic—man is free to reject even strong appeals of desire—but if it takes place, it is not unexpected. The will that now proceeds to practical action belongs to the same disposition of character that previously found aesthetic enjoyment in the vision of a hedonistic state.

A person more under the influence of the higher will has a different sense of what brings genuine satisfaction. This person may well be enticed by a powerful poetic statement of a hedonistic existence; it richly embellishes and supports his own moments of hedonistic flight from aristocratic character. But, by virtue of his predominant orientation of personality, the hedonistic vision is likely also to create uneasiness. He senses in it the expression of an ignoble, incomplete, and ultimately miserable state of soul, one in which he has sometimes participated.

For a person in whom will of an immoral type is strongly entrenched and in whom imagination attuned to that will is continuously reinforcing the same orientation of character, it may be quite difficult to change. Even a cultured individual of predominantly sound character will remain to some extent sus-

---

1. Irving Babbitt, *Democracy and Leadership* (Boston: Houghton Mifflin, 1952), 192-93; hereinafter referred to in the text as "DL."

ceptible to the stirrings of his lower will, especially if it finds expression in vibrant, luxuriant poetic vision. Plato feared the influence of wrongly inspired poets on souls still lacking in ethical maturity. Babbitt suggests that in the relatively good man, too, the imagination can become the ally of secret drives, which, in his better moments, he would not indulge. If a person lets himself be drawn into intuitions which play upon and expand his more ignoble self, his imagination will help him conceal his moral qualms. These become portrayed, perhaps, as symptoms of a ridiculous and narrow-minded "bourgeois" puritanism. The now dominant desire, by contrast, is depicted as the manifestation of a higher freedom, above such petty notions of responsibility. A powerfully endowed imagination may paint even diabolical drives in alluring images. Were it not for man's ability to fashion the potentialities of his own lower self in aesthetically enthralling ways, that self would have little power to influence men of culture. The more creative a person's intuition, the greater its influence, for good or evil.

It is pertinent here to explain one sense in which the higher will can be described as an "inner check." When ignoble hedonistic intuition is pulling an individual into itself or into practical action, he may be suddenly stopped by moral uneasiness. What Babbitt calls the inner check is the transcendent Good breaking into consciousness by arresting incipient activity. It affords man an opportunity to reconstitute his intentions. What begins as a negative act, as moral censuring of a present intention, may in the next moment assert itself positively. In a person of some habitual responsiveness to the higher will, the latter may be given the opportunity to articulate itself in imagination, for example, in the intuition of the ultimate misery of the hedonistic life as the defeat of the promise of happiness. At best, this means the purging of the previously dominant lower imagination and with it the sustaining lower will.

In most men the interplay of will and imagination does not often result in intuitions of a particularly poetic type. The imagination usually works in spurts and at the mercy of pressing practical needs. In the poetically inclined and gifted person,

on the other hand, the imagination may detach itself from service to impulses of the moment and swell into an elaborate,
finely harmonized vision of life. In art, intuition synthesizes
possibilities of human existence according to the aesthetic
requirement of beauty. Still, it must not be overlooked that,
even in the aesthetic intensification of art, intuition is at the
same time will. It emanates from an underlying disposition of
character. The work of art is the expression of a personality
whose sense of reality is the result of innumerable acts of will
in the past which have led the artist to explore some possibilities of experience and neglect many others. The disposition of
character and sensibility which has been built up over the years
now selects the material for the aesthetic creation. By virtue of
his past willing, the artist is particularly sensitive to some potentialities of human life, less sensitive to others. We know the will
by its fruits in imagination.

Babbitt insists that, although art must have a special aesthetic
integrity and coherence to be truly itself, what is poetically
expressed can differ greatly in value. Art can be more or less
profound, or truthful, in its statement of life's possibilities—
truthful not in an intellectual sense but in an intuitive sense.
Art ranges from works which capture with depth and fullness
the essence of human existence, with its anchor in a universal
moral order, to works of a trivial and superficial type or of positively distorting vision. Some richly poetic works exclude or
disfigure elements of reality. For instance, it is not uncommon
for man to crave refuge from everything mundane and uncomfortable. The individual sometimes allows himself to be intox-
icated by his imagination. He loses himself in *das Fabelhafte*. Intuitions that might disturb the escapist vision of a pleasant, rosy
existence are not allowed to enter the poetic synthesis. The will
at the root of the intuitive creation excludes what is not pleasing to it. Most works of art reflect some such more or less
deliberate contraction or distortion of reality, betraying the bias
and selectivity of the will that created it. Truly great works of
art, by contrast, are open to all of what life may contain. This
requires a will permitting contemplation of the more disturb-
ing and painful dimensions of experience, as well as the poten-

tialities for pleasure and happiness.

A person accustomed to finding the meaning of existence in passing pleasures will tend to express in his art possibilities of experience consonant with that sense of what life has to offer. Insofar as he has any intuition of moral responsibility and allows it to enter his poetic vision, he is likely to express it according to his accustomed hedonistic sensibilities, hence in some cynically distorted form. The resulting poem will not convey man's actual moral predicament. The poem will lack what Babbitt calls "centrality." Although the hedonistic intuition may be aesthetically enthralling, it has no depth of vision. To the extent that the poem does not build up an entirely illusory intuition of life, it offers merely fragmentary vision.

If, on the other hand, the hedonistically inclined poet permits the sudden intuiton of the ethical will to expand and deepen so as to come into its own, which assumes that an orientation of will hospitable to that new quality of imagination is asserting itself, his aesthetic vision will undergo a transformation. A different sense of what life may contain begins to arrange the material of intuition. Only an imagination which is sensitive to possibilities of experience in their relation to what is ultimately real—exercise of the ethical will and the happiness it brings—can express the essence of the human condition. This does not mean that all men of good character can also write and appreciate poetry. It does mean that the most penetrating imagination can emanate only from a human soul attuned to the real ethical opportunities and dangers of existence.

What Babbitt calls the moral imagination gives man a sense of the very essence of life, most importantly the moral order of existence. The ultimate reality in which man participates through ethical action he can also know intuitively through this highest form of imagination The moral imagination "imitates the universal." (As will be explained, imitation is for Babbitt *creative* imitation.) While Babbitt insists that great art is never didactic, he also believes it teaches man something about life. Whether it be in the dramas of Aeschylus or Sophocles, the myths of Plato or the poetry of Dante, the moral imagination lets us see deeply into that fundamental structure of life which is ourselves and all humanity. Absorbing a truly great work of art, men say to themselves, "This is truly what life is like!" A drama by Sophocles shows us individual persons and events, but by means of these imaginary characters we intuit the universal nature of human existence. In them we meet ourselves and all other human beings. We are Oedipus when we are ignorant and blind like him; we are Antigone in moments of courage to do what must be done; we are Ismene when courage fails. In sullen moods in which meaninglessness and injustice seem the truth about life, we are Iokaste; we are Creon when power and self-importance go to our head. The drama concretizes for us, presents in aesthetically intensified form, potentialities of all human existence. Intuiting the role and meaning of *hubris* and *nemesis*, we simultaneously intuit the proper attitude of man, *sophrosyne*. The total effect of the drama is to give us an elevated sense of order, proportion and reality. The moral imagination leaves out no essential element of human experience. We are drawn in the direction of "seeing life steadily and seeing it whole." The perspective of the great work of art is not that of the warped and incomplete personality; it is the perspective of the truly integrated moral personality.

But the imagination can also draw man into illusory views of existence. It can hide from him his real predicament and what he needs to do in order to find happiness and peace. It may ignore the duality of human nature and draw the individual into utopian or otherwise questionable expectations. Indeed, men often deliberately seek pleasing illusion. They wish to be deceived. As long as this is merely for temporary relaxation, the effect may not be entirely unhealthy. But such moments of imaginative extravagance may begin to acquire an aura of profound experience of life's deepest secrets and expand into pervasive themes. Babbitt takes as one example the idyllic imagination of Rousseau, which ignores essential aspects of experience. In this manner, men may drift further and further away from the central facts of their existence, although their imagination may at the same time contain fairly accurate views of some particular dimensions of life. Whatever the deficiencies of our imagination, they tend to distort our understanding of reality in general. If they are sufficiently grave and widely shared in society, the practical consequences can be social misery and destruction. A central task of civilization, Babbitt argues, is to expose lower or merely trivial forms of imagination and to make it possible for man to see life more realistically and richly.

Babbitt develops extensively an insight about which the professional philosophers seem to know little or nothing. The imagination in its higher form, he suggests, is man's most important source of humane *knowledge,* a knowledge, to be sure, which is non-intellectual in nature. Through the moral imagination man has an *intuitive* perception of the universal. Babbitt's idea has profound implications for the theory of knowledge. It is pertinent to note that Aristotle is aware that poetry gives a kind of knowledge. As is well known, Aristotle regards poetry as more philosophical than history and as aiming "rather at the universal" (a subject treated further below). It is both curious and revealing that in spite of this fact, interpretations of Aristotle's epistemology uniformly fail to consider the *Poetics* as a part of his theory of knowledge. This failure is symptomatic of underestimating the important aesthetic ingredient in the process of knowledge. This book aims to demonstrate that the role of the imagination must be a central subject in any adequate epistemology.

It has already been shown that Croce regards intuition as forming a part of the activity of knowing. However, especially before 1917, his understanding of imagination is in one important respect quite different from Babbitt's. An examination of that difference helps to explain the significance of Babbitt's ethico-aesthetical doctrine for the theory of knowledge.

According to Croce, reason always gives truth; otherwise it is not reason. "False reasoning" is a round square. Error is due to the interference with the work of reason by some passion that causes a break in the chain of valid arguments. Error is the absence of thought. This holds true for both philosophical and pragmatic thought. An error in mathematical calculation means that at some point we just did not think. There was a blur and a deceptive hope that the result would still be correct. As applied to the humanistic field, this Crocean theory is open to a fundamental criticism. Croce argues that the work of reason contains within itself, as an integral part, the work of imagination. In order for reason to be always correct, then, its imaginative basis must have the same characteristic. There could be no such thing as a distorted imaginative view of human affairs. Croce's theory of "the practical origin of error"—i.e., the explanation of error as the interruption of cognition by practical passions—must be extended to cover also the work of the imagination. That is to say, the latter must be in its own way infallible as long as it functions at all. Imagination can be stopped by passion, but if it could be perverted, the infallibility of reason would also break down; for intuitive distortion would inevitably infest the reasoning of which it forms a part.

The type of imagination which works independently of the cognitive purposes of reason to create *Dichtung* cannot, according to Croce, ever mislead anyone with regard to the nature of reality. If the imagination is truly poetic, then, by definition, the only "truth" that can be legitimately asked for is *poetic truth;* and poetic truth is but another term for poetry being poetic. To demand of poetry some kind of philosophical truth in addition is unwarranted and mischievous. For Croce, the poetic imagination is a kind of luxury in the economy of the spirit, a function which somehow does not have consequences for the development of experience. Poetry can no more be philosophically false than it can be immoral. In the apparent exceptions to this rule, poetry is no longer just poetry but a mixture of poetry and passion, the latter intruding upon the autonomous functioning of the imagination. To look for morality or philosophical truth in poetry is as senseless as demanding them from geometry, or demanding geometry from poetry.

These are well-known Crocean theses. Analyzed with reference to Babbitt's insights regarding the imagination and to the reasoning in earlier chapters, they can be seen to be highly questionable. Celebrated though they be, Croce's theses simplify the relationships between will, imagination and reason.

Most people have met individuals with a seemingly innate

propensity for misunderstanding everyday situations. One may try to argue with such a person to change his interpretation of some event. "No, Mr. X did not mean what you think he meant, and Mrs. Y had something entirely different in mind than you imagine." But the effort turns out to be pointless. The person produces a stream of arguments for his view which are perhaps quite ingenious but based on yet other misunderstandings. His reasoning may be cool and lucid, as though impeccable and incontrovertible, the details of his argument all fitting into a coherent pattern and mutually supporting each other. You are finally left exhausted and despairing of ever bringing him around to a more accurate perception of the matter. The person may be exceptionally intelligent. Still, in this case he simply fails to grasp the situation. He is somehow not sensitive to all of the relevant facts. Masses of *petites perceptions*, to borrow Leibniz's phrase, do not register in his mind. Why do they fail to register? Croce may be right in asserting that the person does not *want* to take in these interconnected *petites perceptions*, and that some passion stops his imagination from doing so. But it is important to note that as a result *reason may be mistaken.* Even a brilliantly intelligent person may argue himself deeper and deeper into error. The deficiency of the reason is in this case in its intuitive element.

Suppose that a man with this penchant for seeing things as they are not should be a highly intelligent and learned historian. He shows a great skill in arguing his theses and meeting the counter-arguments of his fellow historians. In debates with his colleagues he goes from victory to victory. His colleagues are overwhelmed and talked down. Many are converted to his theories. Others continue to disagree but are finally reduced to silence. In the face of his stream of arguments they can only mutter between their teeth, "And yet the man is dead wrong."

Croce teaches about the historian that he should have plenty of imagination and a capacity for keen philosophical thought. From a Crocean point of view, what could be the defect of the historian just described? Is he insufficiently philosophical? But he may conceivably have some of the skills and the learning of a Bertrand Russell. Then, is he unimaginative? He could well be an excellent novelist reminding us of Zola or Proust or Sartre, or a lyrical poet, having some of the same originality in relation to our times that Wordsworth, Shelley or Swinburne had in relation to theirs. Lack of imagination would thus not explain his shortcomings. What, then, might be wrong? The Crocean account of historical thought leaves one wondering.

Reading the literary works of the historian will probably bring some enlightenment. His versions of historical events are likely to bear a striking resemblance to the sort of *Dichtung* he produces. If Wordsworth and Shelley had written historical accounts of the French Revolution, Arcadian haze and Promethean revolt would almost certainly have "colored the news." Similarly, "realists" will stress the darker, more unpleasant side of life, whether they write fiction or history. There is abundant evidence that an author is all of a piece. In the light of these observations, the weakness of Croce's theory can be defined as not recognizing that the imagination may be more or less truthful and often distortive. Croce's flat rejection of such a notion forbids him as literary critic to state some very important facts about writers and works under review. Or he smuggles these facts in under a false label, branding as a purely "aesthetic" defect what is really blindness to moral truth. He will say about an author whose vision of life is superficial that his imagination is uneven and meager. But, like a Rousseau, the writer may, on the contrary, be remarkably imaginative. The trouble is that he uses his poetic gifts to lead himself and others into mazes of illusion.

As a young man Croce tied himself to the theory that a rich poetic imagination cannot be used to express largely false views of life. He clung to this theory in spite of ever-growing evidence to the contrary. Babbitt, by insisting on the existence of imaginative distortion of life, calls much of Croce's philosophy and modern aesthetics into question. His argument is epistemologically arresting, for if philosophy or history relies on imagination and the latter can present illusory vision, the resulting ratiocination may lead deeper and deeper into error, no matter how splendidly the philosopher or historian writes or how keenly he argues emerging points of theory. The works of Marx,

Engels and Lenin can be criticized on many grounds, but perhaps their most fundamental deficiency is lack of what Babbitt calls ethical imagination. Babbitt stresses that at the root of one-sided or warped theories of life are distorting qualities of imagination, inspired by corresponding qualities of will. With such a defect a thinker is helpless. Encyclopedias of learning, powers of ratiocination that would dwarf a Euclid, cannot save him from drifting into illusion. And errors in the perception of the nature of man and society can have terrible consequences: wars, tyranny and suffering without end.

Epistemology can learn from Babbitt that for a person to be receptive to truth, his intuitive-volitive orientation must predispose him toward reality. No amount of argumentation will overcome a faulty theory of man and society unless the arguments are designed to undermine the imaginative construction dear to the heart which energizes and gives appeal to the theory. Babbitt addresses in depth a problem later seen by Eric Voegelin. Discussing a "resistance to truth," Voegelin writes, "The reasons why the various ideologies were wrong were sufficiently well known in the 1920s, but no ideologist could be persuaded to change his position under the pressure of argument. Obviously, rational discourse, or the resistance to it, had existential roots far deeper than the debate conducted on the surface."[2] In exploring these "existential roots" Babbitt formulates a solution to a problem that has baffled philosophers. Eliseo Vivas, in an assessment of Bertrand Russell, admits to being at a loss to explain how Russell could be at the same time a "technical philosophical genius" and a political "imbecile." "It cannot be explained, for it does not advance our understanding to be told that it happens every day: that geniuses have often been damned fools and often mischief-making fools at that."[3] This inability to account for the possible coexistence of formal brilliance and distorted views of life points to a gaping hole in the theory of knowledge and more generally in the

---

2. Eric Voegelin, *Anamnesis* (Notre Dame: University of Notre Dame Press, 1978), 6.
3. Eliseo Vivas, "A Good Guy? A Bad One?," review essay in *Modern Age* (Spring 1968), 174.

understanding of human nature. With that deficiency philosophy is poorly equipped to define the requirements for protecting and strengthening civilization. But where Vivas expresses puzzlement, Babbitt speaks with authority.

Part One of this book has drawn liberally from Croce's substantial accomplishments in technical philosophy. The criticisms of Babbitt deduced from Crocean insights have perhaps made Babbitt seem less than perspicacious in a few areas. Yet, unless Croce's ideas be joined to Babbitt's central doctrines and revised accordingly, they may well represent a fiddling while Rome is burning. It is time to affirm and substantiate by further argument that, when it comes to defining the most basic needs of civilization, Babbitt's weaknesses and omissions are of secondary importance. Croce's failure to recognize the existence of the moral imagination and the possibility of imaginative distortion, on the other hand, dangerously obscures these urgent needs. In his theory of the relationship between will and imagination Babbitt offers a penetrating diagnosis of the decline of Western society and a strategy for recovery. At the core of the decline he sees a corruption of the imagination and with it moral character. Babbitt's ideas in this area and their relevance for epistemology will be examined at greater length.

Technical philosophy plays an indispensable role in the life of the spirit. But the work of perfecting its concepts is properly informed by and placed in the service of wisdom.

Chapter 10
Intuitive Wisdom and Illusion

The new theme of imaginative truth and untruth requires a second look at some questions treated in earlier chapters. The previous comments on Babbitt's view of the "imagination" as related to "perception" and "reason" were largely negative (see Chapter 4), concerned as they were with demonstrating the untenability of a pragmatic understanding of these concepts and the need for finding their categorial basis. In that context it was not taken into account that Babbitt had in view purposes of his own to which justice was not done by drawing attention to imperfections in his technical philosophy. His primary purpose was not to provide precise definitions of the mentioned terms but to show how man can work his way out of imaginative error and attain imaginative truth.

It is helpful, in reconsidering Babbitt's notion of "imagination" and "reason," to illustrate his line of reasoning with some concrete examples. His view should be kept in mind that at the basis of our outlook on life lies an intuitively constituted vision of reality. The individual holds and develops this intuitive whole in an "inner monologue" by means of linguistic symbols. "Words govern the imagination." (DL, 192)[1] Consider a young rebellious individual. He has built up his intuition of the world out of whatever experience he has had. Among other things, he has encountered a great many evils in his society— some of them real enough, some of them only apparent but subjectively experienced as real. Now suppose the outlines of the ideology of Communism reach him from somewhere. The

1. **Irving Babbitt,** *Democracy and Leadership* (Boston: Houghton Mifflin, 1952), 192-93; hereinafter referred to in the text as "DL."

phrase "the evils of capitalist society" takes hold of his imagination. Until that moment the young rebel has looked upon defects and instances of misery and unhappiness around him and in himself as so many disconnected items. Now they are suddenly drawn into a new imaginative unity and seen to form part of a pattern. Other words—"exploitation," "alienation," "class war"—expand and diversify the emerging vision of life. As the terms are acclimatized in the youth's imagination by finding concrete referents in his own experience, they more or less subtly reconstitute his view of reality. The phrase, "the classless society," stirs in him what Babbitt calls "the idyllic imagination." The young rebel remembers idyllic aspects of his own experience, in real life or in works of fiction. Now he becomes aware of their resemblance to what is vaguely promised in that haunting phrase, "the classless society." His own vision of that future society is constituted by drawing together these likenesses. The imagination unifies previously more or less disconnected items by instituting *likenesses and analogies*. The result is an interpretation of his own experience as related to the promised society. The antithesis of that goal, the nightmare of capitalist society, is intuited out of the dark and unpleasant experiences of his past.

The words "likenesses and analogies" have been employed because they figure prominently in Babbitt's description of the imagination. Babbitt speaks not only of "conceiving" likenesses and analogies (which is synonymous with "instituting" them) but also of "perceiving" or "seizing" them. The latter is a "mimetic" ingredient in his language. His terminology may seem to indicate a relapse into an antiquated aesthetics, for words like "perceiving" or "seizing" tend to obscure the creative role of the imagination, implying that the likenesses and analogies were there before the act of imagination. In a sense they actually were there before, as even the Coleridgean theory will admit. The young man of the example was certainly aware of the likenesses and analogies of his previous idyllic experiences before he came under the influence of Communism. But at this latter stage the creative vision comes into play—now his imagination *conceives* or institutes new likenesses between the experiential material and the tenets of the new faith. These likenesses did not exist before the creative act of conceiving them. The former likenesses and analogies could be said to be "perceived" or "seized," as they were already familiar, but not the latter. However, a more subtle view emerges as one inquires into the origin of those likenesses and analogies of which it has been said that they were perceived or seized. Were they not on earlier occasions conceived themselves? Our idyllic experiences, for example, were shaped by poetry, fiction, painting and music which helped to raise our dumb and inarticulate feelings to the level of conscious experience. The words of our mother tongue served the same function. Acts of the imagination once conceived those likenesses and analogies which, on becoming familiar or habitual, are said to be perceived.[2]

The young rebel's Communist vision of the world is of course in part valid historical thought. But it is pieced out with fancies which can be traced back to a sometimes willful neglect of those aspects of historical reality which do not easily fit the sympathies and antipathies that find expression in his imaginative construction of the world. The Communist is likely to feel uncomfortable, for example, dwelling on the apparent ability of many so-called "capitalists" to show genuine humaneness and in general to transcend their own "class." Considerations of this type pose a threat to the vision. The task of the critical intellect, Babbitt says, is testing visions as to their reality. But it is in the nature of the ideologue to be reluctant to have his vision really tested. An individual of this type may be voluble when among sympathizers or among people who can be easily converted, but in the presence of a truly well-informed person he can be expected to "clam up" and avoid genuine discussion. The vision is too sacred to be submitted to searching analysis. Beneath a surface of intellectualism is discovered a familiar phenomenon, romantic anti-intellectualism. (Some reluctance to confront uncomfortable elements of reality is of course a tendency in all human beings, regardless of their ideo-

2. The intention of this argument is not to deny an extra-mental reality.

logical biases.)

Consider instead a person who is genuinely trying to work his way towards a truer perception of reality. The word "truer" is the appropriate one, for, as Babbitt insists, truth is a matter of degrees; no one sees life steadily and sees it whole. The person of this illustration has a greater willingness than the ideologue to subject his favorite "visions" and "ideas" to the sobering analysis of reason. What are the "facts" with a view to which he can check his imaginative sense of reality? Specific historical facts, warrantably ascertained by approved scholarly methods, must certainly play a role in revealing elements of illusion or simple inaccuracy. But in the end what serves as a corrective to the person's vision of life is his entire experience of human existence. This experience has been acquired through the previous cooperation between his creative imagination and his critical reason—a process that has gone on in him since childhood. It has resulted in whatever knowledge of men and the world that he possesses. Reading has of course furnished him with a great deal of the material used in that ongoing cooperation between imagination and reason. If his reading has been wide enough, he will be able to follow Goethe's famous advice that "one should always oppose to the aberrations of the hour the masses of universal history." If he is not a scholar, the "masses of world history" will be limited to that section of contemporary, perhaps chiefly local, history he knows well, although the remoter "masses" have also seeped into his interpretations of life in ways he cannot account for himself. The very language he has learnt is charged with them.

When the intellect comes into play, its function, says Babbitt, is to resolve the imaginative synthesis into its elements and to ask for their status within the context of reality. The elements unified into an imaginative vision may be so far apart and different that the vision has little to do with reality and is fantastic. To return to the earlier illustration, the grievances of the young Communist, when carefully investigated, may turn out to be partly justified, partly due to sheer misunderstanding of the workings of the market economy and democratic processes. A close analysis of "cause and effect" in the world criticized and rejected by the Communist may give him pause.[3] Similarly, his idyllic imagination may have picked out from real life certain situations and cases of conduct, which, when realistically analyzed, can hardly support his dreams of what human beings and human life might become. Going backwards, as it were, and scrutinizing the elements that have been drawn together into the imaginative vision, the analytical intellect "tests the creations of the imagination as to their reality," in Babbitt's phrase. Such critical examination is necessary, for "the imagination gives unity but not reality." It gives us a *Weltanschauung*, but no guarantee that the *Weltanschauung* is tenable. On close inspection, the dissimilarities between the elements that have been unified by the imagination may turn out to be much more pronounced than the similarities. In such cases, the "likenesses and analogies" are more truly chimeras.

The validity of Babbitt's arguments in these matters is not really diminished by his failure to arrive at a categorial logic and precise definitions of "imagination" and "reason." For his own special purpose—describing how we get out of illusions and move closer to imaginative truth—Babbitt's philosophically rather simple terminology is adequate.

By-passed in earlier chapters was a comment made by Babbitt about Coleridge. Read outside the context of Babbitt's modes of thought, this comment concerning Coleridge's distinction between a "primary" (i.e., historical) and a "secondary" (i.e., fictional) imagination might seem a scandalous misunderstanding. Babbitt writes, "One cannot . . . be wholly satisfied with the definition of 'the primary imagination' as 'a repetition in the finite mind of the eternal act of creation in the infinite I AM.' This would seem to be an invitation to the romantic to exalt himself to the level of deity before making sure of the validity of his imaginings apart from his emotions." (OBC, 129)[4]

3. The words "cause and effect" are put within inverted commas, because they are only metaphors. Human processes are far from disconnected and chaotic, but they cannot be explained by application of the laws of physical, or even biological, science.

4. Irving Babbitt, *On Being Creative* (New York: Biblo and Tannen, 1968), 129; hereinafter referred to in the text as "OBC."

It might be objected to Babbitt that by "the primary imagination" Coleridge means perception of reality, while the "secondary imagination" is the medium of the poets; Coleridge is speaking of the construction (or rather the reconstruction in knowledge) of the real world in which we live, but Babbitt mistakenly applies his words to the imaginative creations of individual poets. Such a criticism of Babbitt does not do him justice. Cannot the "perception of reality," that is, the "primary imagination" of, say, a Communist be distorted, so that he had better make sure of "the validity of his imaginings apart from his own emotions"? He should hardly be encouraged to consider himself infallible and, as it were, exalted to the level of the deity. Neither should those who criticize such persons trust uncritically what *they* take to be "perception of reality." Coleridge is repeating a Kantian doctrine. Kant seems to have been quite sure that reality in the sense of the common world is the world of Newtonian physics. The knowledge of this world, or the approximation of knowledge among the unlearned, is constructed in the finite minds by a repetition of "the eternal act of creation in the infinite I AM." Yet, as is better understood nowadays, physical science can never become quite sure of what its "reality" is. Also outside of physics, Newtonian or modern, knowledge of man and society is rarely beyond dispute. Babbitt's criticism of this aspect of Coleridge's doctrine is well taken.

But the distinction between primary and secondary imagination needs to be examined in more depth. Outside of natural science, the reality with which man's primary imagination is concerned is historical experience. The knowledge of history, or what is taken to be such, is in one respect an imaginative construction—in some extreme cases obviously a misconstruction—and it is never wholly free from illusion even in the case of wise men. In what way, then, does history differ from poetry, the primary from the secondary imagination? Babbitt's line of argument seems in danger of making them coalesce. One obvious difference is that the historian's intention is different from the poet's. We are historians whenever we try to know about the world in which we act. (Babbitt could have supplemented his practical criterion of reality with Croce's criterion of historical reality.) We are poets—if not creators of poetry at least re-creators of it—when our intention is that of imaginatively constructing or re-constructing a world which is not identical to the one in which we act practically and which we therefore name real.

This distinction between two intentions might seem incompatible with the fact that many poets, perhaps all, teach us about human life. A true poet clearly is not guided by didactic intent, but he does want to show us something. The "something" invariably turns out to be an aspect or potentiality of human experience. This seems to make the intention of the poet not dissimilar to that of the historian. And yet the difference is more than a matter of degree, for the claim of the historian is that things actually happened the way he says they did, whereas the poet has set out to create *Dichtung*. The latter may enlighten us about life, but it does so indirectly. Both men have to be imaginative, but the imagination of the historian is checked by a sort of facts that the poet can disregard. The poet's imagination must also be "true to" something—an emerging awareness of some dimension of human experience—but this poetic loyalty to experience is very different from "truth about" individual historical persons or events.

The distinction between "poetic truth" and "historical truth" is rather widely accepted, but vaguely so. Outside of Croce's books the subject is rarely treated at any length. American treatises on aesthetics, in particular, tend to ignore "poetry *versus* history," in spite of Aristotle's emphasis on this distinction. Instead they dwell somewhat monotonously on "poetry *versus* science." Although Croce's *Aesthetic* has perhaps been more widely read than any other book on the subject, he is alone among major thinkers, if an outsider like Babbitt is disregarded, in emphasizing "poetry *versus* history." This is primarily because the vast majority of philosophers (as R.G. Collingwood complained in his *Autobiography*) pay little attention to the theory of history. Croce deals adequately with this subject up to a point. Missing in his thought is the idea of the distorting or perverting imagination. If practical emotions (feelings of hatred, etc.) seem to distort the historian's imagination, Croce explains, what really happens is that they stop it. Croce applies this analysis to poetry as well as history. He is strangely loath to admit that extreme and perverting practical emotions may predominate in the material of poetic expression, so that ethical and intellectual control of the emotions is almost absent, and that the result may still be truly poetical. As Babbitt insists and amply illustrates, there is such poetry. The historian's imagination is exposed to the same danger. To be sure, there are degrees of imaginative distortion. The enthusiasm of the French Revolution, whether expressed in poetry or history, was of course far nobler than the totalitarian cults of this century. But even the former contained an element of inhuman envy and hatred of the nobility combined with illusions about the natural goodness of "the people." This more or less corrupting imagination was often admirably poetical, as for instance in much of Wordsworth and Shelley.

Croce affirms the "independence" of poetry from truth and morality in a simplified manner. He consistently confuses the moral standards of censors and police courts with the interest of civilized and sensitive critics and readers in moral truth. Some works of poetry may contain fairly accurate pictures of human life, avoiding, among other things, the complementary illusions of Rousseauistic romanticism and so-called realism. Other works may present precisely such misleading visions of human existence. Croce brushes considerations like these aside as "moralism" and "intellectualism" and as irrelevant to literary criticism. Starting in 1917 Croce substantially revised his position, but he still held that imaginative creations, if truly imaginative, cannot contain erroneous views. The imagination as such, and therefore poetry insofar as it is poetry, is always impeccable from the point of view of truth and morality. It follows that errors in historical judgment cannot be attributed to a perverted imagination. Unless they be due to practical intrusions stopping both the imagination and the thinking of the historian, the errors result from defects in the conceptual apparatus applied by the historian to his material. And philosophy is for Croce always conceptual philosophy. He denies the existence of "philosophy" in the sense of an imaginative, non-conceptual grasp of life. For Babbitt, this type of awareness of reality is fundamental to man's view of the world. Croce's important affirmation of the interdependence, indeed, the identity, of history and philosophy must be reelaborated if in philosophy is included the "philosophy" of imaginative insight. Knowledge of life, and not least of the moral essence of human existence, we owe first of all to the imagination, even though its knowledge has to acquire conceptual form to become philosophy. Because it neglects the role of "philosophy," Croce's theory of knowledge can be said to suffer from excessive intellectualism.

Ever since Aristotle, the distinction between prose and poetry has tended to take on a philosophical meaning. Prose contains poetry, but it differs from pure poetry by subordinating imagination to thought. History is, of course, prose. An account of what Alcibiades did is tethered to philological fact. Prosy conceptual clarification of the implied philosophical criteria or of the classificatory terms used are not out of place in works of history, but are rather in many cases inevitable. Admitting this, one must also insist that the quality of the historian's imagination is decisive for his conceptual reasoning. The judgment of reason is enhanced or distorted depending on the quality of the imaginative "philosophy" that informs and directs it. In assuming that *all* knowledge is conceptual, Croce underestimates the influence of imagination and the danger of conceptual distortion.

Babbitt reconciles elements of classical and modern aesthetics. He stresses that art is imagination and not some kind of rationality, but he also argues that the imagination, if disciplined with reference to an ethical center, may express intuitive wisdom. Babbitt is critical of Schiller's encouragement of the notion that one can escape neoclassical didacticism only by eliminating purpose and allowing free imaginative play. He views Schiller as preparing the way for "the divorce of art from ethical reality." (RR, 47)[5] Babbitt recognizes in Schiller the man "an essential

5. Irving Babbitt, *Rousseau and Romanticism* (Austin: The University of Texas Press, 1977), 47; hereinafter referred to in the text as "RR."

nobility of spirit" (OBC, 185) and concedes his aesthetics is not easily categorized. But it finally lacks an "adequate criterion for distinguishing between a legitimate and an illegitimate play of the imagination." (OBC, 153n) The absence in Schiller's discussion of the sublime of references to an ethical *frein vital* makes it difficult to distinguish his view of poetry from the romantic craving for the unlimited and immeasurable. In the end Babbitt does not think his conception of great art includes that type of intuitive wisdom that Babbitt calls "a direct perception of the universal." It is possible to argue that Coleridge, in his awareness of an ethico-religious dimension in art and beauty, is beginning the work of synthesis that Babbitt believes to be necessary. Coleridge develops a version of the philosophical principles of the Germans of which Aristotle's *Poetics* are made to seem a natural outgrowth. Coleridge recognizes a creative imagination expressing non-rational wisdom. Among his precursors, besides the moralist Baumgarten, one may point above all to Lessing, who gropes his way towards a reconciliation of Aristotle and the first glimmerings of modern aesthetics. Coleridge pursues Lessing's aim in a more conscious manner, bringing to it a philosophical depth made possible by Kant and his successors. The task of reconciling classical and modern aesthetics took a major step forward with Babbitt, but his seemingly indiscriminate denunciation of romanticism has caused careless readers to mistake him for a neo-classical reactionary. The needed synthesis is expressed in the title of Eliseo Vivas's *Creation and Discovery* (1955), creation standing for the new theory of the imagination, discovery for what is still valid in the Aristotelian idea of imitation. Vivas and others unfortunately misunderstand Babbitt so badly that there has been no fruitful continuity in the task at hand. It is clear Babbitt himself is not blameless. He put the worst interpretation on the German ingredients of Coleridge. He avers that "transcendentalism is a doctrine that mixes about as well with that of Aristotle as oil with water"—and this he could write in spite of Coleridge, who proves the very opposite. Only if by "transcendentalism" is meant a pantheistic cult of nature, which is what Babbitt arbitrarily takes the term to mean, can his assertion be defended. Babbitt rightly points out that Wordsworth's peasants often look less like persons than an "emanation of the landscape." (RR, 122) If Reason, in the sense of *Vernunft*, is interpreted as sentimental communion with God-Nature and as a view of human beings colored by this pseudo-religion, then there is truth also in the following passage: "Coleridge and others who wished to avoid the charge of having substituted emotionalism for thought adopted the nebulous German metaphysical distinction between a higher synthetic reason *(Vernunft)* and the uninspired analytical understanding *(Verstand)*. Practically the abdication of the keen discriminations of the understanding, however uninspired, is the abdication of thought." (OBC, 61) Babbitt fortunately does not present this analysis as the whole truth about Reason and Understanding. As a student of Plato, with his distinction between *nous* and *dianoia*, and Plotinus, not to speak of the mystics of the East and West, he is well aware that the distinction between types of reason can assume a great many forms. This is probably why he uses the term "nebulous." Recognizing genuine spirituality in Emerson's poem "Brahma" and in the phase of Hindu religion that it expresses, he also knows that pantheism does not have to be the subrational melting into nature of many of the romantics. And perhaps better than anybody else he knows that the term "mysticism" has been used to group together experiences which are very different from one another. He writes, for example, "If Blake is a mystic then Buddha must be something else." (RR, 126)

Whatever the context in which the distinction between Reason and Understanding occurs, a common trait can usually be discerned: Reason is viewed as synthetic and as an awareness of wholes, whereas the Understanding is seen as analytic and as breaking up wholes into parts. Thus it is hardly surprising that, as in Babbitt, the romantic communion with nature should become associated with Reason, and that the activity of breaking up imaginative visions into constituent parts and discovering chimeric traits should become associated with the Understanding. Yet, according to Babbitt himself, wholes need not be chimeric. Reason may give reality, and the fragmenting

Understanding may give illusion, unless it be followed by a return to the reality of Reason which re-synthesizes what has been broken into pieces.

Is then the synthetic function of imagination the same as the synthetic function of Reason? Babbitt raises but does not go into the issue. He always speaks about "analytic reason." Croce argues that in one sense the synthetic vision of the imagination and the synthetic vision of the Reason are the same: Reason gives conceptual form to concrete intuition. All rational unification of experience is thus at the same time intuitive unification. If this view is not satisfactory to the champion of "analytic reason" (a phrase Babbitt keeps repeating), he does not provide an alternative. Surely, he cannot mean that *all* synthesis, in every field from poetry and philosophy to physics, can be attributed to the "imagination." The meaning of the latter term would be so broad as to be unmanageable. The subject of conceptual synthesis will be reintroduced below.

Fully in possession of the idea of the creative imagination, Coleridge also begins the task, deemed so important by Babbitt, of distinguishing between different qualities of poetic intuition. Coleridge breaks up the Wordsworthian vision and identifies chimeric elements. His critical principles, based in large part on a comparative study of Aristotle and the Germans, are applied with great skill. His criticism is nevertheless incomplete by Babbittian standards. It is paradoxical that after his many justifiable criticisms, Coleridge should in the end turn around and give this assessment of Wordsworth: "Lastly, and pre-eminently, I challenge for this poet the gift of imagination in the highest and strictest sense of the word." Coleridge shares with Wordsworth an emotional attachment to romantic pantheism and the closely related idea that the imagination always expresses truth. This attachment creates in Coleridge a tension. His criticism of Wordsworth makes him uncomfortable, and he does not carry it through to its logical conclusion. He wants to believe that Wordsworth's imagination is of the highest type and that it gives magnificent expression to the pure intuitions of the "practical reason," that is, of religious faith. The intuitive deficiencies are due to the intrusion of mere Fancy.

Coleridge writes, "In the play of fancy Wordsworth, to my feelings, is not always graceful, and sometimes recondite. The likeness is occasionally too strange, or demands too peculiar a point of view, or is such as appears the creature of pre-determined research rather than spontaneous presentation. . . . But in imaginative power he stands nearest of all modern writers to Shakespeare and Milton; and yet in a kind perfectly unborrowed and his own."[6] Babbitt expresses doubts about this "kind perfectly unborrowed and his own." In part it represents a subtly perverted type of imagination. The inspiration of the early Wordsworth, Babbitt contends, is mostly quite different from that of higher religion; it is really romantic pantheism.

In *Aids to Reflection* (1825), Coleridge rejects pantheism and has some qualms about his earlier estimate of the religious quality of Wordsworth's early poems. Referring to the pantheistic tendency of the day, he writes that there are many who, "to use the language, but not the sense or purpose of the great poet of our age," would substitute for the Jehovah of the Bible "A sense sublime / Of something far more deeply interfused." Individuals of this disposition have been "educated to understand the divine omnipresence in any sense rather than the only safe and legitimate one, the presence of all things to God."[7]

Coleridge's earlier association of the highest "imaginative power" with romantic pantheism might seem venial. But according to Babbitt nothing is more dangerous to the health of civilization than intuitive perversion within what man takes to be his highest spirituality. Even subtle imaginative distortion in this sphere can powerfully affect his outlook on life as well as his whole orientation of character. Coleridge's view of Wordsworth's imagination in *Biographia Literaria* has had a profound influence on English-American opinion. Babbitt writes, "Coleridge has been followed in this view by so many and such weighty authorities that, in suggesting that Wordsworth's imagination is not after all of the highest type, I am, like Dr. Johnson in his attack on the three unities, appalled by my own

6. S.T. Coleridge, *Biographia Literaria* (London: J.M. Dent and Sons, 1975), 271.
7. S.T. Coleridge, *Aids to Reflection* (Port Washington, N.Y.: Kennikat Press, 1971), 347-48.

temerity.'' (OBC, 75) The substitution of romantic pantheism for religious dualism is for Babbitt not a matter to be taken lightly; and Coleridge's estimate of Wordsworth in *Biographia Literaria* has probably done incomparably more to promote such a substitution than *Aids to Reflection* to counteract it.

Keeping the imagination a source of intuitive wisdom rather than dangerous illusion is a never-ending task. The primary intellectual need of the modern world, Babbitt contends, is to expose certain qualities of imagination pervasive in society which distort the essence of human existence and draw man into behavior destructive of his happiness. Without the revival of the moral imagination in the mind of Western man, reality will elude him, and he will bring destruction on civilization.

Chapter 11
The Way
to Reality

This book has argued that philosophical reason works on the basis of intuition. Chapters 9 and 10 have also found ample justification for Babbitt's view that the imagination may contain falsehood as well as truth. If he is correct, reason will be able to form reliable judgments only in proportion as man is able to free himself from illusory imaginative visions dear to his heart. A theory of how the latter task can be accomplished must consequently form an integral part of any adequate theory of knowledge. The problem of reality, Babbitt argues, cannot be solved on abstract, intellectual grounds as assumed by most epistemological theories. This chapter will examine further his view that reality must be achieved first of all through imagination and actual conduct. While Babbitt holds an exaggerated opinion of the shortcomings of modern theories of knowledge as represented by Kant, he legitimately reacts against failures to understand the role of imagination and will in leading man towards reality.

Coleridge distinguishes between the "primary imagination," the power which constitutes the common world of everyday experience, and the "secondary imagination," which creates the separate, purely imaginative worlds of the poets. Thus formulated, the distinction is in one way adequate but in another way misleading. The individual "worlds" of the poets always contain references to the common world in which we act. Even more important, we owe our deepest insights into this common world to the truly great and wise visionaries. Their works, the *symbols* of the secondary imagination, are means or instruments in building up our experience of the common world. They are indispensable to the working of the "primary imagi-

nation." The latter would be impotent without the light streaming forth from them. If the secondary imagination becomes
distorted, the primary imagination will also suffer perversion.
And if the former moves closer to reality, the latter will keep
it company. Babbitt's greatest accomplishment is probably his
clear perception of this relation and of its connection with the
problem of will. His solution to the epistemological problem
in so far as the knowledge of man and society is concerned follows from this perception.

According to Babbitt, modern philosophy is bankrupt, an
opinion that Whitehead later voiced in the Lowell Lectures of
1925 at Harvard. In Babbitt's view, philosophy, in spite of some
limited achievements, lacks an all-important insight, one that
would inaugurate a truly effective humanistic education.
Although the severity of Babbitt's judgment of modern philosophy must be questioned, not even Benedetto Croce, for all the
merits of his historical epistemology, provides a clear understanding of the role of the imagination in constituting man's
grasp of reality or a corresponding method for reeducating perverted imaginations.

An obscure remark on "appearance and reality" in the
Introduction to *Rousseau and Romanticism* points to the need
deemed central by Babbitt:

Man is cut off from immediate contact with anything abiding and therefore worthy to be called real and condemned
to live in an element of fiction or illusion, but he may . . . lay
hold with the aid of the imagination on the element of oneness that is inextricably blended with the manifoldness and
change and to just that extent may build up a sound model
for imitation. One tends to be an individualist with true standards, to put the matter somewhat differently, only in so far
as one understands the relation between appearance and
reality—what the philosophers call the epistemological problem. This problem, though it cannot be solved abstractly and
metaphysically, can be solved practically and in terms of
actual conduct. Inasmuch as modern philosophy has failed
to work out any such solution, it is hard to avoid the conclusion that modern philosophy is bankrupt, not merely from

Kant, but from Descartes. (RR, 8-9)[1]

The theme of the bankruptcy of modern philosophy is taken up again in the final chapter of the volume, but there Babbitt is equally provocative and hard to understand. We are told that "Kant himself is in his main trend a rationalist [of the Enlightenment]. The epithet critical usually applied to his philosophy is therefore a misnomer. For to solve the critical problem—the relation between appearance and reality—it is necessary to deal adequately with the role of the imagination and this Kant has quite failed to do." (RR, 281)

To understand Babbitt's meaning, it should be kept in mind that the book as a whole contrasts the knowledge of genuine ethico-religious insight with various more or less illusory views of life, especially of the romantic and "realist" varieties. The symbols of the latter two viewpoints are not based on the experience of actual conduct. They give mainly appearance and do little to lead man towards reality. Mediaeval Christianity, on the other hand, is viewed by Babbitt as containing real knowledge, even though the symbols in which it was conveyed were often made rigid by strictly literal belief. When the critical spirit challenged literal belief, the proper task was to conserve the deeper knowledge enshrined in the dogmas and to restate it in a form acceptable to critical thought. Babbitt agrees with Voegelin that rejection of hardened dogmas does not pose a threat to, but helps to preserve, ethico-religious truth. Its symbols, while not literally true, express a profound and inexhaustible reality which can be explored more and more fully. According to Babbitt, insights attained through the reinterpretation of ethico-religious symbols should form the basis in the modern world for revised modes of life and social arrangements, and above all for a new education. Reinvigorated imagination and will in mutually supportive interaction should direct man towards a deeper sense of reality. This is how the epistemological problem can be solved "practically and in terms of actual conduct." We may be condemned as humans to live

1. Irving Babbitt, *Rousseau and Romanticism* (Austin: The University of Texas Press, 1977), 8-9; hereinafter referred to in the text as "RR."

in a world of symbols, but we can reach out for symbols preg-
nant with reality. The inevitable negative accompaniment of
such a program is incessant criticism of symbols containing
more error than truth. To the extent that men achieve truthful
symbols, they are building up ''a sound model for imitation.''
More intelligibly put, they are finding concrete modes of ordering their lives, individually and in social cooperation, which
are directly experienced as conducive to happiness and a
heightened sense of reality.

Even if the work of discerning sound and unsound symbolisms is done with a fair amount of success in scholarly treatises, the troubles of Western society are not ended. The
essential insights need to be made effective in education. An
important question raised by Babbitt is whether the necessary
revival of moral seriousness can be built upon truths that are
understood to be symbolic and not literal.

> The truths on the survival of which civilization depends
> cannot be conveyed to man directly but only through
> imaginative symbols. It seems hard, however, for man to ana-
> lyze critically this disability under which he labors, and, facing
> courageously the results of his analysis, to submit his imagi-
> nation to the necessary control. He consents to limit his
> expansive desires only when the truths that are symbolically
> true are presented to him as literally true. The salutary check
> upon his imagination is thus won at the expense of the criti-
> cal spirit. The pure gold of faith needs, it should seem, if it
> is to gain currency, to be alloyed with credulity. (RR, 280)

Literal belief tends to bear fruit in a well-ordered society. This
kind of society in turn tends to produce the critical spirit, a questioning of dogma, and then an anarchical undermining of the
bases of society. Is it necessary to run through this cycle? Babbitt thinks not. The critical spirit, properly understood, is not
incompatible with ethico-religious insight. For one thing, belief
may transcend philosophy, which regards ethico-religious truth
as symbolic. Modern men who prefer to rely solely on philosophy should refrain from assertions that there is nothing
beyond it. ''Many other things are true, no doubt, in addition
to what one may affirm positively; and 'extra-beliefs' are in any

case inevitable." (DL, 225)[2] Few educated Christians, for their part, would deny that an element of "credulity" is part of the history of Christianity. This admission suffices for the purposes of Babbitt's argument. He would have Western man rebuild the moral and religious bases of civilization in a spirit of non-denominational openness. The religions of the Far East should also be studied seriously. The aim is a truly ecumenical philosophical wisdom—what Walter Lippmann, in a book inspired by Babbitt's principles, called a "public philosophy." Such wisdom will not be looked upon by learned representatives of any of the higher religions as a threat but rather as a welcome and partial statement of their respective teachings. Man *as a philosopher*, however, knows no religious truth that is not symbolic.

But high imaginative truth is found not only in the teachings of the religions. Styles of more secular or worldly life have been developed by mankind which can also be apprehended imaginatively and seen to contain reality. The classical tradition was born among the Greeks, assimilated by the Romans at their best and revived in the humanism and neo-classicism of later times. Confucian humanism is a similar tradition in the Far East. Men were initiated into these traditions less by intellectual processes than by entering imaginatively into the styles of life which society practiced and held up for emulation. These styles of life were manifested in the type of manners, dress, dance, music, architecture, sculpture and poetry that were approved and admired. Together they expressed the classical spirit. The general mode of life of a civilization conveys a concrete knowledge of the meaning of human existence which is imaginative and non-conceptual. Watching and listening to a fine pianist playing Mozart, one is aware of a splendid mastery of spirit over matter, not only in the music but in the skill of the pianist, acquired through a lifetime of practice. This performance may be compared to the sort of recent music that comes close to howls of animal passion, the manner and dress of the performer being consonant with the music. No doubt,

2. Irving Babbitt, *Democracy and Leadership* (Boston: Houghton Mifflin, 1952), 225; hereinafter referred to in the text as "DL."

the latter performance may be art in the Crocean sense of adequate expression. The skill of the performer has perhaps been laboriously acquired, but he carefully hides this fact in order to make the music seem an outburst of primal passion. Both experiences convey in a non-conceptual way a view of human existence. They each contain a "philosophy" of life. The "philosophy" imparted by the former is the supremacy and value of the ordering spirit. The latter imparts a primitivistic cult of the expansive passions. Both performances are symbolic. Just as a paleontologist may reconstruct an entire animal from a single bone, so two very different civilizations, two qualities of life, may be perceived as focused and concretized in the two performances.

Babbitt's solution to the epistemological problem, then, is to move closer to truth above all by training the imagination, which is intimately related to the will. This is done negatively by unmasking perversions, thus in a manner ridding our minds of them, positively by discovering and absorbing the visions of the imaginative master-minds and the more or less profound elements of truth found in artists of lesser distinction. The general life of high civilization imparts a sense of what life ought to be. Conceptual, intellectual activity must of course form a part of this process; keen analysis is needed to discover both truth and distortion in works of history and poetry. Yet mere theory is grey and will itself be distorted, unless it is supported by the insights of the imagination. The only truth that can powerfully influence our conduct is the living concrete insight of the imagination. Intuition of the happiness and reality of moral action tends to call forth practical willing having the same quality. Similarly, a person growing in moral discipline can more easily identify with and be illuminated by the experience of the moral imagination. In the most favorable circumstances, character and imagination reinforce each other in the good life. Training of the moral imagination is thus inseparable from the training of moral character.

The central subject of the new education should be the philosophical study of works of the imagination. Babbitt follows Matthew Arnold, who shows in *Literature and Dogma* how the Bible can be taught as illuminating literature without presupposing dogmatic beliefs in the pupils. The education toward reality should be at the same time philosophical and "philosophical" (i.e., intuitively philosophical). Of course, working out this solution is not just an individual concern but a matter of creating a new cultural *milieu*.

The intellectual element in the conjoint training of imagination and character Babbitt calls criticism, which means philosophical history. Kant seems not to have even an inkling that such a dual training might be the proper approach to truth. This is what Babbitt has in mind when saying that the epithet "critical" usually applied to Kant's philosophy is a misnomer. The weakness of Kant's system is his blindness to the possibility of imaginative truth and his attendant narrow rationalism:

One can indeed put one's finger here more readily perhaps than elsewhere on the central impotence of the whole Kantian system. Once discredit tradition and outer authority and then set up as a substitute a reason that is divorced from the imagination and so lacks the support of supersensuous insight, and reason will prove unable to maintain its hegemony. When the imagination has ceased to pull in accord with the reason in the service of a reality that is set above them both, it is sure to become the accomplice of expansive impulse, and mere reason is not strong enough to prevail over this union of imagination and desire. Reason needs some driving power behind it, a driving power that, when working in alliance with the imagination, it gets from insight. To suppose that man will long rest content with mere naked reason as his guide is to forget that "illusion is the queen of the human heart"; it is to revive the stoical error. (RR, 46-47)

The religious and humanistic imagination contains profound poetic truth about human life. The purpose of art, according to Babbitt, is to show us what life truly is. Kant does not see the possibility of such a purpose. He attributes to art only a *Zweckmässigkeit ohne Zweck*. Strictly speaking, this is a contradiction in terms. Nothing can be *zweckmässig* except in relation to some purpose, even if it be only an easy and pleasurable apprehension of purpose. But such an aim is surely the lowest function of art, and dwelling on it exclusively is aestheticism. Great art has a higher function, that is, a higher purpose, in the economy of the spirit. It reveals to us the world as acted upon by the transcendent ethical will. Only the symbols of great art have the healing power of helping us out of our idiosyncrasies and illusions and out of the collective perversions of our time and place. They alone help us towards a more truthful perception of that common reality which is known through the primary imagination. The closer we come to truth, the better the eternal I AM is realized within us. We are dialectical beings, in which the I AM is working to realize itself in victory over the flux of mere idiosyncrasy. Babbitt is fond of quoting the philosopher of the Over-Soul. In his essay on "Nominalist and Realist," Emerson writes, "I am very much struck in literature by the appearance that one person wrote all the books; as if the editor of a journal planted his body of reporters in different parts of the field of action, and relieved some by others from time to time; but there is such equality and identity both of judgment and point of view in the narrative that it is plainly the work of one all-seeing, all-hearing gentleman."[3]

According to Babbitt, the central aim of education and self-education is to lead man out of individual, local and temporal "zones of illusion" and to attain *"centrality of vision."* In Kant's philosophy we have centrality of vision on rather easy terms: the transcendental Self is realized within us as soon as we have grasped the world of Newtonian physics. For Kant, progress consists in extending the mechanical explanation ever further into areas like organic life which can still be dealt with only by the *reflektierende Urteilskraft.* If the Utopia of mechanical science were ever attained—which is impossible as there will never be a "Newton des Grashalms"— we would know the thing-in-itself (at least according to the neo-Kantian interpretation of the *Marburger Schule* of Cohen-Natorp-Cassirer). Babbitt is not primarily interested in the sort of centrality of vision that can be attained through physical science. He is concerned chiefly about humanistic and religious truth, and his aim is the sort

3. Ralph Waldo Emerson, *The Selected Writings of Ralph Waldo Emerson* (New York: Modern Library, 1950), 439.

of ultimate centrality of vision that such insight can bring.

Babbitt's theory of the imagination, as related to the question of truth and error, gives new depth to the understanding of the process of knowledge. In the language of German philosophy, the aim of the imagination might be described as finding ever more adequate symbolisms for understanding human life. But this statement of the task assumes the existence of less adequate or, in straightforward language, erroneous and misleading symbolisms. Philsophies rooted in pantheism of some kind do not like such negative language; they would assume the positive value of whatever exists. Most important among the pioneers of a modern philosophy of symbolism is probably Ernst Cassirer. But Cassirer is loath to admit that symbolism may lead man into error. His is another version of the romantic view observed in Croce, that the imagination as such is somehow always impeccable.

While there are significant weaknesses in Kant, notably his neglect of degrees of imaginative insight and truth, Babbitt is not on strong ground questioning the term "critical" as a proper epithet for Kant's philosophy. If Kant does not provide a satisfactory critique of the imagination, he has written important critiques of other human activities. Indeed, his idea of "synthesis a priori" may be the decisive step towards the redemption of modern philosophy, pointing the way more generally towards the justification of modernity. Babbitt, in furnishing his own doctrine of imaginative truth and falsehood, is contributing to a philosophical edifice already under construction. He draws attention to the incompleteness of the edifice and supplies an essential missing element. Modern civilization may be threatened with bankruptcy, as Babbitt believes, but, if his own analysis is correct, this bankruptcy is due primarily to the corruption of the modern imagination, and only indirectly to the failings of technical conceptual philosophy. Perhaps serious modern philosophy—seriousness measured by its willingness to deal with questions of value—has done fairly well within its own limited sphere. The failure of modern intuitive "philosophy" should hardly be laid at the doorstep of the philosopher Kant.

Chapter 12
Imaginative Perception
of the Universal

All human self-understanding and interaction presuppose the synthetic activity of an intuitive Self joining all particular selves. Without the more or less developed intuitive grasp of our common humanity and common world, experience would shatter into chaotic dispersion. The conceptual synthesis of reason presupposes and incorporates the pre-logical synthesis of intuition. In art of the kind that Babbitt calls moral imagination the intuitions of ordinary life are greatly intensified and enriched. Such art gives a heightened awareness of the essence of existence. Reality is not grasped by some intellectual abstraction from individual phenomena. As has been shown previously, the empirical "data" forming the material for generalizations are pragmatically extracted from an already constituted intuitive whole. The personages of great art have reality, not because they represent general ideas of the human, but because they express directly, embody in themselves, the nature of life. These personages are concrete, fully human individuals in whom we experience more deeply ourselves and all humanity. We penetrate the universal through the particular.

Babbitt uses the term "imaginative perception of the universal" to describe concrete intuitive experience of the essential reality of life. If the universal is for Babbitt ultimately a moral reality, a sense of what life should really be like, practical willing is but one aspect of human activity. The moral will draws man's other faculties, imagination and reason, into its support. To grasp the universal is to see all the aspects of the human, but in relation to the purposes of the ethical will. A part of this vision is recognizing that failures to live up to this "law for man" are punished by individual and social misery.

Babbitt has less to say about the fact that, having grasped the universal imaginatively, or realized it in practice, men may proceed to formulate it conceptually, as did Aristotle, for instance, in the *Nicomachean Ethics*. As philosophers we can formulate in concepts—"higher will," "lower will," etc.—activities which the poet conveys in an intuitive manner. Croce's approach to the universal was at first purely conceptual and philosophical: We can know the universal only through concepts. Not until 1917, and then conceivably under Babbitt's influence, did he admit that there can be an "imaginative perception of the universal."

Croce distinguishes different categorial structures within the universal. Together they form the universal in the singular. These basic categories of human activity are:

1) an ethical will, aiming at the good and trying to keep in subordination
2) a lower will, which may operate independently but even so has an intrinsic standard: efficiency;
3) imagination, with an intrinsic norm of success: adequate expression;
4) perception of reality, aiming at historical knowledge in the widest possible sense, or knowledge of concrete reality;
5) reflective awareness of these categories, or philosophy.

Of these, 4 and 5 coalesced when Croce passed from his early *Estetica* to his *Logica*. History and philosophy are really different emphases within one and the same activity. Both aim at a knowledge of reality, the former being knowledge primarily of its individuality-multiplicity-change-concreteness, the latter being knowledge primarily of its universal dimension, that is, of the mentioned categories. The categories are intrinsically ends or aims to be achieved: goodness, efficiency, beauty, truth. As aims, they are, and they are not, realized: they *are being* realized. Human activites are "dialectical" in a sense which makes formalistic logic—the static alternative of "is" or "is not"—inapplicable to them.

The term "category of human activity" denotes a mode of human life which is present (at least to some extent) in every human society and individual, no matter how primitive, even if the reflective awareness of this same activity (or the fifth/fourth mode of activity) has not yet progressed very far. The different modes of activity are universals of which concepts may be formed. The activities exist prior to the concepts. Man was an imaginative being before he formed a concept of "the imagination," and so on. There is a distinction to be drawn between "category" as an existential mode of activity and "category" as a concept in which this mode of activity is reflectively perceived. It will be apparent from the context in which of these two senses the term "category" is used.

In addition to *philosophical concepts* of categories of activity or aspects of these activities there are *pragmatic concepts* (or concepts of the Understanding; or fictional concepts; or "pseudo-concepts"), which are either mathematical or classificatory. They are inspired by the practical will (whether or not ethically inspired) for limited utilitarian purposes.

To summarize, philosophy is for Croce the conceptual perception of the nature of the human consciousness *(spirito)*, or, differently put, the thinking of the categorial structure of experience. It is equally correct to use the plural and call philosophy the conceptual perception of the universals, which together form the universal in the singular.

If Babbitt is correct, the existence of a non-conceptual awareness of the universal (or universals) must also be recognized. Before 1917 Croce ruled out the possibility of such intuition. The first paragraph of his *Aesthetic* reads as follows: "Knowledge has two forms: it is either *intuitive* knowledge or *logical* knowledge; knowledge obtained through the *imagination* or knowledge obtained through the *intellect*; knowledge of the *individual* or knowledge of the *universal*; of *individual things* or of the *relations* between them: it is, in fact, productive either of *images* or of *concepts*." (A, 1)[1] Intuition (imagination) gives individuality and nothing but individuality. Croce upheld this sharp division between concepts and intuitions not only with regard to the *universalia* of philosophical thought but also with regard to the *generalia* of classification. "Intuitions are: this river,

---

1. Benedetto Croce, *Aesthetic* (2nd. rev. ed.; London: Macmillan, 1922), 1; hereinafter referred to in the text as "A."

this lake, this brook, this rain, this glass of water; the concept is: water, not this or that appearance and particular example of water, but water in general, in whatever time or place it be realized; the material of infinite intuitions, but of one single constant concept.'' (A, 22)

This division would appear to be untenable. How can anyone be intuitively aware of "this glass of water" without the classificatory concepts of "glass" and "water" somehow being present in the intuition? Can "this river" be perceived or imagined in total absence of the classifications "river" and "water"? Croce is strangely reticent on this point in his *Aesthetic* and remained so in his later work, providing only hints of an answer. For an intelligible statement of what Croce doubtless had in mind one may turn to passages in John Dewey. According to Dewey, the results of previous classifications are absorbed into immediate perception. At this stage they can no longer be called "concepts," as they are no longer conceptually held but have been transformed into intrinsic qualifications of the perceived material:

In the situation which follows upon reflection, meanings are intrinsic; they have no instrumental or subservient office, because they have no office at all. They are as much qualities of the objects in the situation as are red and black, hard and soft, square and round. And every reflective experience adds new shades of such intrinsic qualifications. In other words, while reflective knowing is instrumental to gaining control in a troubled situation (and thus has a practical or utilitarian force), it is also instrumental to the enrichment of the immediate significance of subsequent experiences.[2]

Elsewhere Dewey explains the same idea as follows:

Knowing is itself a kind of action, the only one which progressively and securely clothes natural existence with realized meanings. For the outcome of experienced objects which are begot by operations which define thinking, take into themselves, as part of their own funded and incorporated meaning, the relation to other things disclosed by thinking.

2. John Dewey, *Essays in Experimental Logic* (Chicago: University Chicago Press, 1916), 17.

There are no sensory or perceived objects fixed in themselves. In the course of experience, as far as that is an outcome influenced by thinking, objects perceived, used and enjoyed take up into their own meaning the results of thought; they become ever richer and fuller of meanings.[3]

The view that conceptual meanings are "absorbed" into intuition is implicit in Croce's notion of the "circularity" of human experience: the materials of new intuitive vision are all the previous desires, perceptions, dreams and *thoughts*, of a person's life; and these materials, including ideas, are "transfigured" into elements of the new intuition. The "concepts" no longer function as concepts in the intuition. They are objects of conceptual thought only when the mind concentrates on their definitions. When the mind dwells on individual appearances they are transformed into qualifying traits of these appearances. When in a painting or a novel we are aware of "this woman" or "this child," our mind is absorbing the individual phenomenon. No intellectual energy is spent on the definition of "woman" or "child." Words are used in poetry not as vehicles for concepts but as suggestions of qualifying traits—traits which are usually individualized to the utmost in that they belong to this or that person or object. The problem of how to define "anger" may occupy us as conceptual thinkers, but when in some concrete situation we hear the words, "John was angry," our mind does not busy itself with finding a definition of anger. Our attention is immediately concentrated on *John's* anger, on *his* particular way of being angry. We do not take the time to reflect on the full meaning of "angry," which would involve defining the term or recalling a definition already in existence. Still less do we, like scientists, consider the appropriateness of subsuming John's conduct under a definition. In the attempt to grasp John's anger, the word-meaning is limited to suggesting a *sensed* and *individualized* qualification of John's state of mind and conduct. The sensed qualification is not lifted out of its individualizing context and considered *per se* and in abstraction, which would be

3. John Dewey, *The Quest for Certainty* (New York: Minton, Balch an Co., 1929), 167-68.

a reflective act transforming it into a concept. Natural speech is in this sense non-conceptual and purely aesthetic. The meaning of a word is its contribution to building up an intuitive whole: "John (this particular John) was (in this particular situation) angry (in the personal way in which John and nobody else is angry)." A stream of words has its meaning in the total intuition they convey, which is not a sum of separate conceptual word-meanings, united by a plus-relation.

Croce's view about intuition and natural speech as non-conceptual and concerned merely with the individual was none-too-clearly stated in the *Aesthetic*. The argument regarding non-conceptuality is hardly open to criticism, provided "conceptual" and "non-conceptual" are understood as Dewey understands them. But what about Croce's view that what is intuited is "mere individuality"? This view seems incompatible with recognizing the presence of "qualifying traits" in the intuitions, for a *sort* of universality is thereby admitted as inherent in the intuitions. Although shorn of conceptual significance and almost disappearing in the individualized phenomena, enough sensed generality remains to permit the use of general words like "water," "woman," "child," "anger," etc. If Croce's view were interpreted to mean that the individuality of the intuitions is absolute, his theory would be untenable.

The "intrinsic qualifications" do not always originate in the manner described. Sometimes they originate within intuition itself, which creatively conceives likenesses. Classificatory concepts may be created after an intuition by fixing one's reflective attention on the likenesses, by naming them, trying to define them and thereby turning them into abstract constants. A permanent "give and take" goes on between the intuitive and conceptual modes of consciousness, concepts being transformed into qualia and qualia being turned into concepts.

The illustrations have thus far been classificatory concepts, but the same line of argument can be applied to philosophical concepts, that is, when attention is shifted from *generalia* to *universalia*. There exists an imaginative awareness of *universalia*, a poetic wisdom or "philosophy" which is distinct from philosophy proper. It took Croce many years to arrive at this

Babbittian conclusion, this in spite of the fact that the conclusion would seem almost inevitable given Croce's view that language is basically non-conceptual and aesthetic. He did not make much of the non-conceptual universality inherent in intuition, because for years he saw no point in so doing. But in the chaotic Europe of 1914 and later Croce saw an increasing need for revival of the classical spirit. A reinstatement of conceptual *raison* as the governing element in poetry would have been a reactionary abandonment of what is valid in romantic aesthetics. Instead, intuitive wisdom as inherent in the imagination *as such* became a new interest of his. This concern came to the fore in a paper published in 1917 on "The Character of Totality." By "totality" Croce means the whole of the Spirit, including the ethical will, as intuited in great art. *All* the categories of life are present in the representation of such art. As for the "practical interests" (i.e., factors of a volitive nature), Croce would have the artist assert them all *(farli valere tutti insieme nella rappresentazione)*, which means that man's moral self should be among the "interests" expressed. Knowingly or unknowingly confirming Babbitt, Croce writes, "If the moral force is, as it certainly is, a cosmic force and queen of the world . . . it dominates by its own power; and art is the more perfect, the more clearly it reflects and expresses the development of reality; the more it is art, the better it shows the morality inherent in the nature of things."[4]

Croce's idea may be explained with reference to Emerson's Over-Soul and Coleridge's "infinite I AM," expressing itself in and joining all individual selves. In great works of art I meet myself, you, and all of us, because these works are symbols of the great I AM governing the cosmos. In the experience of great art I do not *think* these things conceptually but *sense* them intuitively.

Every genuine artistic representation is itself and the universe, the universe in that individual form, and that individual form as the universe. In every poetic accent, in every imaginative creation, there lies all human destiny—all the

4. Benedetto Croce, *Nuovi saggi di estetica* (Bari: Laterza, 1920), 131; hereinafter referred to in the text as "NSE."

hopes, the illusions, the sorrows and joys, the greatness and the wretchedness of humanity, the entire drama of Reality, that grows and develops perpetually upon itself, suffering and enjoying. It is therefore unthinkable that artistic representation may ever affirm the mere particular, the abstract individual, the finite in its finiteness. (NSE, 126)

. . . to confer *artistic* form upon an emotional content is to confer upon it at the same time the imprint of *totality*, the cosmic afflatus; and in this sense universality and artistic form are not two but one. (NSE, 128)

These ideas were familiar to Coleridge and Emerson and in general to idealistic philosophers from Plotinus to Hegel. In his *Aesthetic* Croce had given this tradition a bad name, calling it "mystical aesthetics." He had developed an aesthetics of his own which severed art from truth and goodness. Arguably, he gave up this "heresy" in 1917. It appears that Croce was returning home after an experiment, by no means unfruitful, of straying from the fold. In any case, his new ideas brought him very close to the older idealism. In a sense I am you, he, and all those actors that strut and fret their hour upon the stage. We are the *Sartor Resartus* forever in new clothes. What is intuited in great poetry is the infinite I AM impersonating itself in diverse shapes. An artistic landscape, too, is a state of soul; and the higher, ethical intuitions may or may not be vitally present in that state of soul. Universal Life has many aspects and potentialities, and there is room in art for idylls as well as tragedies.

"Mystical aesthetics" rests upon a type of perception which, according to Croce before 1917, simply does not exist. "This activity, called in antiquity *mental or superior imagination*, and more often in modern times *intuitive intellect or intellectual intuition*, was held to unite the characters of imagination and intellect in an altogether special form. . . . Intellectual intuition has sometimes been considered to be the true aesthetic activity." (A, 65) Even in the 1917 essay Croce rejects the idea of "intellectual intuition," but he gives no reasons for so doing in this essay or in his subsequent writings.

A change in a person's philosophical ideas should, according to Croce himself, be reflected in his historiography. Yet, his own history of aesthetics seems to have remained unchanged. Given Croce's new insights, should not an element of truth be discerned, for instance, in Strabo's view that poetry is "a first philosophy which educated young men for life" and which had therefore always been a part of education? (A, 161) In aesthetic theories scorned by Croce as "intellectualistic" there is often just beneath the surface that awareness of imaginative truth which was to be rediscovered by Croce himself. If there is justification for treating Kant's excessive rationalism as largely a surface phenomenon, should one not apply the same consideration to intellectualistic aesthetics? After 1917 Croce no longer had any real grounds for disposing of Plotinus and of Plato's *Symposium* and *Phaedrus* as mere "mystical" errors. They were strangely fruitful errors. And they recur in modern times whenever the dignity of art is asserted. Winckelmann's revival of these "errors" had an immensely stimulating effect on the great age of German literature. Croce's own account of Hegel's "mystical aesthetics" in the *Aesthetic* suggests its importance. Croce points out that for Hegel the aim of art is presentation of truth in a sensible form. "Art contains no universal as such," but it contains the universal "individualized and converted into a sensible individual." (A, 300) (The "universal" is, of course, the World-Spirit, the Over-Soul, the eternal I AM.) It is known that Croce became dissatisfied with his own early account of the history of aesthetics. But the splendid intellectual energy of his younger days had apparently failed him. He was a mind divided, reluctant to draw the consequences of his insights of 1917, and his history of aesthetics was never revised.

The great aesthetic tradition had become impotent in Hegel's version. He retained the insight that there is a kind of truth in art, but in the idealistic tradition with its strong pantheistic leanings, the complementary insight that false and illusory worldviews are also held imaginatively was submerged. This promoted an uncritically tolerant attitude (like Coleridge's view of Wordsworth). An *omnium gatherum* inclusiveness was cultivated. Hegel enumerated types and periods of art (Oriental, Classical, Modern or Romantic). He put them all on the same level and showed scant interest in evaluating the achievements within each period. Only very dimly did Hegel see that the moral will and the imagination develop together as man tries to move closer to reality. In as much as the absence of this idea is the "bankruptcy" of post-mediaeval philosophy, as Babbitt says, the "central impotence" of the Kantian system of which Babbitt speaks is also that of the Hegelian system: Hegel did not see that the imagination is a source of baleful falsehoods as well as truth, and he lacked a method for working one's way out of the former towards the latter.

After 1917 Croce had an opportunity to reform the idealistic tradition precisely in the manner that was urgently needed. He was rediscovering this tradition because of his sympathetic interest in twentieth century anti-romanticism. He perceived that "now, after a century and a half of romanticism," a reaction against it was justified. "We see in fact that in France, and also here and there elsewhere, a discussion is going on regarding a return to classicism," and "the attitude, generally considered, is legitimate, because justified by present historical conditions." He also saw what Babbitt knew well, that the so-called realistic school "was itself also, by derivation and character, romantic." Romanticism is the "malady by which the great body of modern literature is afflicted." If this malady "does not abate, and if, on the contrary, it grows still more in the immediate future and becomes more complicated, this will mean that a still longer ordeal is inevitably in store for our *travagliata e travagliante* society." (NSE, 133-35)

Croce's discovery that art "offers an entirely intuitive universality, formally different from the universality which is conceptually thought or used as a category of judgment" (NSE, 130) has been sharply contradicted by an enthusiastic Crocean, G.N.G. Orsini. In *Benedetto Croce: Philosopher of Art and Literary Critic* (1961), Orsini objects to Croce's revised aesthetics that "Intuition is now defined as knowledge of the 'indistinction of the particular and the universal,' and it is hard to see what that thing can be except a confused blur." If the object of intuition becomes universal, "then there is a serious conflict with the previous doctrine, and it becomes impossible to distinguish any longer intuitions and ratiocinations.''[5] Orsini asserts this to be the case without argument. He wrongly believes that Croce's original view had been that intuition is always of the ''individual'' uncontaminated by any element of universality, and he thinks Croce made a mistake in abandoning that view. As has been shown, this is a simplistic interpretation of Croce's earlier theory. Croce cannot simply have denied Kant's famous formula that ''intuitions without concepts are blind.'' Instead, he revised Kant to the effect that intuitions would be blind but for the work of *language*. Poems and novels are constructed with words, and the meanings of words (except proper names) are a kind of universals. Not surprisingly, Orsini does not try to give an account of Croce's theory of language, which is the most difficult part of the *Aesthetic*.[6]

Defining art as intuition of absolute individuality is to turn it into mere *flatus vocis* and to leave meaning and coherence unexplained. As the universal elements in art are not conceptual, they must be intuited universals. For Orsini ''it is hard to see what such a thing can be except a confused blur.'' And yet it is difficult to see how one could read a novel or a poem without having an awareness of a texture of universal meanings inhering in the artistic vision one is reconstructing.[7]

Why does Orsini turn against his admired *maestro* in this particular matter? At least a part of the explanation may be found

5. G.N.G. Orsini, *Benedetto Croce: Philosopher of Art and Literary Critic* (Carbondale, Il.: Southern Illinois University Press, 1961), 216; 213.

6. The task of explaining Croce's theory of language should be attempted only by philosophers capable of comparing Croce to other major philosophers of language within calling distance of his thought. John Dewey has already been cited. Ernst Cassirer and Theodor Litt should also be pondered by anyone trying to understand how universal word-meanings can be married to individual phenomena, how *das Allgemeine*, the universal, can appear in two different forms, intuitive (*anschaulich*) and conceptual. See Folke Leander, ''Über einige offene Fragen, die aus der Philosophie der symbolischen Formen entspringen: Cassirer—Croce—Litt,'' in Paul Arthur Schilpp (herausg.), *Ernst Cassirer* (Stuttgart: W. Kohlhammer Verlag, 1966) and Theodor Litt, *Das Allgemeine im Aufbau der geisteswissenschaftlichen Erkenntnis* (Leipzig: Hirzel Verlag, 1941), 17-18.

7. Anyone who thinks that the language of music conveys no intuited universality should read Confucius, Plato or Schopenhauer or the modern treatment of the subject in the final chapter of Susanne Langer, *Philosophy in a New Key* (New York: New American Library, 1951).

in non-philosophical considerations. Orsini is acutely aware that Croce's new emphasis is bringing him embarrassingly close to the critics of Rousseau and romanticism, in fact, is making him one of them. In the first decades of this century Croce was hailed by the aesthetes for liberating them from "intellectual intuitions," from the demand for moral truth. But his criticism became ever more "humanistic" in Babbitt's sense of the term. The result was a desire by the aesthetes to get rid of Croce. His merits as a philosopher had never been fully understood in these circles and thus had little to do with his early popularity. He was brushed aside when he turned against modernist poetry.

Orsini's not untypical sensitivities can be illustrated by quoting a passage from Croce's 1917 essay together with Orsini's comment. Croce writes,

Women hold Bacchantic revels in modern literature because men themselves have become aesthetically somewhat effeminate; and a sign of this effeminacy is the lack of shame with which men exhibit all their miseries and weaknesses, and that frenzy for sincerity (which as a frenzy is insincere, but a more or less clever simulation), which endeavors to get credit for itself by means of cynicism, according to the example that was first given by Rousseau. And as the sick, the seriously ill, often resort to remedies which instead of alleviating their sickness only aggravate it, so there have been during the whole of the nineteenth century and in our own day numerous attempts to effect a restoration of form and style, the impassivity, the dignity, the serenity of art and pure beauty; these things, sought for their own sake, provided fresh evidence of the deficiency that was felt but which was not therefore made good. (NSE, 134)[8]

8. It may be noted that, although Babbitt would not have contradicted Croce on the influence of women, he held the view that in an age like ours women are on the whole ethically superior to men. "If women are more temperamental than men it is only fair to add that they have a greater fineness of temperament. Women, says Joubert again, are richer in native virtues, men in acquired virtues. At times when men are slack in acquiring virtues in the truly ethical sense—and some might maintain that the present is such a time—the women may be not only men's equals but their superiors." *Rousseau and Romanticism* (Austin: The University of Texas Press, 1977), 131; hereinafter referred to in the text as "RR."

Orsini comments, "The last sentence should show clearly that Croce, although like Babbitt denouncing Rousseau as the fountainhead of emotionalism, did not fall into the camp of doctrinaire classicism. Nor did he fall then into moralism, for he compared moralistic art with pornography, to the detriment of the former: 'obscenity in art, which is the object of scandal among Puritans, is only one instance of immorality in art, nor is it necessarily the worst, for the foolish exhibition of virtue, which makes virtue herself look foolish, seems to me almost worse.'"[9]

There seems to have been an unwritten law in American literary scholarship that derogatory assertions about Babbitt do not need to be substantiated by quotations or other evidence. One wonders how Orsini could get the idea from Babbitt's books that Babbitt stands for "doctrinaire classicism." Babbitt actually devotes pages and chapters to criticize, sometimes almost to ridicule, the neo-classicists of the seventeenth and eighteenth centuries. Can a champion of the Coleridgean theory of the imagination be classified as a "doctrinaire classicist"? To argue that Babbitt stands for "moralism," Orsini would have to explain away passages in his books like the following:

Like the pseudo-classicist, [the romanticist] inclines to identify high seriousness in art, something that can only come from the exercise of the ethical imagination at its best, with mere preaching, only he differs from the pseudo-classicist in insisting that preaching should be left to divines. One should insist, on the contrary, that the mark of genuinely ethical art, art that is highly serious, is that it is free from preaching. Sophocles is more ethical than Euripides for the simple reason that he views life with more imaginative wholeness. At the same time he is much less given to preaching than Euripides. He does not . . . interrupt the action and the exhibition of character through action in order to "jaw philosophy." (RR, 164)

There are passages in Dante which are less imaginative than theological. Passages of this kind are even more numerous in Milton, a poet who on the whole is highly serious. It is in

9. Orsini, *Benedetto Croce*, 219.

general easy to be didactic, hard to achieve ethical insight.
(RR, 272)

The spontaneity of true poetry is marred by what Babbitt calls
"clogging intellectualism." (RR, 170) So much for his alleged
"doctrinaire classicism" and "moralism." In general, those
who have written on Babbitt and More in this vein seem to have
taken one another's unsubstantiated assertions on authority.

Croce combines a sharply critical attitude toward Rousseau
and romanticism with an even greater hostility to what the
Italians term "decadentism," the tendencies represented by
Marinetti, d'Annunzio, Mallarmé, Valéry and others. He sees
these tendencies as examples of the older romanticism sink-
ing to an ever lower ethical and artistic level. Again, Croce is
in dangerous proximity to Babbitt, and Orsini is ill at ease:
"Croce's lack of appreciation for the poetry of some of the great
names of the modern Parnassus, such as Mallarmé and George,
may be due to a shortcoming of his individual sensibility. Every
critic, as Croce has acknowledged late and early, has his limitations. . . ."[10] Orsini's apology for Croce is that "no man can
be young twice." But is any apology called for?

The existence of an obscure and largely unintelligible poetry
poses a serious problem for Crocean aesthetics. The latter
assumes that it is always possible, given sufficient patience and
mental agility, to reproduce the aesthetic visions of other persons. What has been created by the human spirit must be intelligible to the human spirit. Croce notes that the difficulties to
be overcome may be of many kinds. For instance, "Where the
tradition is broken, interpretation is arrested; in this case, the
products of the past remain silent for us. Thus the expressions
contained in the Etruscan or Mexican inscriptions are unattainable. . . . But the arrest of interpretation, as that of restoration,
is never a definitely insurmountable barrier; and the daily
discoveries of new historical sources and of new methods of
better exploiting the old, which we may hope to see ever
improving, link up again broken traditions." (A, 126) The difficulty faced by someone trying to understand modernist poetry
is the programmatic extreme individualism of the poets. One

10. *Ibid.*, 281.

of the aspects of this movement that is analyzed by Babbitt is color-audition.

If we go through the testimony of people in the habit of seeing sounds and hearing colors, we shall find that to one the flute seemed red, to another sky-blue; for one the trumpet was scarlet, for another green, and so on. In his celebrated sonnet Arthur Rimbaud declares that the vowel *a* is black, *e* white, *i* red, *u* green, *o* blue. To René Ghil, however, the vowels suggest very different colors, *o*, as he maintains, being not blue but red; a point disputed by these "exquisite invalids," as Anatole France calls them, "under the indulgent eye of M. Mallarmé." Here as elsewhere the last stage of romantic suggestiveness is an incomprehensible symbolism. Attempts such as were made at Paris a few years ago to found a school of art on color-audition must remain forever vain. Color-audition and similar phenomena have little bearing on the higher and more humane purposes of art. For the critic of art and literature they are interesting and curious, but scarcely anything more. They concern more immediately the student of psychology and medicine, and in some cases the nerve-specialist. (NL, 182-83)[11]

Croce simply rejects the more extreme products of this school as not being poetry at all. Yet, given his own view of poetry, one wonders how he can be so sure. The fact that we do not understand is not proof that there is nothing to understand. Perhaps we have failed to enter sympathetically into the poet's state of mind. Perhaps by practice we can acquire the ability to experience *o* as blue when reading Rimbaud and as red when reading René Ghil. And can we ever say with certainty about poetry more difficult than that of Mallarmé that it is not true *intuizione*, true art? But in many cases Croce decides it is not. Babbitt, too, judges much of this alleged poetry not to be real art, but unlike Croce he does so in full accord with his own first principles. These poets, he argues, have removed themselves too far from centrality of vision, which is one of his two criteria of art (the other being intuitive coherence). A poem may or may

11. Irving Babbitt, *The New Laokoon* (Boston: Houghton Mifflin, 1910), 182-83; hereinafter referred to in the text as "NL."

not contain a poetic vision, an act of expression in Croce's sense, but if it lacks centrality it has no particular humane significance and can be safely ignored. It is not worth our while to perform experiments on ourselves to experience *o* as red or blue, if the reward is a vision of minimal interest. On purely Crocean grounds, on the other hand, it is hard to see how it can be denied that various Rohrschach visions are "intuitions." If Orsini (assuming he is not just playing to the gallery of American aesthetes) sees beauty in some poems discarded by Croce, the Babbittian humanist will shrug his shoulders, for he is interested in poetry that has some centrality of vision, and the greater the centrality, the greater his interest.

The unwillingness of most modern aestheticians to consider the ethical content of art leads Babbitt to stress that question in his own work. Observers insufficiently attentive to Babbitt's arguments have concluded that for him the only value to be expressed in art is ethical. One interpreter generally sympathetic to Babbitt has suggested that according to Babbitt literature is "ethics 'touched by emotion'."[12] This is a misunderstanding. Babbitt regards literature not as ethics but as imagination, and as such it must meet the aesthetic criteria of all genuine poetry. Also, poetry cannot be confined to ethical intuition. With its characteristic freshness, art should express a wide range of possible experience. In Babbitt's words, "Art of course cannot thrive solely, or indeed primarily, on the higher intuitions; it requires the keenest intuitions of sense." What is distinctive about Babbitt's aesthetics is his view that "if art is to have humane purpose, these intuitions of sense must come under the control of the higher intuitions." (NL, 227) This does not mean that great art somehow dismisses or ignores the variety of human experience. What distinguishes great art is that it intuits this multiplicity in its most significant aspect, that is, in its bearing on what ultimately completes human existence. Without this sense of proportion, art must present more or less unreal, twisted or trivial visions of life.

12. Austin Warren, *New England Saints* (Ann Arbor: University of Michigan Press, 1956), 154.

Deeply pessimistic, cynical, or utopian views of the world reveal in their own way the self-serving, confining orientation of the will that carries them. Poetry which is not sensitive to the real terms of life may still capture acutely and vividly some elements of existence. It may give fine expression to feelings of absurdity and despair. The ethical imagination is certainly not unfamiliar with such states. But in the ethical imagination bursts of fragmentary insight found in lesser works of intuition are absorbed into a more comprehensive vision which deepens and completes the intuition of the Whole that they render only imperfectly. Feelings of absurdity and despair are affirmed and expressed by the higher imagination, but through it such feelings are seen more deeply and clearly as the manifestations of life lacking ethical order. The ethical imagination synthesizes the vast and varied potentialities of human experience by creatively subsuming and arranging them under the intuition of that power in the world which makes for happiness.

What has been superficially interpreted as aesthetic moralism or didacticism in Babbitt is in fact his opposition to art that distorts life or loses its fullness. He knows, certainly as well as his critics, that art has its own aesthetic needs, which are different from those of moral action and philosophy. He is fully aware that art discovers new and sometimes unexpected potentialities of existence, thus liberating man from ever threatening routinization and entropy. But primary among the things that the highest form of imagination creatively expresses is the ethical purpose at the core of human life, thwarted or realized. Babbitt writes: "To assert that the creativeness of the imagination is incompatible with centrality or, what amounts to the same thing, with purpose, is to assert that the creativeness of the imagination is incompatible with reality or at least such reality as man may attain." (RR, 203) The aestheticism of *l'art pour l'art* detaches art from that deeper stratum of order and direction in life and leaves the imagination "more or less free to wander wild in some 'empire of chimeras'." (DL, 147)[13]

---

13. Irving Babbitt, *Democracy and Leadership* (Boston: Houghton Mifflin, 1924), 147; hereinafter referred to in the text as "DL."

It is possible to turn to the literary credo of Peter Viereck for a succinct expression of what is also Babbitt's aesthetic theory. Viereck rejects both "soap-box poetry" and formalistic virtuosity. "Why confine poetry to this false choice between Agitprop and furniture polish? We have a third alternative: not the moral preachiness of didacticism, but the moral insight of lyrical humanity." Poetry without an ethical center is poetry without genuine humanity. Devotees of aestheticism do not understand, Viereck writes, that "you will capture beauty only by seeking more than beauty." Beauty which does not express our essential humanity tends to lose also its beauty. "What dehumanizes, de-lyricizes."[14]

A poetic vision, whether created or recreated by us, draws our whole personality into itself. If we have some moral character, a part of our experience of the poem is the reaction of our higher will to the intuition of life presented in it. To the extent that the intuition ignores or violates the concerns of the higher will and is censured by the moral uneasiness of our participating self, a dissonance mars the aesthetic vision. If, by contrast, the poem successfully renders the presence of the higher will in the world, the intuition expresses our deepest humanity and pulsates in harmony with reality itself. For a mature literary critic to take account of these reactions of his aesthetically participating self has nothing to do with narrow-minded moralistic censorship. The critic is providing a statement regarding the imaginative depth of the poem.

After 1917 there seemed to be plain sailing for Croce towards a full recognition that perverted imagination does exist. But Croce was emotionally too attached to his old doctrine. To the extent that poetry bears the imprint of objectionable romantic tendencies, it is not real poetry, he asserts; these tendencies are unaesthetic outcries of passion inhibiting the work of the imagination and never becoming a part of it. There can be no unethical imagination. "The foundation of all poetry is the moral personality, and since human personality finds its com-

14. Peter Viereck, *The Unadjusted Man* (Westport, Conn.: Greenwood Press, 1973), 288-89.

pletion in morality, the moral conscience is the foundation of all poetry.''[15] The foundation of *all* poetry! The difficulties of such a view have already been discussed. Croce did proclaim his adherence to the anti-romantic critique, but his heart was not quite in it. Nor has this aspect of his thought exerted any appreciable influence.

Thus, in the end, Babbitt remained isolated. He alone among major thinkers sets up "centrality of vision" as a necessary complement to the Crocean "adequacy of expression." Babbitt alone effectively asserts a dualistic theory of art as against the Crocean monistic theory. Babbitt is able to rehabilitate that "intellectual intuition" which Croce had rejected. He simultaneously avoids the modern pantheistically perverted versions of such intuition and goes straight back to Plato and Aristotle. In *The New Laokoon* Babbitt expresses his disagreement with the *Estetica* of 1902: "As [Croce] defines it, form is a mere aspect, the inevitable result, as it were, of true expression. Art has to do solely with the fresh intuitions of sense. . . . The higher, or so-called intellectual intuitions, Signor Croce denies." (NL, 223) To Babbitt, "form" is the presence of the ethical imagination, or of "the intellectual intuitions."

> But though form thus limits and circumscribes, we should not therefore regard it as something inert, mechanical, external. . . . The law of human nature as distinct from the natural law [of physical nature] is itself a law of concentration; only this law should be held flexibly and not formally, and this feat, though difficult, is not impossible with the aid of those higher intuitions at which Signor Croce sneers. . . . (NL, 226-27)

I myself have associated the higher intuitions with Plato. But I might just as well have associated them with Aristotle; for it is a fact that should give us pause that the master of analysis no less than the master of synthesis puts his final emphasis on these intuitions. Indeed, the form this insight assumes in Aristotle is often more to our purpose, especially in all that

15. Benedetto Croce, *Ultimi saggi* (Bari: Laterza, 1935), 10; hereinafter referred to in the text as "US."

relates to art and literature, than the form it assumes in Plato. For example, in describing the region that is above the ordinary intellect Aristotle says that though itself motionless it is the source of life and motion, a conception practically realized one may say in Greek sculpture at its best. . . . (NL, 228-29)

Associating Aristotle's Unmoved Mover, as the object of "intellectual intuition," with the theory of poetry may cause some surprise, as the Unmoved Mover is not mentioned in the *Poetics*. According to a well-known passage, poetry differs from history as well as philosophy by dealing "rather with the universals" (μᾶλλον τὰ καθόλου; *Poetics*, 1451ᵇ7). The "rather" can be interpreted as denoting the non-conceptual and intuitive way in which universals are present in poetry. Aristotle's text has "universals" in the plural, whereas Babbitt speaks of "imaginative perception of the universal." Babbitt thereby stresses the idealistic implication of poetry as more philosophical than history, the universals being identical with the universal to the philosophical mind. The Aristotelian preference for types, for normalcy, for *generalia*, need not be dwelt on here: the poet should avoid introducing anything exceptional and unusual that would distract attention from the essentials of the drama. But it may be asked whether Babbitt is justified in associating "intellectual intuition" and the Unmoved Mover with Aristotle's statement concerning the "universals" of Greek drama. It is a question of what can be concluded if the *Poetics* is interpreted within the context of Aristotle's philosophy as a whole. When he speaks about the "universals" of Greek drama, there is no reason to assume that he is excluding the apex of the pyramid, which is Pure Form. An intuitive sense of the Divine is present both in the tragedian and his public. In knowledge, Aristotle holds, "the soul is in a way all existing things,"[16] the knowing mind becoming identical with the forms known. "God is within us" is a corollary of the theory of knowledge. Active reason participates of Divinity; it has "cognizance of what is noble and divine, either as being itself

16. Aristotle, *On the Soul*, 431ᵇ 20.

also actually divine, or as being relatively the divinest part of us.''[17] It alone is immortal and eternal.[18]

Babbitt can safely assume that the Unmoved Mover is in a sense within man: ''The affirmation of a human law must ultimately rest on the perception of a something that is set above the flux upon which the flux itself depends—on what Aristotle terms an unmoved mover. Otherwise conscience becomes a part of the very flux and element of change it is supposed to control. In proportion as he escapes from outer control man must be conscious of some such unmoved mover if he is to oppose a definite aim or purpose to the indefinite expansion of his desires.'' (RR, 132) ''According to the ancient Hindu . . . the divine is the 'inner check.' God, according to Aristotle, is pure Form.'' (RR, 123)

A Christian would say that in creating their works the great poets have at least an obscure sense of the reality of God and of divine government of the world. Aristotle, in saying that poetry is more philosophical than history, hardly omits from the connotation of ''philosophical'' any reference to that Divine which he tried to formulate conceptually in his doctrine of pure Form. The apex of the pyramid of *ta katholou* is closely related to Plato's *Agathon*, the Good of the *Republic*. In any case, this is the realm in which Babbitt seeks an anchorage for those ''intellectual intuitions'' which are ignored in Croce's aesthetics.

Babbitt is of course well aware that the Greek thinkers conceived of the mentioned spiritual processes as strictly intellectual. His own reinterpretation of them as alogical and intuitive implies that the Greeks were unable to state clearly something they nonetheless had in mind.

The phrase imaginative insight is, I believe, true to the spirit of Plato at his best, but it is certainly not true to his terminology. Plato puts the imagination (φαντασία) not only below intuitive reason (νοῦς) and discursive reason or understanding (διανοια), but even below outer perception (πίστις). He recognizes indeed that it may reflect the operations of the

17. Aristotle, *Ethics*, 1177^a 15.
18. Aristotle, *On the Soul*, 430^a 23.

understanding and even the higher reason as well as the impressions of sense. This notion of a superior intellectual imagination was carried much further by Plotinus and the neo-Platonists. Even the intellectual imagination is, however, conceived of as passive. Perhaps no Greek thinker, not even Plato, makes as clear as he might that reason gets its intuition of reality and the One with the aid of the imagination . . . . (RR, 307-308n)

Thus when Babbitt takes over the term "intellectual intuition" to denote the capacity of the imagination to conceive truth in an altogether intuitive manner, he is reinterpreting the term and, as it were, excavating its deeper meaning, hidden under a surface of intellectualism.

Babbitt differs from his admired Greek sages in that he emphasizes the potential wisdom of the imagination, whereas they stress exclusively the wisdom of the reason. He agrees with them in viewing the search for truth as a struggle against blinding passions, but, according to Babbitt, the passions blind men by perverting their imaginations. Contemplative truth, in so far as men can attain it, is for him first of all imaginative insight. Similarly, he conceives of morality as primarily an activity of the higher will, not reason. His criticism of Greek rationalism is that it does not sufficiently recognize the nature and importance of what is alogical in man's inner life.

As often happens when intellectual challenges are mounted, Babbitt may be carrying his criticism too far. He is certainly right to question the Greek tendency to over-intellectualize the elements of the moral life and the search for reality, but he also appears to underestimate the function and power of conceptual philosophy in its own sphere. The comparative analysis of Babbitt and Croce has shown that the two thinkers travel much of the road together. In his *Logica,* Croce develops significant insights which Babbitt is predisposed to miss because of an over-reaction to Greek and Western rationalism. But in his understanding of the imagination as leading man toward the universal, or into illusion, Babbitt chooses a road of his own which takes him considerably closer to the truth in very important respects.

Chapter 13
Will, Imagination and Reason

The intricacy of the relationships between will, imagination and reason has necessitated a slow and sometimes circuitous approach to the epistemological issues of this book. The stage has been reached at which the emerging epistemological synthesis of Babbitt's and Croce's respective contributions can receive a more definite form. Some arguments will be added fully to explain why Babbitt's ideas concerning will and imagination are central to the theory of knowledge.

It has been shown that Babbitt agrees with Croce in sharply separating theoretical knowledge and will, in conceiving of the relation between them as circular in a certain sense, and in distinguishing between a higher, ethical will and a lower will. But the two men also differ in important ways. Babbitt has an elaborate theory of imaginative truth and error, a theory which has far-reaching consequences for how we understand the acquisition of knowledge. What Babbitt can add to the Crocean theory of knowledge forces its reelaboration. Croce's epistemology has a certain classical simplicity and beauty, but it does not fully account for the interplay of the human faculties. The needed philosophical addition can be summarized as follows: The less active and effective the ethical will within an individual, the more distorted will be his self-knowledge and general historical-philosophical knowledge; his desires will pervert his imagination, and because reason works upon the basis of intuitive insight, his reason will tend to become incapacitated.

Croce is of course quite aware of the dependence of knowledge upon will, but he does not appreciate the extent to which it depends on the *moral* government of the will. He has nothing to say on this subject in that part of *The Philosophy of the*

Practical in which the circular relation of knowledge and will is explained, and here for a good reason. In this part of the book he is writing about will in general and postponing the distinction between ethical and non-ethical (merely "economic") will. But when dealing with the latter subject he does not return to the circular relation of cognition and volition. As a result, nothing is said in the book about the importance of morality for developing a true view of life. The problem of will as related to degrees of imaginative truth and error is ignored. Croce explains that we may be blind to some things because we do not want to see them or because sheer laziness makes us inattentive. But he does not go into the crucial matter of how such inattentiveness, when due to *moral* laziness, may seriously and perhaps disastrously affect our view of life in every field of knowledge, whether conceptual or non-conceptual.

Babbitt, by contrast, concentrates on the moral basis of imaginative truth and error. This criterion of interpretation enables him to discover relationships in history which Croce overlooks. Rationalism in ethics, as defined by Babbitt, includes inadequate appreciation of the role of ethical volition and ethical imagination in the search for truth and reality. By this definition Croce is too rationalistic. Babbitt has much to say on this subject in the chapter "Europe and Asia" in *Democracy and Leadership.* He argues that European civilization is characterized by a rationalistic tendency, whereas the attitude of the great Orientals—Christ, Buddha, Confucius—was rather one of ethico-religious voluntarism. The Western tendency came to the fore in the Socratic-Platonic identification of knowledge and virtue. The contrast with "voluntarism" was by no means clear-cut, for knowledge (*episteme, sophia*) was conceived by Socrates and Plato in such a way as to include a great deal of the "voluntaristic" attitude toward life and, accordingly, of the insights of the ethical imagination. Pure ethical rationalism can be studied better in certain philosophies of the Hellenistic era: "The truth is that the Greeks, on their emancipation from traditional standards, slipped rather rapidly into mere rationalism, and mere rationalism, whether in the Stoical or Epicurean form, showed its usual inability to control the expansive lusts of the human heart. . . . [I]n assuming that right will follows upon right knowledge, the Stoic . . . conceived that he was a true Socratic; if herein he missed the true Socratic spirit, one is forced to conclude that this spirit was rather easy to miss.'' (DL, 173-74)[1]

The assumption of ethical rationalism is that purely conceptual, philosophic thought is enough to ensure right conduct. Babbitt stresses continuous exercise of the higher will and the attendant development of ethical imagination. The Stoics are prone to assume that if you have understood the Stoic philosophy and constantly keep it in mind, right conduct will follow. In practice, the Stoic will be a mind divided: the imagination will become the accomplice of his momentary desires and pull him in another direction than prescribed by his Stoical theory. Croce blinds himself to the possibility that the imagination could exert such an influence. His hostility to the suggestion that there should be a continuous inner moral censorship of the activities of the imagination is well known. The Crocean attitude is similar to that of the Stoic in that it displays over-confidence in assiduous ratiocination. Babbitt is more realistic in stressing the inability of reason to withstand the concerted pull of the desires and the imagination. Conceptual philosophy may tell the Stoic that he is doing wrong, but another part of his personality may enjoy this activity. He will understand Ovid's famous lines only too well: *''Video meliora proboque, deteriora sequor.'' ''Nitimur in vetitum semper, cupimusque negata.''* (DL, 172) Aristotle insists in his protest against over-emphasis on conceptual intellection in Socrates-Plato that there is no substitute for the training of character. The education of the will, Babbitt argues, should go hand in hand with the education of the imagination. The latter helps the individual to discover the moral life *in concreto*. Only after he has begun to acquire experiential knowledge of the happiness of the good life and a distaste for its opposite, has the time arrived for emphasis on conceptual moral philosophy. The Stoics are much too optimistic in their

---

1. Irving Babbitt, *Democracy and Leadership* (Boston: Houghton Mifflin, 1952), 173-74; hereinafter referred to in the text as ''DL.''

view that diligent ratiocination can ensure a good life.

The Stoic bases his optimism primarily, we soon discover, not, like Rousseau, on faith in his instincts, but on faith in reason. To *know* the right thing is about tantamount to doing it. Reason and will thus tend to become identical. The Stoics themselves conceived that in this matter they were simply following in the footsteps of Socrates. The whole question is, as a matter of fact, closely allied to the Platonic and Socratic identification of knowledge and virtue; and this again brings up the great point at issue between European and Asiatic as to the relation of intellect and will. The chief religious teachers of Asia have . . . asserted in some form or other a higher will to which man must submit in his natural self (and in Asiatic psychology intellect belongs to the natural self). . . . (DL, 167-68)

What does not belong to the natural self in the Asiatic view is the ethico-religious will. Lacking this notion, the Stoics have no idea of how this higher will should be cultivated in education. Also, they know little about the daughter of and guide to this will—the ethical imagination. Stoicism therefore tends to begin education at the wrong end, believing that men's conduct could be transformed by imparting to them the correct philosophical ideas. The Stoics inevitably discover, in themselves and others, that virtue is not so easily acquired. Hence their melancholy: "The melancholy of the Stoic is the melancholy of the man who associates with the natural order a 'virtue' that the natural order does not give, and so is tempted to exclaim at last with Brutus, that he had thought virtue a thing and had found that it was only a word." (RR, 241)[2]

The "natural order" which does not give the virtue expected by the Stoic is in this case the activity of reason, unaided by the higher will and the moral imagination. Christianity introduces the awareness of a higher will, superior to the natural self and superior even to the reason that is part of the natural self. Christianity gives a voluntaristic emphasis to education and assigns to conceptual enlightenment a subordinate role. It

2. Irving Babbitt, *Rousseau and Romanticism* (Austin: The University of Texas Press, 1977), 241; hereinafter referred to in the text as "RR."

also perceives that the training of character cannot be effective without letting the imagination dwell on certain symbols. Grace, restoring a fallen will, and faith are closely related. The ethico-religious will (grace) and the ethico-religious imagination (faith) are complementary in the building of character. "Christianity supplied what was lacking in Greek philosophy. It set up doctrines that humbled reason and at the same time it created symbols that controlled man's imagination and through the imagination his will." (DL, 175)

According to Babbitt, "if one wishes to get at a Christian's views of man's will the best method is frequently to ascertain his views of God's will." (DL, 319) The voluntaristic *motif* is clearly visible in Saint Augustine, Duns Scotus and Occam. Scotus develops the thesis that "will is superior to intellect" *(voluntas superior intellectu)* in both God and man. Occam affirms in a still more uncompromising fashion that God's will is absolute. God does not will something because it is just, but it is just because He wills it. (DL, 320-321) Such a doctrine contains truth also about man, Babbitt holds, when, as in Buddhism, God is identified with man's higher will. Valuation proceeds ultimately from this higher self, not from the cognitive side of human nature. Moral standards emanate from a "higher immediacy" of autonomous valuation: "If there is no principle of unity in things with which to measure the manifoldness and change, the individual is left without standards and so falls necessarily into an anarchical impressionism. Now Buddha like a true Asiatic discovers this unifying principle, not in intellect, but in will. Though he assigns an important role to intellect, since he is himself highly analytical, this role is after all secondary and instrumental. . . . Buddha is for reducing theory to a minimum." (DL, 170) Moral standards are in a sense the conjoint creations of the imagination and the intellect. But the final acceptance or rejection of particular norms thus formulated is an activity of the higher will. It was shown in Chapter 1 that for Babbitt the ultimate criterion of reality is the happiness or peace that comes with exercise of the ethico-religious will. All particular standards are transcended by the evaluating power itself. This will inspires the search for ever better norms. If actions and standards are good, they are so because the higher self, like Occam's God, wills them; the higher self does not will them because they have been deemed good.

The sense in which ethical will has primacy over intellect should be examined further. Babbitt agrees with Buddha and Christ, as he understands them, that the unifying principle of human life is will. But he also claims to state a philosophical *truth* when saying, "the unifying principle is will." What status has this truth? It seems obvious that *knowledge* of the truth is also an ordering, unifying power. And if that is the case, there is one type of unification of life in terms of action and another in terms of conceptual intellection. If the question is raised, which one has primacy, the issue is whether a higher dignity belongs to unification *sub specie bonitatis* or to unification *sub specie veritatis*. Babbitt's view is that in the end goodness is a higher value than truth. Conceptual intellection is subordinate, for by itself it would be capable of leading man neither to truth nor goodness. The primacy of ethical will *(voluntas superior intellectu)* is the primacy of an awareness without which man would be the helpless victim of his lower inclinations. Without this awareness, he would not be in a position to understand his fellow men or himself, as he would lack the most important organ of humanistic knowledge, "the imaginative perception of the universal." In Christianity, grace, restoring the fallen will, and faith, vivifying the spiritual vision of the believer, can be seen as aspects of the same spiritual process. *Mutatis mutandis* the same spiritual activity may exist in the non-believer. Unification of life *sub specie bonitatis* means unification through the higher will and ethico-religious "vision," whereas unification *sub specie veritatis* means the development of a coherent conceptual philosophy.

Unlike Croce, Babbitt is not content with several supreme values, each supreme in its own sphere and yet related to the others in a nexus of equality. Moral goodness, Babbitt holds, is the end of life; it is in goodness that we find happiness and peace. Philosophical truth is supreme and autonomous in its own sphere of cognition, but this value is ultimately instrumental to goodness. So are beauty and efficiency. Common sense observation tells us that the thinker must often interrupt his thinking because he has other and more urgent duties. The same is true of the artist. Unless we let moral duty take precedence and put our various activities in the service of the moral good, we shall be left in the end with a gnawing sense of leading meaningless lives. This feeling tends to shatter all concentration and every sound sense of proportion. Even *sub specie veritatis* we must subordinate *veritas* to *bonitas*. The latter is thus the *ultimate* principle of reality and order. But as such it needs and demands the cultivation of truth, beauty and practical efficiency in their own internally autonomous spheres. *Bonitas* can become the more fully realized the more it is supported by these other activities.

Some of Babbitt's utterances concerning the relationship between will and knowledge may seem to contradict one another. They fall into a coherent pattern as soon as his central idea is understood: "One may well come to agree with certain great Asiatics, in contrast at this point with the European intellectual, that the good life is not primarily something to be *known* but something to be *willed*. There is warrant for the belief that if a man *acts* on the light he already has the light will grow." (OBC, xxxv-xxxvi)[3] This view might seem to be contradicted by another passage: "It is not enough to put the brakes on the natural man . . . we must do it intelligently. Right knowing must here as elsewhere precede right doing." (RR, 282) But the contradiction is only apparent. A man should act on "right knowing." In this sense, right knowing does precede right doing. But if he acts in this manner, the light will grow, and in this sense right doing precedes right knowing. Determining the relationship between knowing and doing is not a parallel to deciding which comes first, the hen or the egg. Croce agrees with Babbitt that there is no relation of compulsion between "the theoretical basis" of action and the action. Action may or may not supervene; it is free, not caused. When Babbitt says, "*if* a man acts on the light he has," that "if" is far from a certainty. In the moment of action a sudden defalcation of the

3. Irving Babbitt, *On Being Creative* (New York: Biblo and Tannen, 1968), xxxv-xxxvi.

moral will may occur; the individual may sink into moral laziness. Why? The question is a misplaced causalistic question demanding a causalistic answer. The fictions of natural science are not applicable. *If* the man acts on the light he has, it will grow—yes, but the "if" breaks the analogy with the hen and the egg. In spite of the most favorable "theoretical basis," the individual may choose immoral actions not conducive to growing light.

Another apparent contradiction can be found in some of Babbitt's passages regarding the epistemological problem. He has already been quoted to the effect that the main task of the post-mediaeval world is to work out a knowledge of human nature and social life which moves man from appearance to reality. Yet in other passages, expounding his ethical voluntarism, Babbitt seems to reject emphasis on the epistemological problem as an intellectualistic error: "Some of the difficulties inherent in any attempt to treat the problem of the One and the Many primarily as a problem of knowledge appear in the Platonic theory of ideas." (DL, 170-71) "The real emancipation of intellect got fairly under way with the Renaissance. . . [Men] were inclining once more, like the ancient Greeks, to look on life primarily as a problem of knowledge." (DL, 178) Again there is no contradiction. What Babbitt rejects is not attention to the problem of knowledge but the attempts to define this problem in abstract, merely intellectual terms. A distinction has been developed here between philosophy proper and intuitive "philosophy," truth and "truth." The solution to the epistemological problem is for Babbitt the cultivation of "the imaginative perception of the universal." His position can be stated in the famous lines of Keats, though not precisely in the sense Keats meant them:

"Beauty is truth, truth beauty,"—that is all
Ye know on earth, and all ye need to know.

The intuitive truth of the ethical imagination is the basis for all other knowledge. The truth-beauty Babbitt has in mind is at once the reward for ethical discipline and the inspiration of such activity. Although Babbitt does not explicitly address the matter, he would probably agree that good philosophy must admit the primacy, and ultimacy, of intuitive "philosophy." Secondly, philosophy will lack practical influence, unless it be immediately translated into "philosophy." The way to truth is a way of life which develops the entire human personality under the guidance of the sense of goodness. One-sided concentration on intellection is bound to make man miss precisely what he claims to seek—the truth. As an example Babbitt takes Plato's theory of ideas in so far as it is mere intellectualism and not also imaginative spiritual vision. Babbitt is well aware that an injustice is done to Plato by thus abstracting his intellectualistic side from the whole of his teaching. But this experiment makes it possible to demonstrate the nature and consequences of intellectualism carried too far. Exaggerated emphasis on ratiocination leads Plato into a world of conceptual abstractions and gets him involved in almost insuperable difficulties when it comes to finding the way back to concrete reality. "The attempt to deal intellectually with the relation of the unity to the manifoldness would seem to lead to difficulties of the kind Plato has himself set forth in the second part of his 'Parmenides.'" (DL, 171)

For many centuries after Plato philosophers were going to rack their brains with the problem of *methexis,* participation. The problem of how to get from mere intellectual abstraction back to the concrete becomes especially acute in the case of the most important idea of all, that of the good. According to Babbitt, a real solution can be reached only by shifting the primary emphasis from thought to action, from the "good" as a concept to the good as willing. Good willing becomes realized *in concreto* and achieves in action what the theory of the *Parmenides* and similar doctrines cannot understand. *"Das Unbeschreibliche, hier ist's getan."* In Crocean language, one has to transfer the attention from good as a concept to good as a *potenza del fare,* which is an intuited good. Babbitt has an illuminating passage on how ethico-religious voluntarism was introduced into the West:

> This problem as to how to escape from mere abstraction appears in the case of the chief idea of all—that of the good or of God which also coincides with what is most exalted in

man. The word that stands for the idea of the good is the word par excellence, the logos. One can follow to some extent the process by which the Greek conception of the logos was transmitted through intermediaries like Philo Judaeus to the author of the Fourth Gospel. The specifically Asiatic element in the Christian solution of the problem of the logos is the subordination, either implicit or explicit, of the divine reason to the divine will. By an act of this will, the gap between a wisdom that is abstract and general and the individual and particular is bridged over at last; the Word is made flesh. The human craving for the concrete is satisfied at the essential point. The truth of the incarnation . . . is one that we have all experienced in a less superlative form: the final reply to all the doubts that torment the human heart is not some theory of conduct, however perfect, but the man of character. Pontius Pilate spoke as a European when he inquired, 'What is truth?' On another occasion Christ gave the Asiatic reply: 'I am the way, the truth, and the life.' (DL, 171-72)

After the concrete acts of will comes the historical-theoretical awareness of the acts of will. The theory of Christian voluntarism was worked out by Saint Augustine. A philosophical difficulty was that Christian dogma made a separate person of that higher will which in Buddhism is viewed as man's own higher Self. One might have thought that Babbitt, who avoids dogmatic creedal commitments, should have felt the need to give a systematic conceptual account of the incarnation of the good will in concrete good actions. Considering Babbitt's dualism and the general tendency of his thought, it would have been natural for him to attempt a dialectical account of experience, one which absorbs what is valid in Hegel while rejecting pantheistic, monistic implications. But Babbitt does not recognize this opportunity in logic. Incarnation seems to him intellectually incomprehensible; it is *"das Unbeschreibliche."* He retreats to the doctrine of the *Parmenides* regarding *methexis.* He implicitly accepts the kind of Greek intellectualism which on his own showing should rather be abandoned. Good actions, he says, are paradoxical to our reason. Can there then be no theoretic account of good actions, a *veritas* concerning them? The logical argument of this book has been that something must be wrong with a "reason" which disputes facts of which we are unmistakably aware. This so-called "reason" blasphemes *Veritas* to her face. "Reason" alleges that the facts are paradoxical because they violate the principle of "A = A." But *Veritas* answers that the facts are dialectical; abstracted from complementary considerations ("A = A *and* non-A"), "A = A" is the principle of sophistry.

To undialectical reason, good actions are cases of *methexis* and hence logically impossible. It should be clear from the arguments of this book that such an abstract reason is ill-equipped to participate in philosophical debates about human existence. When formalistic-pragmatic reason interferes with and attempts to replace genuinely philosophical self-knowledge, it tears elements out of context, reifies what is dynamic and living, and juggles the resulting abstractions. In philosophy proper, pragmatic reason is a mountebank. *Veritas*, genuinely philosophic reason, can take heart and lift her head, not in pride but in modest self-confidence. Man is theoretically aware of goodness, truth, beauty, and prudence as they are "incarnated" in their respective categories of action. Philosophic *Veritas* is precisely this awareness. The law of her being is a deeper logicality than what is formulated in the conventional formulae "A = A" and "A is not non-A"—as if the alternative of "is" and "is not" exhausted logic and there were no meaning in concepts like "becomes," "grows," "develops," "makes itself into." Aristotle's actual philosophizing about man, society and nature, which is usually quite sensitive to life's element of change and development, rises above those of his comments on logic which point in the direction of "A = A," a formula incongruous with his own concepts. The dialectical mind of philosophical reason discovers riches unknown to formalistic, reifying logic from Aristotle to Bertrand Russell.[4] Reason is not so impotent in humane knowledge as Babbitt, in the wake of traditional logic, assumes it to be.

Babbitt speaks in his essay on *The Dhammapada* about "that

---

4. Aristotle is of course a thinker of a different stature than Bertrand Russell.

dualism which is the scandal of reason and is nevertheless one of the immediate data of consciousness.'' (D, 107)[5] How does Babbitt *know* that dualism is a ''datum'' (or, as he might rather have said, a category of experience) unless something in him perceives and judges it to be such? How does he *know* that the ''word becomes flesh,'' that the universal can shape the flux of individuality, unless he can *know* the world of historical multiplicity? The latter knowledge is not just of abstract ''forms''; it includes an immediate awareness of individuality. So it is, says Babbitt, but it is a scandal to reason! One of the purposes of this book has been to refute such a conception of reason. Babbitt's own conceptual elaboration of ''the immediate data of consciousness'' exemplifies the work of philosophical reason.

The Platonic *nous* is clearly in close proximity to what Babbitt calls imaginative perception of the universal. Plato's strong tendency to conceive of what is highest in man in terms of ''reason,'' and of reason in terms of universal ''forms,'' may have inhibited his insight in some areas, but it did not stop him from seeing deeply and imaginatively into the essence of human existence. It should be noted in the present context that there is at least the limited warrant for associating the highest power with reason that the latter continuously takes theoretical account of intuitive insight.

It has already been mentioned that Plato's own work contains important partial correctives for his proneness to intellectualize the problems of life. ''Incarnation'' as the solution to problems that confuse us theoretically is pre-figured in his writings. The proposed dialogue on the *Philosopher* remained unwritten (perhaps because Plato, despite attempts at liberation, remained ensnared like a new Laokoon in the coils of an abstract, ahistorical logic). But as Paul Elmer More writes in *Platonism:* ''Plato has done for us better than his promise. If the picture of the philosopher as an abstract ideal was not drawn, he has left us in the character and lineaments of Socrates an immortal portrait of philosophy incarnate in a living historic

5. Irving Babbitt, ''Buddha and the Occident,'' in *The Dhammapada*, translated and with an Essay on Buddha and the Occident by Irving Babbitt (New York: New Directions, 1965), 107; hereinafter referred to in the text as ''D.''

man.'"[6] More's comment points back to the previous theme, the imaginative perception of the universal. What did Socrates represent to all of his friends on whom he made such an indelible impression? Was he above all a teacher of philosophical concepts, an intellectual more inventive and incisive as a reasoner than the other theorists in the Athenian agora? He certainly did help his interlocutors to perceive conceptual universals more clearly. But perhaps he had an influence stronger still fostering their non-conceptual awareness of those universals. It might even be argued that for Socrates conceptual thought was a means rather than an end. More may be right in saying that Socrates taught what he stood for most effectively by *incarnating* it. His words did not simply manifest a process of conceptual intellection. They were also the expression of a noble personality sharing richly in the universal. Such teaching, unlike technical philosophical clarification, may come home even to those who are not markedly brilliant.

There is a sense in which great poetry creates human types which become unforgettable treasures in the memory of mankind. It would seem that in the following passage, which criticizes non-aesthetical intrusions in art, Croce has this meaning of "type" in mind: "To typify would signify, in this case, to characterize; that is, to determine and to represent the individual. Don Quixote is a type; but of what is he a type, save of all Don Quixotes? A type, so to speak, of himself. Certainly he is not a type of abstract concepts, such as the loss of the sense of reality, or of the love of glory. An infinite number of personages can be thought of under those concepts, who are not Don Quixotes. In other words, we find our own impressions fully determined and realized in the expression of a poet (for example in a poetical personage). We call that expression typical, which we might call simply aesthetic." (A, 33-34)[7] Croce rejects concepts of the Understanding (that is, pseudo-concepts) dressed up in flesh and blood so as to resemble human beings. He makes this even clearer in the next section of the *Aesthetic*,

6. Paul Elmer More, *Platonism* (2nd. rev. ed.; Princeton: Princeton University Press, 1926), 303.
7. Benedetto Croce, *Aesthetic* (2nd. rev. ed.; London: Macmillan, 1922), 33-34.

which is devoted to allegory. It is less clear in what sense he is prepared to accept the words "type" and "symbol." The reader gets the impression that he wants to ridicule the whole idea of types. Don Quixote is said to be the type—of all the Don Quixotes. But this idea is anything but ridiculous. What it means is that Don Quixote is the type of all of us in certain moods and attitudes in which we recognize ourselves in him and him in us. Through him we learn something about ourselves, and about life in general. A plethora of examples may be used to illustrate this same point which is sharply contradicted in the *Aesthetic*. In spite of the difference of sex, male readers may find in themselves something of the heroic Antigone and the timid Ismene. Female readers may find buried somewhere in themselves a potential tyrannical Creon. Othello, Lear and Hamlet are not only personages in Shakespearean drama. Their attitudes and actions and their consequences are sometimes visible also on the stage of everyday life, where we are all actors. These configurations of action and suffering are no less "typical" in the same non-conceptual sense than are the mentioned literary personages. That poetry aims "rather at the universal" can also be expressed by saying that it aims at the typical, in the non-conceptual sense.

When Croce forbids us to call the Muse a teacher, he autocratically expels a notion which has been felt to contain a truth ever since the days of the early Greeks. Throughout the ages men have perceived that art at its best has something to tell us about reality. They have also sensed, as Plato did, that poetry sometimes manages to paint vice in alluring colors and make virtue look ugly and disgusting, giving distorted pictures of the origins and consequences of both. Down the centuries there has been overwhelming commonsensical agreement that this is often so, even if aesthetic and epistemological theory has not given a satisfactory account of the fact. According to Croce, what centuries have assumed to be a function of art simply does not exist. For all the strengths of his aesthetics even before 1917, it must be said that the Croce who has been celebrated by the aesthetes as a liberator of art lacks an insight of crucial importance to the welfare of human society.

Probably the greatest of Babbitt's accomplishments, made possible by his deeper sensitivity to the ethical dimension of human activities, is his incisive and subtle understanding of the relationship between moral character and imagination in the search for reality. Like Croce, he is well aware of the creative nature of the imagination. But he joins to that insight a clear recognition that the imagination contains opposing potentialities. The great poets of the human race show us the universal and pull us toward peace and reality. But often the Muse succumbs to our lower passions and entices us into behavior destructive of our happiness and hold on reality.

Babbitt's notion of the imaginative perception of the universal refers to the intuitive unification and deepening of human experience resting on and inspiring ethical will. But just as discovery of reality has an ethical and intuitive dimension, so is there an intellectual unification and deepening of experience. Croce has shown that there is a historical-philosophical perception of life which takes conceptual account of our practical and intuitive activities and of itself. An immediate awareness of the categories of human life is knowingly or unknowingly presupposed in all merely pragmatic intellectual activity. The more or less general classifications produced by pragmatic reason could not exist without knowledge of the more fundamental order and continuity of life from which pseudo-conceptual thought excises convenient fragments. Philosophy is not an intellectual abstraction from "empirical" particulars or the contemplation of merely abstract universals. In the human consciousness, the particular and the universal exist together. The universal without the particular would be empty and the particular without the universal mere dispersion. Philosophical knowledge is indistinguishably synthetical and analytical. New philosophical insight is a cognitive act in which concrete experience looks more deeply into its own categorial structure.

If Babbitt is generally much less perceptive than Croce in his treatment of the subject of reason, his ethico-aesthetical doctrine is nevertheless a decisively important contribution to the theory of knowledge and to the understanding of the nature of conceptual insight. Croce has shown that conceptual thought works on the basis of intuition. But because he lacks Babbitt's sure grasp of the ethical imagination, he simplifies the nature of that dependence. Incorporating Babbitt's ideas into the theory of knowledge, one must stress that only if reason relies upon the most penetrating intuition, truly sensitive and open to the different aspects of human reality, can its concepts achieve truth and comprehensiveness. Reasoning that builds on distorted imagination may be formally brilliant but will present illusions. The remedy is not abstract counter-argument but a turning of the whole personality. Because Croce does not recognize the danger of imaginative distortion, he exaggerates the possibility of clear conceptual vision. If acceptance of Croce's categorial logic brings with it a needed new faith in reason, and perhaps also a temptation to premature certainty regarding the nature of reality, one effect of Babbitt's ethico-aesthetical doctrine is to induce intellectual humility.

Babbitt's explication of the relationship between imagination and will, as joined to Croce's logic, demonstrates the ultimate dependence of philosophical knowledge on moral character. Both Croce and Babbitt reject the Socratic view that virtue is knowledge. But although Babbitt is critical of the Greek tendency to intellectualize the key problem of reality, his ideas suggest a reelaboration of a profound truth which is imperfectly stated in its Socratic version. While virtue and knowledge are not the same, the deepest and most comprehensive grasp of reality rests on the will of the moral personality and the intuitive vision that it makes possible.

Index

47*n*; 45, 46, 49, 68, 70, 79, 80, 82, 87, 91, 118
Cusa, Nicolaus of, 71

D'Annunzio, Gabriele, 198
Dakin, A. Hazard, 48*n*, 49*n*
Dante, 152, 197
Democracy and Leadership (Babbitt), 13–14, 29, 79–80, 101, 208
Democritus, 67
Descartes, René, 25, 71, 177
Dewey, John: on Bradley's logic, 98–99; on man's intuition of the Whole, 99; on relationship between imagination and reason, 188–90; on science as concrete action, 115; on the nature of thought, 88; parallels to Babbitt, 49; 48, 49, 98–99, 195*n*
Dhammapada, The (Buddha/Babbitt), 14, 217–18
Dialectic, Hegelian, 52
Dialectical logic, 100–107, 119–32, 216–17
Don Quixote: as a "type," 219–20
Dualism: epistemological basis for, 119; *versus* romantic pantheism, 173–74

Eleatic logic: defined, 98
Eliot, Charles W., 13
Eliot, T.S.: influenced by Babbitt, 34; misunderstands Babbitt's "inner check," 33–34, 36, 38; 12, 38, 40*n*
Emerson, Ralph Waldo, 54, 55, 63, 66, 171, 182, 191, 192
Engels, Friedrich, 158
Epistemology: of natural science, 73–75, 77
Essay on Man, An (Cassirer), 117, 118
Estetica (Croce), 68, 186, 203
Ethical rationalism: criticized, 209–11
Ethics: its relationship to knowledge, 18, 19; primarily dependent on will/imagination, 209–12; related to knowledge, 26
Euclid, 158
Euripides, 197
Experience: artificially restricted conceptions of, 25–26
Experience and Nature (Dewey), 49

Fichte, Johann Gottlieb, 57, 62, 86–87
Filosophia della pratica (Croce), 50
Fischer, Kuno, 110*n*
Foerster, Norman, 30*n*, 48*n*
Formtrieb, 56–57
France, Anatole, 199

Galileo, 71
Gentile, Giovanni: on reification, 101; mentioned, 46, 47*n*
George, Stefan, 198
Ghil, René, 199
Giese, W.F., 66*n*
Goethe, Johann Wolfgang von, 72–73
Grattan, C. Hartley, 31*n*, 32*n*
Great Chain of Being, The (Lovejoy), 50

Hallowell, John, 20
Hamlet, 220
Happiness: defined, 32; distinguished from pleasure, 27
Hartley, David: his sensationalistic materialism, 54
Hazlitt, Henry, 32
Hegel, Georg Wilhelm Friedrich: his aesthetics criticized, 193–94; quoted, 131; 17, 47, 86–87, 101, 105, 107, 110, 118, 121, 192, 193
Hemingway, Ernest, 12
Heraclitus, 70
Higher will (inner check): analyzed, 29–37; as basis of community, 29–30, 34–35, 36–37; as ultimate criterion of reality, 42; experienced directly, 43; compared with Christian doctrine of grace, 37, 40–41; its religious and humanistic manifestations, 41–42; 25, 26, 148–149
Historicism: as explicated by Croce, 134–144; not incompatible with the universal, 126
History: as study in self-knowledge, 110,
History of Europe in the Nineteenth Century (Croce), 46
Hobbes, Thomas, 125
Hoeveler, David, 14, 50*n*
Homer, 92